About the Editors

Harry Harrison was born in Stanford, Connecticut, in 1929 and now lives in San Diego, California. Apart from enjoying an enviable reputation as one of the best writers on the science fiction scene, he is also an experienced editor, anthologist, translator and trained cartoonist. Harrison's style leaps from the humour of his STAINLESS STEEL RAT to the splendid combination of fantasy and s.f. found in CAPTIVE UNIVERSE and in the DEATHWORLD trilogy. (All available in Sphere Books.)

Brian Aldiss was born in Norfolk in 1925 and now lives with his family in Berkshire. Voted by the British Science Fiction Association as Britain's most popular science fiction writer and awarded the Ditmar for being the Best Contemporary Writer of s.f., he has also won a Hugo for HOTHOUSE and a Nebula for THE SALIVA TREE. (Both available in Sphere Books.)

'The Harrison/Aldiss series is the one, when all is said and done, that one must read to stay up to date in s.f.'—*Locus*

Also available in Sphere Books

THE YEAR'S BEST SCIENCE FICTION Nos. 1-5

The Year's Best Science Fiction No. 6

Edited by HARRY HARRISON
and BRIAN ALDISS

SPHERE BOOKS LIMITED
30/32 Gray's Inn Road, London WC1X 8JL

First published in Great Britain in 1973
by Sphere Books Ltd.

Set in Linotype Times

Printed in Great Britain by
Hazell Watson & Viney Ltd.
Aylesbury, Bucks

ISBN 0 7221 4355 9

CONTENTS

INTRODUCTION

HARRY HARRISON

Will success spoil science fiction?

This is a real worry that, while it doesn't keep me awake at nights, still gnaws at my consciousness more and more these days. Despite a good deal of Cassandra-muttering, SF is a large and continually growing field of literary endeavor. Each year brings an increase in the number of books published over the preceding year. (I carefully refrain from saying *better* books because that is a different concern which we shall get to in a moment.) The Science Fiction Book Club appears to have tripled its membership as well. While the American "literary establishment" still considers SF a lower form of life, the United States schools do not and, at the last reckoning, there were over two hundred college courses in the subject. There are far more classes at intermediate level—no one knows exactly how many—because teachers find science fiction an extremely valuable field with which they can teach other disciplines. Reading skills in particular; SF is the *only* kind of reading that students do voluntarily.

So the science fiction express roars on into the future, brass gleaming and wheels rattling. But what kind of cargo is there behind those chromium doors? It is my firmly held belief that much of what is labeled SF is not only of inferior quality—but is something else all together, as different as chalk is from cheese. Both have their place in the economy but, to carry the image just a bit further, when I am hungry for cheese I do not wish to sink my teeth into chalk.

In order to tackle this problem correctly we are going to have to ask just what science fiction is. I wanted a pragmatic, not a theoretical answer to this question, so I asked the members of the SF class that I teach at San Diego State University. It is a graduate course; most of the class members are practising teachers, a good number of them teach high school SF courses. Each one wrote in one sentence what he thought SF was and we abstracted out all the vital descriptive words. The same words were repeated often enough to show agreement. I have put these together into a description that embodies these words and concepts. It is a little inelegant and rough hewn but I believe it contains the pragmatic description I was after.

Science fiction is that part of literature which deals with the effects of science and technology upon individuals and societies. It extrapolates change into the future.

There are other elements which we can hold aside for the moment; such as the fact that all stories contain a philosophy of some kind, and that SF may be the mythology of the machine age. It is the basic concept of science fiction that is under consideration, because very much of what is now published with the SF label is not science fiction at all. For support in this argument I turn to Anthony Burgess. Burgess is a fine writer, an excellent critic, a friend in the greater field of English letters who does not look down on our particular corner of it. He writes:

"I'd always understood that SF . . . was part of the main literary stream, not a railed-off preserve."

I agree. There are stories in this anthology from the science fiction magazines and the original anthologies. There are also selections from *New Statesman*, *Sierra Club Bulletin* and an author's collection of short stories. SF is where you find it. Some writers do it almost exclusively, others, like Burgess himself, write it when the story to be told demands the use of this idiom. This is what I am for. What I am against is bad fiction of any kind, and particularly bad science fiction. What I dislike as well is clique-ism, the tendency of some writers in this field to spiral in ever tighter circles about each other, writing fiction that may be good but is usually bad, and to claim at the same time that it is science fiction—when it is really nothing of the sort. It contains none of the elements mentioned in the earlier definition. Burgess puts it even more strongly when he writes:

"But there is a whole generation of SF writers—I have had them in my writing courses at American universities—who think they're not concerned with art but something better: truth, or the salutary warning, or the rape of the mind, or something. They scorn what they term artsy-smartsy junk."

Which brings me full circle to my original point; will success spoil science fiction? To which I can answer now—it will if we let it. We can dilute our efforts until the SF stands for "speculative fiction" and the science will have completely gone. And if we do that we are dead for we will have lost the only strength we have. SF can survive sword and sorcery, Star Trek, Tolkien, comic books, almost anything that grows out of the parent stock or is related to it in some way. The one thing that science fiction cannot survive is the unending production of stories and books that have nothing at all to do with the awareness of science and its role today and in the future. I ask the writers to stop writing it, the publishers to stop printing it. I ask the up-and-coming writers to examine their work in the light of this, and to work with the idea that *intent* is not enough. If science fiction does not have *content* as well it condemns itself at the least to frivolity, at worst to destruction. If these writers are in any doubt as to what I am talking about, I ask them to look at the *Graphics* in this anthology, at the admirable cartoon by Lichty. This is a wry joke because it hurts when you laugh. Science fiction is not all fiction any more. What was mad speculation a few years ago is now part of history. This is not a plea for the predictive power of SF, which I feel is overrated. It is instead the suggestion that science fiction writers remember that the human brain is the only new thing in the universe, that this brain can, did and will alter the environment and life in every way. If this awareness is not behind a science fiction story—well, then it is not a science fiction story.

I feel that this present volume reflects that awareness. Here are the stories from the calendar year of 1972 that are both good science fiction *and* good fiction. For some reason the stories in *New Worlds 3* were all copyrighted in 1971, although the book was published and copyrighted in its entirety in 1972. This sort of thing is best ignored; suffice to say that the stories are the best I could discover that were published during this year. There have been no restrictions placed upon me by length or source, and I again thank the publishers for giving me a completely free hand. As always my good and old friend Brian W. Aldiss has scouted the SF sources outside the

United States and discovered many a fine story that I would otherwise have missed. The final choice, as always, has been mine. Once again it has been a good year, and a good time to be alive in science fiction.

HARRY HARRISON

IN THE MATTER OF THE ASSASSIN MEREFIRS

KEN W. PURDY

Here is a chillingly humorous look at a courtroom of the future by the former contributing editor of Playboy *and all-time automobile expert. (His book* Kings of the Road *has been continuously in print since 1952.) It is a pleasure to welcome him back; he last appeared in these pages with "The Dannold Cheque"* in The Year's Best Science Fiction No. 3. *Most unhappily this will be his last appearance; he died in June, 1972.*

The judge enters the courtroom. Think of him as a man of middle age: a hundred and twenty-five or so. Being a judge, he has no name. See him going into the bench. (Nothing in the law is more fascinating than its persistence in looking backward; indeed, is not the law in its entirety based on backward-looking, the search for precedent? So we still call it the bench, although it is only a cube of flexibo big enough for one man, and judges wear around their necks a scrap of black, relic of the robes of ancient times. Such is the nature of things.) So, he enters, he sits, the bench rises soundlessly halfway to the ceiling, he stares down upon us, implacable, merciless, and he speaks.

"The matter before this court," he says, "is the trial of the assassin Merefirs. The gavel has fallen."

The persecutor is Dafton, flat-faced as a door, reedy, impalpable, a century of mediocrity behind him. His assignment is a doom-cry for Merefirs: Dafton draws only certainties, and has for years, since a boy barely sixty, a year out of law school, pinned him to the wall in an easy and insignificant first-degree mopery case. Well, legally insignificant, but alas for poor Dafton, a son of the then Regent was a principal, and Dafton's career was forever blighted. Such is the nature of things.

"If the court will but indulge us," Dafton says, "the state

will briefly review the crime for which the abominable Merefirs is to be put to maceration.

"Azulno, or perhaps I should say, as all who were living on that tragic day know, the Regional Eminence Fallet was, while in the performance of his public duty, namely and to wit, the dedication of the 101st National Euthenic Unit, in this mega, made dead by the assassin Merefirs. Of the commission of the crime, azulno, there is no shred of question: the affidavits of 246,744 actual witnesses have been deposited with this court, and I may say that I myself did see, before the said affidavits were put under seal, a convincing sampling of them. There can be no doubt that they are genuine affidavits in every particular. Further, the Media Communicative Authority has verified that on that day, indeed at the relevant millisecond, 196,593,017 citizens, and a lesser but still weightily significant number of humans, and rather more than a million subhumans, in the categories of slaves, servants, sexers and so on, experienced the tragedy on the telfee. The assassin Merefirs is guilty beyond all question, and it is a mark of the mercy of the present Eminence that the state requires that his punishment be merely the mild one of six-hour maceration. Fibular disintegration would be a more fitting punishment, if I may intrude a personal view, and . . ."

The judge clears his throat, a sound for all the world like the death rattle of a foggus.

"You may intrude nothing, fool," he says. "You should yourself have been macerated decades since. Proceed."

(Here we see the clear thread of modern jurisprudential connection with the ancient Anglo-Saxon law: the judge as impartial arbiter, friend of no one, no one's foe.)

"If it please," Dafton says, "I most humbly agree. The state rests."

The judge speaks.

"We will hear, briefly," he says, "the attorney for the despicable Merefirs."

This is Terravan, the legendary Terravan, savior of lost causes, snatcher from the brink, whose tongue, they say, is gold—and all the rest of him, too. Merefirs, a mere civil servant, could not afford the price of a nod from Terravan, much less a five-minute appointment with him. Terravan has taken the case without fee and out of sheer bravado because no one else in this mega, or any other, would have the temerity. It is a hopeless case, and not only that . . . the assassination of a Regional Eminence? Any other lawyer would well know that if by wild chance he won an acquittal, exsanguination within twenty-four hours would be the very best he could expect. Terravan is beyond all that, being famous, rich, and deeply knowledgeable, as we say, as to where the bodies are buried. Such is the nature of things.

So Terravan rises, a short, heavy, feral-looking man, barely a century old, full of fire and ferocity.

"If it please," he says, "I will not contest the statement of Persecutor, uh, hm-m-m, Persecutor, ah, yes, Dafter, Dafton. My client, the assassin Merefirs, did in fact kill, or make dead, the Eminence Fallett. Of course he did, and with premeditation, with every intention. His sole purpose in attending the dedication was to strike down the Regional Eminence, and he did strike him down.

"But that is not the point, as I shall make clear. I call to witness the assassin Merefirs."

Two men in the ruby-red uniform of warders wheel him in, strapped nude to the witness-stretcher. From the bright life-support box at the head of it the usual wires and tubes lead into him and out of him, serous fluid pump, heart-actuator, oxygen supply, renal filter, waste-exhaust, and so on. When they have him in place at the foot of the bench, they switch the litter to upright, and there he stands, more or less, clamped. The spectators spontaneously applaud, and I must say I myself join in. From head to toe, Merefirs is spectacularly multicolored, and the pattern of the bruises, from the merest blush of pink through mauve and yellow to deep purple, clearly shows, as if he had been signed, the work of the famous chief warder Toddi. Toddi's preliminary witness-beatings are the despair of his competitors, and well they may be. Aesthetics aside, however, Merefirs does not look well. As a human person, he does not look well. He is by no means whole, various parts of him are missing, his head is notably lumpy—he simply does not look well, although I must say I have seen witnesses in much less important cases, matters of mere civic accident, for example, who were worse off. But, to be sure, they had been in hands other than Toddi's. And I knew even before he spoke into the microphone that his voice would be strong and firm. Toddi can spend a day and a night at his work, and yet, the witness will always be able to speak clearly. It's a kind of art, I suppose. But I mustn't digress.

Terravan puts his client through the standard preliminaries, age, birth lab, citizen class, and all that.

"Now then, assassin," he says, "when you made dead the Eminence Fallett, your weapon was not a desiccator, a defbro, a B-kel or any other common killing device, is that true?"

"That is true," Merefirs says.

The judge speaks.

"Terravan," he says, "every idiot in the planetis knows he did not use a common weapon. You are wasting my time. I will remind you—once—that my patience is not unlimited."

"I humbly thank you," Terravan says. "And if no common weapon, assassin, what did you use?"

"I used a crossbow," Merefirs says.

"Describe it."

"The crossbow was a weapon of the ancients on the planet Earth," Merefirs says, "a sophistication of the plain bow, which was a piece of wood—a fibrous material that once grew wild—bent by a cord, throwing a second piece of wood called an arrow. The crossbow came to its full flower in the Sixteenth Century, Earth Reckoning, so there are few who know of it now."

"Why, assassin, did you choose this obscure weapon?"

"Because I could be almost sure that no one would recognize it as a weapon. Therefore, I could freely carry it, and easily approach the Regional Eminence."

"Tell me," Terravan says, "how could you be sure that this primitive device would be effective in your foul purpose?"

"A crossbow of the ancient Earthians," Merefirs says, "would throw an arrow through a thick piece of strong wood and through a man behind it. Also, it would hit an object as small as the palm of a man's hand at a long distance, say a hundred tontas. It seemed in every way suitable for my purpose, and so I built a crossbow on the patterns of the ancients, known to me through study."

The judge interrupts.

"So you admit, wretch, that you read, you studied, as you say, outside the curricula prescribed for Class II citizens?"

"Yes."

Terravan waits for the judge to speak again. He will not.

"So you made ready your weapon, you approached to within twenty-five tontas of the Eminence and you killed him," Terravan says. "Why?"

"Because he was a heretic," Merefirs says.

A gasp, a rustling of whispers runs through the courtroom.

"Animal!" the judge says. "It is not enough that you assassinated the Regional Eminence, you now defame his memory. This trial is over. The sentence imposed by the persecution is now confirmed. The gavel has . . ."

"If the court please!" Terravan shouts. His voice booms through the room. Clever man! And quick! If the judge had pronounced the word "fallen" the trial would in fact have been over, and no appeal would have been possible.

"I most humbly beg the pardon of the court," Terravan says. "I throw myself upon your mercy, O Judge. But I must, in fulfillment of my obligation as defender of this despicable criminal, say to you that the question of the Regent's orthodoxy or the lack of it does in fact go to the heart of the matter, and I pray leave to develop it. I can cite ample precedent."

"Terravan," the judge says, "one day, you will outrage this court past tolerance. You are a proceduralist. Your obsession with the rights of the accused, as against the rights of the persecution, will eventually, and properly, bring you to the macerator."

"I humbly agree with the court," Terravan says, not being an idiot.

"Against my will, and against all reason," the judge says, "I will be generous. You may attempt to cite precedent."

"I thank you. I cite the case of State versus Hamill, 1186/6V, Archive 29, Volume 617, Page 113, in which the court found that the clearly heretical belief of the defendant in monogamous male-female relationship bore directly upon his crime, even though that crime was most heinous, being in fact arglebub in the first degree."

"You reach a long way for your precedent, Terravan," the judge says. "State versus Hamill . . . that was in the year 2125. You cite ancient history."

"True, O Judge," Terravan says. "But—you will forgive my making an absurdly obvious observation to so learned a jurist as yourself—for the record I must point out that the verdict of the court in State versus Hamill was never overturned, and no counterprecedent was ever established."

"An oversight," the judge says. "However, what you say is true enough. You may proceed. Take heed, however. You have been warned."

"I humbly thank you, O Judge," Terravan says. "Tell me, assassin," he goes on, "in what way did you conceive the Eminence to be heretical?"

Merefirs clears his throat. "I appear to be dying," he says. "Perhaps if the oxygen level could be . . ."

One of the warders fiddles with the life-support system.

"Thank you," Merefirs says. "To answer the question, when the Regional Eminence Fallett came to office he did, azulno, appoint me his Primary Postilion, and in this capacity I was privy to his communication core. On the twelfth day of Hobe, in this subera, I learned of his heresy. I was making a routine run-down of the core when I heard the voice of the Eminence—and, I may say, in synch with his image—dictating what was clearly an entry in his private journal. Obviously he had forgotten to null the fansponder. I was shocked by what I heard. I was stunned. I reran the core, and I committed the entry to memory."

"Please repeat it," Terravan says.

"The Eminence said: 'Today I took food with that moron Javil. It was all I could do to appear to eat, realizing that this specimen of evolutionary disaster is Secretary to the Planetary Council. He went on at great length about the Venusian war. He wants me, in my subcapacity as Obliterative Authority, to support his resolution to throw Venus out of orbit. This is flaming nonsense: we will lose at least a million useful slaves. And, truly vomitous, I will of course have to go along with him, and he knows it.' "

"That is the end of the quotation?" Terravan asks.

"Yes."

"You were naturally horrified to find that your superior, a trusted official, would entertain, much less record, such evil concepts?"

The dough-faced Dafton rises. "I suggest to the court," he says, "that the learned Terravan is coaching his witness."

"True," the judge says. "Furthermore, I warn you, Terravan, do not outrage this court by attempting to present your bestial client in the role of savior of the state, armed in righteous wrath. I warn you!"

"Not at all," Terravan, says, "but I will point out that the Eminence did in fact support the Javil resolution, and that the planet Venus, azulno, was in fact deorbitized. Therefore, the Eminence's private reservations did constitute heresy and he was in fact a heretic."

"Terravan," the judge says, "this has nothing to do with the case before us. Your client, a loathsome sneak who abused his place of privilege by memorizing his superior's journal entries, heretical or not, still acted illegally in assassinating the Eminence. Your point is totally irrelevant."

"I beg to disagree, O Judge," Terravan says. "I will cite further precedent. In the year 1139, Earth Reckoning, the Second Lateran Council, a duly authorized, although secular, governing body of the time, formally outlawed the crossbow as a weapon, forbidding its use except—and this goes to the heart of the matter—except against the infidel. The term 'infidel' was understood to mean one who did not profess the accepted faith, in this case Christianity, one of the ancient religions. To be classified an infidel one did not need to reject the entire faith in its every tenet: the rejection of the smallest part of it would suffice. Clearly, therefore, an infidel was a heretic. And clearly the Eminence Fallett, in rejecting the official policy of this planetis, the Venusian deorbitizing, was heretical."

"And what of it?" the judge says. "If the Eminence was a heretic, he should have been brought to trial and duly macerated in the regular way. All this has nothing to do with the assassin Merefirs."

"Ah, but it does," Terravan says. "For, you see, if the weapon my despicable client used was one that might legally be used upon a heretic, then, in using it, he committed no illegal act!"

There is no sound in the courtroom. No one draws breath. The audacity of it! The sheer brilliance of the man! And now, seeing the balance tip, he presses on.

"I can cite further precedent," he says. "While the crossbow passed from general use as a military weapon after the Battle of Marignano, in 1515, E.R., it persisted as a hunting and target weapon, on Earth, well into the Twenty-first Century. And in the Twentieth Century, in one of the American principalities, called Usa, it was again outlawed, this time as a hunting weapon. In other words, it was forbidden to be used against animals, but, most significantly, not specifically forbidden to be used against men. I argue that this further strengthens my contention that, in killing the Eminence Fallett with a crossbow, the assassin Merefirs did not act illegally."

Dafton comes to his feet. "I too have studied the precedents," he says, "and I would point out to Terravan that it is not wholly true that the principality of Usa forbade the use of the crossbow against animals. In its final form, just before World War III, Usa consisted of fifty-two individual subdivisions, called states, and only fifty-one of them forbade the crossbow."

He sits, looking desperately pleased with himself.

The judge looks at him with obvious loathing. "You are a formidable antagonist in a court of law, Dafton," he says. "Terravan is no doubt terrified. But, nevertheless, perhaps he will be able to go on. You have more to say, Terravan?"

"I rest my case, O Judge," Terravan says.

"The court finds as follows," the judge says. "The Regional Eminence Fallett was a heretic. The assassin Merefirs killed him. But by his choice of weapon, Merefirs, standing upon the precedents cited by his counsel, is found not guilty of assassination, although he did assassinate. So much for that.

"Azulno, the common statutes of the planetis forbid disclosure by a civic servant of material made known to him in the course of his duty. To breach this statute is, upon the arguments and precedents here cited by Terravan, clearly heretical. Thus, Merefirs is a heretic. He should therefore be indicted upon that charge, tried and macerated. However, in the light of what we have learned today . . . Warder, do you understand the workings of this weapon, this crossbow?"

"Me, O Judge?" the bigger of the two warders says.

"You, idiot!" the judge says.

"Yes, O Judge, in a way I do understand how the thing works."

"Good. You may demonstrate," the judge says.

The warder takes the crossbow from the exhibition rack. He stands it on the floor, puts his right foot into the stirrup and his hands on the string.

"If it please the court," Merefirs says, "may I speak? The warder should put one hand on each side of the string, not both hands on the one side."

The warder changes his grip, pulls up with all strength until the string falls into its notch.

"Now," Merefirs says, "you lay the arrow—it is properly called a bolt, or a quarrel—into the groove, the blunt end tight against the string."

The warder does that.

"Stand across the room," the judge says, "and let us see if you can strike the assassin Merefirs in the middle of his chest. Have no fear. As Terravan has so convincingly proved to us, you will be committing no crime."

The warder lifts the crossbow, peers down the length of it. Suddenly, almost without a sound, the arrow, short and thick as your thumb, flies across the room, nearly faster than the eye can follow, and buries itself Thump! in Merefirs' gaudy chest. His chin drops. The violet light on the life-support box winks out. A yellow light comes on briefly, and then, the red. The second warder reaches up and flicks off the switches.

"Well done, Warder," the judge says. "Terravan, I congratulate you. You conducted a brilliant and original defense most successfully. Indeed, there is the mark of your success." He nods toward the body of the assassin Merefirs, still upright, a streak of blood leaking out of the black hole where the arrow has gone. "The gavel has fallen."

The bench drops silently to the floor. The judge stands.

"Terravan," he says, "let us take food together."

The warders trundle Merefirs down the aisle under the admiring eyes of the spectators. The miserable Dafton futilely shuffles his papers. The judge and Terravan go off arm in arm, happy as babes. Such is the nature of things.

AS FOR OUR FATAL CONTINUITY . . .

BRIAN W. ALDISS

Very few science fiction stories deal with the arts; fewer still deal with them well. Brian Aldiss is an enthusiastic and knowledgeable collector of watercolor paintings, and an amateur in this medium, as well as that of the written word. He utilizes both talents in this brief chronicle of another artist, one born just this year.

DAYLING, Orton Gausset (1972–1999).

In a brief transmission, scant justice can be done to this great and still controversial artist. The accompanying holograms will convey Dayling's outstanding qualities better than words.

Illusion and dissolution mark the stamp of his mind. During the last period of his life, Dayling believed himself to be alone in the world, and to have been appointed custodian of the city of Singapore, which he spoke of as one of the world's deserted cities on which the tide was fast encroaching.

His mother was the noted biophysicist, Mary May Dayling. His father was killed in a traffic accident on the day of his birth. Perhaps it was this ill chance, coupled with a peculiar cast of mind, that caused him to become obsessed with the last words of dying men. He came to them, as he came to art and love, precociously early; last words form the titles of all his creations. Once he had access to his mother's art-computer terminal at the age of five, creation seems to have been a continuous process with him, at least until the lost years of his middle period.

His first great work,

THE SUN, MY DEAR, THE SUN IS GOD,

dates from 1979. Its contrapuntal sets of interwoven structures culminating in an attenuated parallelism is a gesture towards representation which seldom recurs—Dayling's is the art of a world beyond mundane perception. Although the work is not well integrated, its daring and light remain attractive and, in its overall spiral movement, it stands as a fitting statement on the painter Turner, whose last words contribute the title and whose life inspired the young Dayling.

MORE LIGHT, MORE LIGHT

Goethe's last words, and related schematically to the item above. More ambitious, less intense, already showing a fine awareness for the new language Dayling was creating. It points its way gropingly towards

GIVE DAYROLLES A CHAIR,

indisputably an early masterpiece, with its mobile non-repeating series of peripheral lights and the first use of that central darkness—speaking of radiance as well as gloom—which later becomes a feature of Dayling's work. No reference here to the external world, unless it be to the basic formal structures of physical phenomena themselves. A certain delicacy about the entire composition reminds us that the words were spoken by the dying Lord Chesterfield.

I HAVE BEEN A MOST UNCONSCIONABLE TIME A-DYING

This work is also known as *Open the Curtains that I May Once More See Daylight*, apparently through some confusion over what the last words of King Charles II actually were. The former title is certainly to be preferred, since this work marks the end of the first stage of Dayling's career; like the three works preceding, it has as its theme light, and the rioting radials suggest a variety of diffusions of light. From now on, the works become more vigorous and coarser, as Dayling masters his life and his medium, beginning with the almost Rabelaisian account of

I COULD DO WITH ONE OF BELLAMY'S MEAT PIES

said to be the last words of one of England's great prime ministers, William Pitt the Younger. Dayling's amazing tumescent forms enter for the first time, as yet not dominant, but certainly in the ascendant. This is a large work, almost the size of the Houses of Parliament, with which it has sometimes jocularly been compared, and for durability Dayling and the computer used daylite, a plastic of their own devising with a semi-fluid core. With daylite, the famous "molten look" was developed, so that in some of the later works in this series, such as the

I WISH THE WHOLE HUMAN RACE HAD ONE NECK AND I HAD MY HANDS AROUND IT,
based on the words of the mass-murderer Carl Panzram, the
IF THIS IS LIFE, ROLL ON GERM WARFARE,
of the Scottish Patriot McGuffie, and the
OF COURSE THE CONFOUNDED GOAT WAS AN EXAGGERATION
of the painter Holman Hunt, one cannot tell whether the forms emerge from obscurity and formlessness or are being pressed back into obscurity and formlessness. Perhaps it is because of this sense of what one critic, André Prederast, has called "cellular oppression" that Dayling has been spoken of as a latter-day Rodin; but Rodin dominated his sculpture; the tentative statement of
AS TO WHICH END OF THE BED IS WHICH . . . would be beyond him. Dayling's morbid preoccupation with death and his sense of humour combined, are complementary, and force him to work always on the verge of disintegration, at the point at which being becomes non-being. Although his approach could scarcely be called scientific, the extent to which he was conversant with current scientific theory is generally apparent, not least in *As to Which End of the Bed is Which . . .*, where the strange tumescent forms of *Bellamy's Meat Pies* have transformed themselves into clouds of virus, life and non-life, fitting symbols of this terminal art.

No artist's art stands apart from his life. At this period, Dayling's love-group broke dramatically apart. The three males and two females who comprised the group had lived in equipoise for some eight years. Dayling suddenly found himself alone.

Now follow the somewhat mysterious years of wandering, when little is known of Dayling's life beyond the facts that he subjected himself to the hallucinatory drug DXB and underwent five years in suspended animation in a clinic in Canton. For the rest, he appeared not to have gone near a computer terminal. His only work from these lost years* is
I'VE HAD EIGHTEEN STRAIGHT WHISKIES—I THINK THAT'S THE RECORD
registered from a monastery in the Sanjak in Jugoslavia.

*The once accepted *Madame, Please Remove Your Lipstick, I can Hardly Hear You* is now known to be a forgery.

Based on the last words of the Welsh poet Dylan Thomas, this small block shows no development and generally marks a return to the more formal tone of *Give Dayrolles a Chair*.

Only in 1995 did Dayling emerge again; he had but four years to live. He was in his twenty-third year and had had both legs and one arm amputated, the better, he said, to concentrate on his art. He settled in Bombay, under the firm impression that it was Singapore. Despite such delusions, his mind was creatively clear enough, and he set to again wholeheartedly, living in a deserted government office, the complete solitary, though in an over-populated city, seen only when he made an occasional midnight march on cybolegs to stare out over the sea, which he believed to be moving in over the land.

His method of work was now more brutal than before. He worked on the daylite himself, leaving the computer to copy the results, to change and eradicate according to open programming. Thus, he was working not with light but with the material itself—a reversion in technique, perhaps, but one which yielded its own unique results. There may always be an area of discussion centring on these last desperate works. Was this reversion a sign of Dayling's failure to adjust to himself and his times? Or is the reversion merely to be regarded as a substitution, remembering that Dayling is the great transition figure, the last major artist spanning the days of the biological revolution, the last major artist to work in inorganic material?

However we answer such questions, there is no disputing the maimed vigour of Dayling's output in his final years: *One World at a Time; On the Whole, I'd Rather Be in Philadelphia; Make My Skin Into Drumheads for the Bohemian Cause;* and *As for Our Fatal Continuity* . . . These are small works, small, dense, and ruinous. All of them speak of fatal discontinuities. All of them have formed the basis since for countless experiments into the new media of semi-sentience.

It may be, as Torner Mallard has claimed, that these final works of Dayling's mark the demise of a too-long sustained system of aesthetics going back as far as Classical Greece, and the beginning of a new and more biologically based structure; certainly we can see that, in the Dadaist titles, as well as in the works themselves, Dayling was undergoing a pre-postmodernist purgation of outworn attitudes, and carrying art forward from the aesthetic arena of balance and proportion to the knife-edge between existence and non-existence.

In his reckless sweeping away of all the inessential props of life, Dayling—by which of course we mean Dayling-and-art-computer—takes the bone-bare universe of Samuel Beckett a stage further; humour and death contemplate each other across a tumbled void. Only the grin of the Cheshire Cat is left, fading above Valhalla.

From *Sculpting Your Own Semi-Sentients:*
A Primer for Boys and Girls. By Gutrud
Slayne Laboratories.

THE OLD FOLKS

JAMES E. GUNN

Past president of the Science Fiction Writers of America, present teacher of SF at the University of Kansas—where he is also preparing a series of fascinating films to be used in teaching science fiction—James Gunn is a man of many parts. But he is first of all a powerful writer as can be seen in this glimpse of an American retirement paradise. Paradise?

They had been traveling in the dusty car all day, the last few miles in the heat of the Florida summer. Not far behind were the Sunshine State Parkway, Orange Grove, and Winter Hope, but according to the road map the end of the trip was near.

John almost missed the sign that said, "Sunset Acres, Next Right," but the red Volkswagen slowed and turned and slowed again. Now another sign marked the beginning of the town proper: SUNSET ACRES, Restricted Senior Citizens, Minimum Age—65, Maximum Speed—20.

As the car passed the sign, the whine of the tires announced that the pavement had changed from concrete to brick.

Johnny bounced in the back seat, mingling the squeak of the springs with the music of the tires, and shouted above the engine's protest at second gear, "Mommy—Daddy, are we there yet? Are we there?"

His mother turned to look at him. The wind from the open window whipped her short hair. She smiled. "Soon now," she said. Her voice was excited, too.

They passed through a residential section where the white frame houses with their sharp roofs sat well back from the street, and the velvet lawns reached from red-brick sidewalks to broad porches that spread like skirts around two or three sides of the houses.

At each intersection the streets dipped to channel the rain water and to enforce the speed limit to 20 m.p.h. or slower. The names of the streets were chiseled into the curbs, and the incisions were painted black: Osage, Cottonwood, Antelope, Meadowlark, Prairie. . . .

The Volkswagen hummed along the brick streets, alone. The streets were empty, and so, it seemed, were the houses; the white-curtained windows stared senilely into the Florida sun, and the swings on the porches creaked in the Florida breeze, but the architecture and the town were all Kansas—and the Kansas of fifty years ago, at that.

Then they reached the square, and John pulled the car to a stop alongside the curb. Here was the center of town—a block of greensward edged with beds of pansies and petunias and geraniums. In the center of the square was a massive, two-story, red-brick building. A square tower reached even taller. The tower had a big clock set into its face. The heavy, black hands pointed at 3:32.

Stone steps marched up the front of the building toward oak doors twice the height of a man. Around the edges of the buildings were iron benches painted white. On the benches the old men sat in the sun, their eyes shut, their hands folded across canes.

From somewhere behind the brick building came the sound of a brass band—the full, rich mixture of trumpet and trombone and sousaphone, of tuba and tympani and big, bass drum.

Unexpectedly, as they sat in the car looking at the scene out of another era and another land, a tall black shape rolled silently past them. John turned his head quickly to look at it. A thin cab in the middle sloped toward spoked wheels at each end, like the front ends of two cars stuck together. An old woman in a wide-brimmed hat sat upright beside the driver. From her high window she frowned at the little foreign car, and then her vehicle passed down the street.

"That was an old electric!" John said. "I didn't know they were making them again."

From the back seat Johnny said, "When are we going to get to Grammy's?"

"Soon," his mother said. "If you're going to ask the way to Buffalo Street, you'd better ask," she said to John. "It's too hot to sit here in the car."

John opened the door and extracted himself from the damp socket of the bucket seat. He stood for a moment beside the baked metal of the car and looked up each side of the street. The oomp-pah-pah of the band was louder now and the yeasty smell of baking bread dilated his nostrils, but the whole scene struck him as unreal somehow, as if this all were a stage setting and a man could walk behind the buildings and find that the backs were unpainted canvas and raw wood.

"Well?" Sally said.

John shook his head and walked around the front of the car. The first store sold hardware. In the small front window were crowbars and wooden-handled claw hammers and three kegs of blue nails; one of the kegs had a metal scoop stuck into the nails at the top. In one corner of the window was a hand mower, its handles varnished wood, its metal wheels and reel blue, except where the spokes had been touched with red and yellow paint and the curved reel had been sharpened to a silver line.

The interior of the store was dark; John could not tell whether anyone was inside.

Next to it was "Tyler's General Store," and John stepped inside onto sawdust. Before his eyes adjusted from the Sunshine State's proudest asset, he smelled the pungent sawdust. The odor was mingled with others—the vinegar and spice of pickles and the ripeness of cheese and a sweet-sour smell that he could not identify.

Into his returning vision the faces swam first—the pale faces of the old people, framed in white hair, relieved from the anonymity of age only by the way in which bushy eyebrows sprouted or a mustache was trimmed or wrinkles carved the face. Then he saw the rest of the store and the old people. Some of them were sitting in scarred oak chairs with rounded backs near a black, potbellied stove. The room was cool; after a moment John realized that the stove was producing a cold breeze.

One old man with a drooping white mustache was leaning over from the barrel he sat on to cut a slice of cheese from the big wheel on the counter. A tall man with an apron over his shirt and trousers and his shirt sleeves hitched up with rubber bands came from behind the counter, moving his bald head with practiced ease among the dangling sausages.

"Son," he said, "I reckon you lost your way. Made the wrong turn off the highway, I warrant. Heading for Winter Hope or beyond and mistook yourself. You just head back out how you come in and——"

"Is this Sunset Acres?" John said.

The old man with the yellow slice of cheese in his hand said in a thin voice, "Yep. No use thinking you can stay, though. Thirty-five or forty years too soon. That's what!" His sudden laughter came out in a cackle.

The others joined in, like a superannuated Greek chorus, "Can't stay!"

"I'm looking for Buffalo Street," John said. "We're going to visit the Plummers." He paused and then added, "They're my wife's parents."

The storekeeper tucked his thumbs into the straps of his apron. "That's different. Everybody knows the Plummers. Three blocks north of the square. Can't miss it."

"Thank you," John said, nodding, and backed into the sunshine.

The interrupted murmur of conversation began again, broken briefly by laughter.

"Three blocks north of the square," he said as he inserted himself back in the car.

He started the motor, shifted into first, and turned the corner. As he passed the general store he thought he saw white faces peering out of the darkness, but they might have been feather pillows hanging in the window.

In front of the town hall an old man jerked in his sleep as the car passed. Another opened his eyes and frowned. A third shook his cane in their general direction. Beyond, a thin woman in a lavender shawl was holding an old man by the shoulder as if to tell him that she was done with the shopping and it was time to go home.

"John, look!" Sally said, pointing out the window beside her.

To their right was an ice-cream parlor. Metal chairs and round tables with thin, wire legs were set in front of the store under a yellow awning. At one of the tables sat an elderly couple. The man sat straight in his chair like an army officer, his hair iron-gray and neatly parted, his eyebrows thick. He was keeping time to the music of the band with the cane in his right hand. His left hand held the hand of a little old woman in a black dress, who gazed at him as she sipped from the soda in front of her.

The music was louder here. Just to the north of the town hall, they could see now, was a bandstand with a conical roof. On the bandstand sat a half a dozen old men in uniforms, playing instruments. Another man in uniform stood in front of them, waving a baton. It was a moment before John realized what was wrong with the scene. The music was louder and richer than the half-dozen musicians could have produced.

But it was Johnny who pointed out the tape recorder beside the bandstand, "Just like Daddy's."

It turned out that Buffalo Street was not three blocks north of the square but three blocks south.

The aging process had been kind to Mrs. Henry Plummer. She was a small woman, and the retreating years had left their detritus of fat, but the extra weight seemed no burden on her small bones and the cushioning beneath the skin kept it plump and unwrinkled. Her youthful complexion seemed strangely at odds with her blue-white curls. Her eyes, though, were unmistakably old. They were faded like a blue gingham dress.

They looked at Sally now, John thought, as if to say, "What I have seen you through, my dear, the colic and the boys, the measles and the mumps and the chickenpox and the boys, the frozen fingers and the skinned knees and the boys, the parties and the late hours and the boys. . . . And now you come again to me, bringing this larger, distant boy that I do not like very much, who has taken you from me and treated you with crude familiarity, and you ask me to call him by his first name and consider him one of the family. It's too much."

When she spoke her voice was surprisingly small. "Henry," she said, a little girl in an old body, "don't stand there talking all day. Take in the bags! These children must be starved to death!"

Henry Plummer had grown thinner as his wife had filled out, as if she had grown fat at his expense. Plummer had been a junior executive, long after he had passed in age most of the senior executives, in a firm that manufactured games and toys, but a small inheritance and cautious investments in municipal bonds and life insurance had made possible his comfortable retirement.

He could not shake the habits of a lifetime; his face bore the wry expression of a man who expects the worst and receives it. He said little and when he spoke it was usually to protest. "Well, I guess I'm not the one holding them up," he said, but he stooped for the bags.

John moved quickly to reach the bags first. "I'll get them, Dad," he said. The word "Dad" came out as if it were fitted with rusty hooks. He had never known what to call Henry Plummer. His own father had died when he was a small child, and his mother had died when he was in college; but he could not find in himself any filial affection for Plummer. He disliked the coyness of "Dad," but it was better than the stiffness of "Mr. Plummer" or the false camaraderie of "Henry."

With Mrs. Plummer the problem had not been so great. John recalled a joke from the book he had edited recently for the paperback publishing firm that employed him. "For the first year I said, 'Hey, you!' and then I called her 'Grandma.'"

He straightened with the scuffed suitcases, looking helplessly at Sally for a moment and then apologetically at Plummer. "I guess you've carried your share of luggage already."

"He's perfectly fit," Mrs. Plummer said.

Sally looked only at Johnny. Sally was small and dark-haired and pretty, and John loved her and her whims—"a whim of iron," they called her firm conviction that she knew the right thing to do at any time, in any situation—but when she was around her mother John saw reflected in her behavior all the traits that he found irritating in the old woman. Sometime, perhaps, she would even be plump like her mother, but now it did not seem likely. She ran after Johnny fourteen hours a day.

She held the hand of her four-year-old, her face flushed, her eyes bright with pride. "I guess you see how he's grown, Mother. Ten pounds since you saw him last Christmas. And three inches taller. Give your grandmother a kiss, Johnny. A big kiss for Granny. He's been talking all the way from New

York about coming to visit Grammy—and Granddad, too, of course. I can't imagine what makes him act so shy now. Usually he isn't. Not even with strangers. Give Grammy a great big kiss."

"Well," Mrs. Plummer said, "you must be starved. Come on in. I've got a ham on the stove, and we'll have sandwiches and coffee. And, Johnny, I've got something for you. A box of chocolates, all your own."

"Oh, Mother!" Sally said. "Not just before lunch. He won't eat a bite."

Johnny jumped up and down. He pulled his hand free from his mother's and ran to Mrs. Plummer. "Candy! Candy!" he shouted. He gave Mrs. Plummer a big, wet kiss.

John stood at the living room window listening to the whisper of the air conditioning and looking out at the Florida evening. He could see Johnny playing in the pile of sand his thoughtful grandparents had had dumped in the back yard. It had been a relief to be alone with his wife, but now the heavy silence of disagreement hung in the air between them. He had wanted to leave, to return to New York, and she would not even consider the possibility.

He had massed all his arguments, all his uneasiness, about this strange, nightmarish town, about how he felt unwanted, about how it disliked them, and Sally had found his words first amusing and then disagreeable. For her Sunset Acres was an arcadia for the aged. Her reaction was strongly influenced by that glimpse of the old couple at the ice-cream parlor.

John had always found in her a kind of Walt Disney sentimentality, but it had never disturbed him before. He turned and made one last effort. "Besides, your parents don't even want us here. We've been here only a couple of hours and already they've left us to go to some meeting."

"It's their monthly town hall meeting," Sally said. "They have an obligation to attend. It's part of their self-government or something."

"Oh, hell," John said, turning back to the window. He looked from left to right and back again. "Johnny's gone."

He ran to the back door and fumbled with it for a moment. Then it opened, and he was in the back yard. After the sterile chill of the house, the air outside seemed ripe with warm black earth and green things springing through the soil. The sandpile was empty; there was no place for the boy to hide among the colorful Florida shrubs which hid the back yard of the house behind and had colorful names he could never remember.

John ran around the corner of the house. He reached the porch just as Sally came through the front door.

"There he is," Sally cried out.

"Johnny!" John shouted.

The four-year-old had started across the street. He turned and looked back at them. "Grammy," he said.

John heard him clearly.

The car slipped into the scene like a shadow, silent, unsuspected. John saw it out of the corner of his eye. Later he thought that it must have turned the nearby corner, or perhaps it came out of a driveway. In the moment before the accident, he saw that the old woman in the wide-brimmed hat was driving the car herself. He saw her head turn toward Johnny, and he saw the upright electric turn sharply toward the child.

The front fender hit Johnny and threw him toward the sidewalk. John looked incredulously at the old woman. She smiled at him, and then the car was gone down the street.

"Johnny!" Sally screamed. Already she was in the street the boy's head cradled in her lap. She hugged him and then pushed him away to look blindly into his face and then hugged him again, rocking him in her arms, crying.

John found himself beside her, kneeling. He pried the boy away from her. Johnny's eyes were closed. His face was pale, but John couldn't find any blood. He lifted the boy's eyelids. The pupils seemed dilated. Johnny did not stir.

"What's the matter with him?" Sally screamed at John. "He's going to die, isn't he?"

"I don't know. Let me think! Let's get him into the house."

"You aren't supposed to move people who've been in an accident!"

"We can't leave him here to be run over by someone else."

John picked up his son gently and walked to the house. He lowered the boy onto the quilt in the front bedroom and looked down at him for a moment. The boy was breathing raggedly. He moaned. His hand twitched. "I've got to get a doctor," John said. "Where's the telephone?"

Sally stared at him as if she hadn't heard. John turned away and looked in the living room. An antique apparatus on a wooden frame was attached to one wall. He picked up the receiver and cranked the handle vigorously. "Hello!" he said. "Hello!" No answer.

He returned to the bedroom. Sally was still standing beside the bed. "What a lousy town!" he said. "No telephone service!" Sally looked at him. She blinked.

"I'll have to go to town," John said. "You stay with Johnny. Keep him warm. Put cold compresses on his head." They might not help Johnny, he thought, but they would keep Sally quiet.

She nodded and headed toward the bathroom.

When he got to the car, it refused to start. After a few futile attempts, he gave up, knowing he had flooded the motor. He ran back to the house. Sally looked up at him, calmer now that her hands were busy.

"I'm going to run," he told her. "I might see that woman and be unable to resist the impulse to smash into her."

"Don't talk crazy," Sally said. "It was just an accident."

"It was no accident," John said. "I'll be back with a doctor as soon as I can find one."

John ran down the brick sidewalks until his throat burned and then walked for a few steps before breaking once more into a run. By then the square was in sight. The sun had plunged into the Gulf of Mexico, and the town was filled with silence and shadows. The storefronts were dark. There was no light anywhere in the square.

The first store was a butcher shop. Hams hung in the windows, and plucked chickens, naked and scrawny, dangled by cords around their yellow feet. John thought he smelled sawdust and blood. He remembered Johnny and felt sick.

Next was a clothing store with two wide windows under the name "Emporium." In the windows were stiff, waxen dummies in black suits and high, starched collars; in lace and parasols. Then came a narrow door; on its window were printed the words, "Saunders and Jones, Attorneys at Law." The window framed dark steps.

Beside it was a print shop—piles of paper pads in the window, white, yellow, pink, blue; reams of paper in dusty wrappers; faded invitations and personal cards; and behind them the lurking shapes of printing presses and racks of type.

John passed a narrow bookstore with books stacked high in the window and ranged in ranks into the darkness. Then came a restaurant; a light in the back revealed scattered tables with checkered cloths. He pounded at the door, making a shocking racket in the silence of the square, but no one came.

Kittycorner across the street, he saw the place and recognized it by the tall, intricately shaped bottles of colored water in the window and the fancy jar hanging from chains. He ran across the brick street and beat on the door with his fist. There was no response. He kicked it, but the drug store remained silent and dark. Only the echoes answered his summons, and they soon died away.

Next to the drug store was another dark door. The words printed across the window in it said, "Joseph M. Bronson, M.D." And underneath, "Geriatrics Only."

John knocked, sure it was useless, wondering, "Why is the town locked up? Where is everybody?" And then he remembered the meeting. That's where everyone was, at the meeting the Plummers couldn't miss. No one could miss the meeting. Everyone had to be there, apparently, even the telephone operator. But where was it being held?

Of course. Where else would a town meeting be held? In the town hall.

He ran across the street once more and up the wide steps. He pulled open one of the heavy doors and stepped into a hall with tall ceilings. Stairways led up on either side, but light came through a pair of doors ahead. He heard a babble of voices. John walked toward the doors, feeling the slick oak floors under his feet, smelling the public toilet odors of old urine and disinfectant.

He stopped for a moment at the doors to peer between them, hoping to see the Plummers, hoping they were close enough to signal without disturbing the others. The old people would be startled if he burst in among them. There would be confusion and explanations, accusations perhaps. He needed a doctor, not an argument.

The room was filled with wooden folding chairs placed neatly in rows, with a wide aisle in the middle and a narrower one on either side. From the backs of the chairs hung shawls and canes. The room had for John the unreal quality of an etching, perhaps because all the backs of the heads that he saw were silver and gray, here and there accented with tints of blue or green.

At the front of the room was a walnut rostrum on a broad platform. Behind the rostrum stood the old man Sally had pointed out in the ice-cream parlor. He stood as straight as he had sat.

The room buzzed as if it had a voice of its own, and the voice rose and fell, faded and returned, the way it does in a dream. One should be able to understand it, one had to understand it, but one couldn't quite make out the words.

The old man banged on the rostrum with a wooden gavel; the gavel had a small silver plate attached to its head. "Everyone will have his chance to be heard," he said. It was like an order. The buzz faded away. "Meanwhile we will speak one at a time, and in a proper manner, first being recognized by the chair.

"Just one moment, Mr. Samuelson.

"For many years the public press has allowed its columns to bleed over the voting age. 'If a boy of eighteen is old enough to die for his country, he is old enough to vote for its legislators,' the sentimentalists have written.

"Nonsense. It takes no intelligence to die. Any idiot can do it. Surviving takes brains. Men of eighteen aren't even old enough to take orders properly, and until a man can take orders he can't give them.

"Mrs. Richards, I have the floor. When I have finished I will recognize each of you in turn."

John started to push through the doors and announce the emergency to the entire group, but something about the stillness of the audience paralyzed his decision. He stood there, his hand on the door, his eyes searching for the Plummers.

"Let me finish," the old man at the rostrum said. "Only when a man has attained true maturity—fifty is the earliest date for the start of this time of life—does he begin to identify the important things in life. At this age, the realization comes to him, if it ever comes, that the individual has the right to protect and preserve the property that he has accumulated by his own hard work, and, in the protection of this right, the state stands between the individual and mob rule in Washington. Upon these eternal values we take our stand: the individual, his property, and state's rights. Else our civilization, and everything in it of value, will perish."

The light faded from his eyes, and the gavel which had been raised in his hand like a saber sank to the rostrum. "Mr. Samuelson."

In the front of the room a man stood up. He was small and bald except for two small tufts of hair above his ears. "I have heard what you said, and I understand what you said because you said it before. It is all very well to talk of the rights of the individual to protect his property, but how can he protect his property when the government taxes and taxes and taxes—state governments as well as Washington? I say, 'Let the government give us four exemptions instead of two.' "

A cracked voice in the back of the room said, "Let them cut out taxes altogether for senior citizens!"

"Yes!"

"No!"

A small, thin woman got up in the middle of the audience. "Four hundred dollars a month for every man and woman over sixty-five!" she said flatly. "Why shouldn't we have it? Didn't we build this country? Let the government give us back a little of what they have taken away. Besides, think of the money it would put into circulation."

"You have not been recognized, Mrs. Richards," the Chairman said, "and I declare you out of order and the Townsendites as well. What you are advocating is socialism, more government not less."

"Reds!" someone shouted. "Commies!" said someone else. "That's not true!" said a woman near the door. "It's only fair," shouted an old man, nodding vigorously. Canes and crutches were waved in the air, a hundred Excaliburs and no Arthur. John glanced behind him to see if the way was clear for retreat in case real violence broke out.

"Sally!" he exclaimed, discovering her behind him. "What are you doing here! Where's Johnny?"

"He's in the car. He woke up. He seemed all right. I thought I'd better find you. Then we'd be closer to the doctor. I looked all over. What are you doing here?"

John rubbed his forehead. "I don't know. I was looking for a doctor. Something's going on here. I don't know what it is, but I don't like it."

"What's going on?"

Sally tried to push past him, but John grabbed her arm. "Don't go in there!"

The Chairman's gavel finally brought order out of confusion. "We are senior citizens, not young hoodlums!" he admonished them. "We can disagree without forgetting our dignity and our common interests, Mrs. Johnson."

A woman stood up at the right beside one of the tall windows that now framed the night. She was a stout woman with gray hair pulled back into a bun. "It seems to me, Colonel, that we are getting far from the subject of this meeting—indeed, the subject of all our meetings—and that is what we are going to do about the young people who are taking over everything and pushing us out. As many of you know, I have no prejudices about young people. Some of my best friends are young people, and, although I cannot name my children among them, for they are ingrates, I bear my son and my two daughters no ill will."

She paused for a deep breath. "We must not let the young people get the upper hand. We must find ways of insuring that we get from them the proper respect for our age and our experience. The best way to do this, I believe, is to keep them in suspense about the property—the one thing about us they still value—how much there is and what will become of it. Myself, I pretend that there is at least two or three times as much. When I am visiting one of them, I leave my check book lying carelessly about—the one that has the very large and false balance. And I let them overhear me make an appointment to see a lawyer. What do I have to see a lawyer about, they think, except my will?

"Actually I have written my will once and for all, leaving my property to the Good Samaritan Rest Home for the Aged, and I do not intend to change it. But I worry that some clever young lawyer will find a way to break the will. They're always doing that when you disinherit someone."

"Mrs. Johnson," the Colonel said, "you have a whole town full of friends who will testify that you always have been in full possession of your faculties, if it ever should come to that, God forbid! Mrs. Fredericks?"

"Nasty old woman," Sally muttered. "Where are Mother and Father? I don't see them. I don't think they're here at all."

"Sh-h-h!"

"I'm leaving my money to my cat," said a bent old woman with a hearing aid in her ear. "I'm just sorry I won't get to see their faces."

The Colonel smiled at her as he nodded her back to her seat at the left front. Then he recognized a man sitting in the front row. "Mr. Saunders."

The man who arose was short, straight, and precise. "I would like to remind these ladies of the services of our legal aid department. We have had good luck in constructing un-unbreakable legal documents. A word of caution, however—the more far-fetched the legatee, though to be sure the more satisfying, the more likely the breaking of the will. There is only one certain way to prevent property from falling into the hands of those who have neither worked for it nor merited it—and that is to spend it.

"Personally, I am determined to spend on the good life every cent that I accumulated in a long and—you will pardon my lack of humility—distinguished career at the bar."

"Your personal life is your own concern, Mr. Saunders," the Colonel said, "but I must tell you, sir, that we are aware of how you spend your money and your time away from here. I do not recommend it to others nor do I approve of your presenting it to us as worthy of emulation. Indeed, I think you do our cause damage."

Mr. Saunders had not resumed his seat. He bowed and continued, "Each to his own tastes—I cite an effective method for keeping the younger generation in check. There are other ways of disposing of property irretrievably." He sat down.

John pulled Sally back from the doors. "Go to the car," he said. "Get out of here. Go back to the house and get our bags packed. Quick!"

"Mrs. Plummer?" the Colonel said.

Sally pulled away from John.

The familiar figure stood up at the front of the room. Now John could identify beside her the gray head of Henry Plummer, turned now toward the plump face of his wife.

"We all remember," Mrs. Plummer said calmly, "what a trial children are. What we may forget is that our children have children. I do my best not to let my daughter forget the torments she inflicted upon me when she was a child. We hide these things from them. We conceal the bitterness. They seldom suspect. And we take our revenge, if we are wise, by encouraging their children to be just as great a trial to their parents. We give them candy before meals. We encourage them to talk back to their parents. We build up their infant egoes so that they will stand up for their childish rights. When their parents try to punish them, we stand between the child and the punishment. Fellow senior citizens, this is our revenge: that their parents will be as miserable as we were."

"Mother! No!" Sally cried out.

The words and the youthful voice that spoke them rippled the audience like a stone tossed into a pond. Faces turned toward the back of the meeting room, faces with wrinkles and white hair and faded eyes, faces searching, near-sighted, faces disturbed, faces beginning to fear and to hate. Among them was one face John knew well, a face that had dissembled malice and masqueraded malevolence as devotion.

"Do as I told you!" John said violently. "Get out of here!"

For once in her life, Sally did as she was told. She ran down the hall, pushed her way through the big front doors, and was gone. John looked for something with which to bar the doors to the meeting room, but the hall was bare. He was turning back to the doors when he saw an oak cane in the corner. He caught it up and slipped it through the handles. Then he put his shoulder against the doors.

In the meeting room the gathering emotion was beginning to whip thin blood into a simulation of youthful vigor, and treble voices began to deepen as they shouted encouragement at those nearest the doors. "A spy!"

"Was it a woman?"

"A girl."

"Let me get my hands on her!"

The first wave hit the doors. John was knocked off balance. He pushed himself forward again, and again the surge of bodies against the other side forced him back. He dug in his feet and shoved. A sound of commotion added to the shouting in the meeting room. John heard something—or someone—fall.

The next time he was forced from the doors the cane bent. Again he pushed the doors shut; the cane straightened. At the same moment he felt a sharp pain across his back. He looked back. The Colonel was behind him, breathing hard, the glow of combat in his eyes and the cane in his hand upraised for another blow, like the hand of Abraham over Isaac.

John stepped back. In his hand he found the cane that had been thrust through the door handles. He raised it over his head as the Colonel struck again. The blow fell upon the cane. The Colonel drew back his cane and swung once more, and again his blow was parried, more by accident than skill. Then the doors burst open, and the wild old bodies were upon them.

John caught brief glimpses of flying white hair and ripped lace and spectacles worn awry. Canes and crutches were raised above him. He smelled lavender and bay rum mingled with the sweet-sour odor of sweat. He heard shrill voices, like the voices of children, cry out curses and maledictions, and he felt upon various parts of his body the blows of feeble fists, their bones scarcely padded, doing perhaps more damage to themselves than to him, though it seemed sufficient.

He went down quickly. Rather too quickly, he thought dazedly as he lay upon the floor, curled into a fetal position to avoid the stamping feet and kicks and makeshift clubs.

He kept waiting for it to be over, for consciousness to leave him, but most of the blows missed him, and in the confusion and the milling about, the object ot the hatred was lost. John saw a corridor that led between bodies and legs through the doors that opened into the meeting room. He crawled by inches toward the room; eventually he found himself among the chairs. The commotion was behind him.

Cautiously he peered over the top of a fallen chair. He saw what he had overlooked before—a door behind the rostrum.

It stood open to the night. That was how the Colonel, with instinctive strategy, had come up behind him, he thought, and he crept toward it and down the narrow steps behind the town hall.

For a moment he stood in the darkness assessing his injuries. He was surprised: they were few, none serious. Perhaps tomorrow he would find bruises enough and a lump here and there and perhaps even a broken rib or two, but now there was only a little pain. He started to run.

He had been running in the darkness for a long time, not certain he was running in the right direction, not sure he knew what the right direction was, when a dark shape coasted up behind him. He dodged instinctively before he recognized the sound of the motor.

"John!" It was a voice he knew. "John?"

The Volkswagen was running without lights. John caught the door handle. The door came open. The car stopped. "Move over," he said, out of breath. Sally climbed over the gear shift, and John slid into the bucket seat. He released the hand brake and pushed hard on the accelerator. The car plunged forward.

Only when they reached the highway did John speak again. "Is Johnny all right?"

"I think so," Sally said. "But he's got to see a doctor."

"We'll find a doctor in Orange Grove."

"A young one."

John wiped his nose on the back of his hand and looked at it. His hand was smeared with blood. "Damn!"

She pressed a tissue into his hand. "Was it bad?"

"Incredible!" He laughed harshly and said it again in a different tone. "Incredible. What a day! And what a night! But it's over. And a lot of other things are over."

Johnny was crying in the back seat.

"What do you mean?" Sally asked. "Hush, Johnny, it's going to be all right."

"Grammy!" Johnny moaned.

"The letters. Presents for people who don't need anything. Worrying about what mother's going to think. . . ."

The car slowed as John looked back toward the peaceful town of Sunset Acres, sleeping now in the Florida night, and remembered the wide lawns and the broad porches, the brick streets and the slow time, and the old folks. "All over," he said again.

Johnny still was crying.

"Shut up, Johnny!" he said between his teeth and immediately felt guilty.

"John!" Sally said. "We mustn't ever be like that toward our son."

She wasn't referring just to what he had said, John knew. He glanced back toward the small figure huddled in the back seat. It wasn't over, he thought; it was beginning. "It's over," he said again, as if he could convince himself by repetition. Sally was silent. "Why don't you say something?" John asked.

"I keep thinking about how it used to be," she said. "He's my father. She's my mother. How can anything change that? You can't expect me to hate my own father and mother?"

It wasn't over. It would never be over. Even though the children sometimes escaped, the old folks always won: the children grew up, the young people became old folks.

The car speeded up and rushed through the night, the headlights carving a corridor through the darkness, a corridor that kept closing behind them. The corridor still was there, as real in back as it was revealing in front, and it could never be closed.

FROM SEA TO SHINING SEA
OR
THROUGH THE ROCKIES AT 31 KNOTS

JONATHAN ELA

The U.S. Army Corps of Engineers are not only Pioneers in wartime but are responsible for canal building in peacetime. Most American conservationists consider that the Engineers, in their canal building rôle, are a power for evil in the world today. When the Sierra Club Bulletin—*the journal of the largest conservation organization—printed the following tongue-in-cheek report about a Cross-Continent Barge Canal it was taken quite seriously by many, including one congressman who considered it "Outrageous!" Science fiction readers are made of sterner stuff and should be able to read this without wincing.*

Conservationists are expressing concern over a proposal just announced to construct a Cross-Continent Barge Canal linking Boston with San Diego. The joint project of the U.S. Army Corps of Engineers and the Atomic Energy Commission would be the largest public work ever constructed in the United States, and would utilize the technology recently perfected by the AEC in its Cannikin explosion on Amchitka Island in Alaska.

The Cro-Con Canal is officially described as "a multiple use project in the highest sense of the term," but it is generally understood in Washington that the major justification for the project is to aid movement of aircraft carriers. Pentagon sources point out that the Panama Canal is too narrow to handle the newer carriers, necessitating enormously expensive and time-consuming voyages around Cape Horn. Plans to construct a new, sea-level canal across Panama have been blocked by Panamanian nationalists and by aroused environmentalists in the United States who have pointed out the

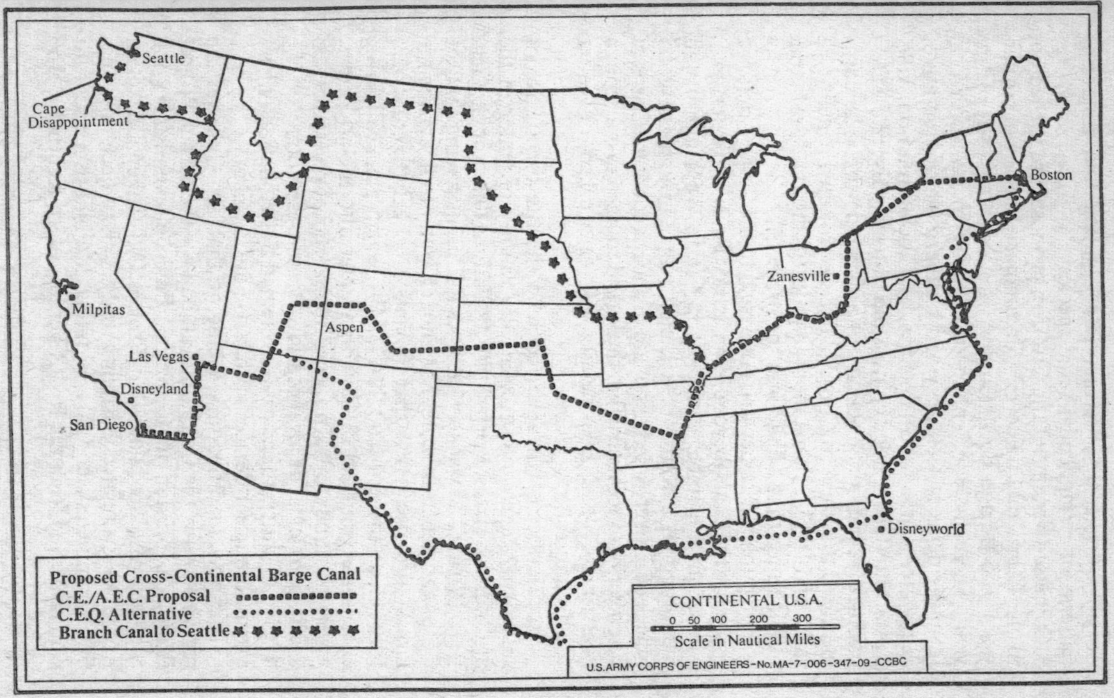

Seattle
Cape Disappointment
Milpitas
Las Vegas
Disneyland
San Diego
Aspen
Zanesville
Boston
Disneyworld
Proposed Cross-Continental Barge Canal
C.E./A.E.C. Proposal
C.E.Q. Alternative
Branch Canal to Seattle
CONTINENTAL U.S.A.
0 50 100 200 300
Scale in Nautical Miles
U.S.ARMY CORPS OF ENGINEERS-No.MA-7-006-347-09-CCBC

possibly disastrous effects on the mating and migrating patterns of certain endangered species.

Supposed benefits of the Cro-Con proposal are spelled out in the Corps of Engineers' "Preliminary Framework Analysis," a 640-page document released on May 18th of this year. These include: enhanced capacity to transport coal from the fields of Kentucky and southern Ohio; creation of deepwater ports for such cities as Cincinnati, Louisville, Tulsa, and Aspen; flood control and water supply; and water-oriented recreational activity of a linear nature. The corps indicated that the Cro-Con Canal has a projected benefit-cost ratio of 1.001 : 1, "thus more than justifying the substantial public funds that will go into the project."

The public "Framework Analysis" fails to give a detailed route for the canal beyond the Charles River at Watertown, Mass., but a member of the Sierra Club's Washington staff has procured a Xerox of a sketch map through the good offices of a disgruntled associate of Jack Anderson. Corps of Engineers' sources warn that the leaked route map is a "rough guesstimate" and that details will be worked out after construction starts.

Early critics of Cro-Con contend the the corps has not sufficiently taken into account the scarcity of water in the arid western states. Corps Public Relations Director Lt. Gen. B. R. "Brute" Thwackem disputes this point, saying that the Corps can generate more than enough water to float even the largest aircraft carriers that the nation is likely to construct. Revival of the dormant NAWAPA water plan will bring enormous quantities of Canadian water into the arid areas, where it can be stored in specially constructed reservoirs. To avoid problems of evaporation, these reservoirs will be located in underground cavities created by detonation of five-megaton nuclear devices in the style of Cannikin.

It is now conceded in Washington that Cro-Con was the real reason for the Cannikin test, and for the earlier Project Rulison explosion in Colorado. Environmentalists in the Midwest also speculate that Project Old Oaken Bucket in Kentucky is a related feasibility study. This project, now one-third completed, consists of filling Mammoth Cave with water diverted from the Red River in eastern Kentucky. The explained justification of Old Oaken Bucket has always been to meet the water supply needs of Cub Run, Kentucky, but local conservationists have never been completely satisfied by this explanation.

Environmental groups have been alarmed that evidently no Environmental Impact Statement, as required under Section 102 (2) (c) of the National Environmental Policy Act, is to be issued for the Cro-Con Project. General Thwackem has given three reasons for this. First, it is argued that there is no conceivable way in which significant environmental damage could occur. Second, corps personnel take the position that NEPA is non-retroactive and that Cro-Con is simply a routine departmental updating of Albert Gallatin's April, 1808, report on proposed domestic improvements, including canals. The corps' argument is that since Gallatin did not have to write an impact statement, neither should they. Finally, the corps argues that the only slight risk of environmental damage would be from the AEC's still novel means of excavation through the use of nuclear devices. The corps feels that for this reason the impact statement is out of its jurisdiction, and should be prepared, if at all, by the AEC. Attempts to reach an AEC official associated with Cro-Con were unsuccessful (although more than 2,000 are said to be employed on the project), but one contact within the AEC's sprawling Germantown, Maryland, headquarters indicated that there are "compelling reasons" for not issuing an impact statement, although he could not divulge them "because of national security considerations."

Conservationists appear to have an ally within the Nixon Administration in the President's Council on Environmental Quality. The CEQ takes the position that it should have been consulted, and is agitating within the Administration to have alternatives considered. The Council finds that some impact from the Cro-Con is likely, and has quickly brought forward a different route. CEQ suggests improving the Intracoastal Waterway along the East Coast, constructing the Ochlawaha (Cross-Florida) Canal, developing the Intracoastal along the Gulf Coast, dredging up the Rio Grande as far as Alamosa, Colorado, cutting due west to Lake Powell, and following the corps proposal from that point. The Council points out that its proposal involves far less construction in areas that do not currently have rivers, and that the portion of the Rocky Mountains that would have to be leveled by nuclear explosions is "much less valuable, estheticwise."

The corps rejects the council's alternative for three reasons. First, it would expose the aircraft carriers to enemy submarines. Second, the CEQ route would have less value for movement of coal, development of inland ports, flood control, mid-continental water sports, and other benefits. Third, the corps proposal is so designed that a branch canal could be extended to Seattle, using basically the Missouri and Columbia Rivers, thus aiding the movement of supertankers from Puget Sound refineries to northeastern markets.

Environmentalists have greeted the Cro-Con announcement with mixed feelings. Some, such as the Sierra Club, have shown initial skepticism, based largely on potential damage to the Grand Canyon. Others, such as the East Birdseye (Indiana) Rod and Gun Club, tend to view the project with favor, as they accept corps ecologists' predictions that the fish will grow fatter in the slack water "because they don't have to work as hard."

It is clearly too early for environmentalists to voice a unified opinion on the Cro-Con Canal, as the facts are not yet all in. Yet the corps has already accused the Sierra Club of "irresponsibility" in "raising baseless questions." "These environmentalists want us to return to the Stone Age," says General Thwackem. "National Security and economic prosperity demand a canal. They've blocked us in Panama and now they want to block us here. But here in the Corps we believe in Cro-Con, just as we believe in America, and no posy-plucker is going to tell us how to run our shop."

With due respect to the General's patriotism and to the desirability of hearing both sides of the question, it nevertheless seems to many environmentalists that the Cross-Continent Canal is a project that bears watching.

WEINACHTABEND

KEITH ROBERTS

Parallel world themes offer a continuing source of interest to both author and reader. One of the classic collections, If It Had Happened Otherwise, *edited by J. C. Squire (Sidgwick & Jackson), has just been reissued—forty years after its original publication. It contains fascinating glimpses of worlds of "if", such as "If the General Strike had Succeeded" and "If Napoleon had Won at Waterloo." A War that is closer to our time, which has inspired a score of stories, a motion picture (*The War Game*), and at least one novel (Philip K. Dick's* Man In the High Castle), *is of course the Second World War. That this theme is far from exhausted is demonstrated by science fiction author-illustrator Keith Roberts.*

The big car moved slowly, nosing its way along narrowing lanes. Here, beyond the little market town of Wilton, the snow lay thicker. Trees and bushes loomed in the headlights, coated with driven white. The tail of the Mercedes wagged slightly, steadied. Mainwaring heard the chauffeur swear under his breath. The link had been left alive.

Dials let into the seatback recorded the vehicle's mechanical wellbeing; oil pressure, temperature, revs, k.p.h. Lights from the repeater glowed softly on his companion's face. She moved, restlessly; he saw the swing of yellow hair. He turned slightly. She was wearing a neat, brief kilt, heavy boots, Her legs were excellent.

He clicked the dial lights off. He said, "Not much farther."

He wondered if she was aware of the open link. He said, "First time down?"

She nodded in the dark. She said, "I was a bit overwhelmed."

Wilton Great House sprawled across a hilltop five miles or more beyond the town. The car drove for some distance beside the wall that fringed the estate. The perimeter defences had been strengthened since Mainwaring's last visit. Watch-towers reared at intervals; the wall itself had been topped by multiple strands of wire.

The lodge gates were commanded by two new stone pill-boxes. The Merc edged between them, stopped. On the road from London, the snow had eased; now big flakes drifted again, lit by the headlights. Somewhere, orders were barked.

A man stepped forward, tapped at the window. Mainwaring buttoned it open. He saw a GFP armband, a hip holster with the flap tucked back. He said, "Good evening, Captain."

"Guten Abend, mein Herr. Ihre Ausweis Karte?"

Cold air gusted against Mainwaring's cheek. He passed across his identity card and security clearance. He said, *"Richard Mainwaring. Die rechte Hand zu dem Gesanten. Fräulein Hunter, von meiner Abteilung."*

A torch flashed over the papers, dazzled into his eyes, moved to examine the girl. She sat stiffly, staring ahead. Beyond the Security officer Mainwaring made out two steel-helmeted troopers, automatics slung. In front of him, the wipers clicked steadily.

The GFP man stepped back. He said, *"In einer Woche, Ihre Ausweis Karte ist ausgelaufen. Erneuen Sie Ihre Karte."*

Mainwaring said, *"Vielen Dank, Herr Hauptmann. Frohe Weihnacht."*

The man saluted stiffly, unclipped a walkie-talkie from his belt. A pause, and the gates swung back. The Merc creamed through. Mainwaring said, *"Bastard. . . ."*

She said, "Is it always like this?"

He said, "They're tightening up all round."

She pulled her coat round her shoulders. She said, "Frankly, I find it a bit scary."

He said, "Just the Minister taking care of his guests."

Wilton stood in open downland set with great trees. Hans negotiated a bend, carefully, drove beneath half-seen branches. The wind moaned, zipping round a quarterlight. It was as if the car butted into a black tunnel, full of swirling pale flakes. He thought he saw her shiver. He said, "Soon be there."

The headlamps lit a rolling expanse of snow. Posts, buried

nearly to their tops, marked the drive. Another bend, and the house showed ahead. The car lights swept across a façade of mullioned windows, crenellated towers. Hard for the uninitiated to guess, staring at the skilfully weathered stone, that the shell of the place was of reinforced concrete. The car swung right with a crunching of unseen gravel, and stopped. The ignition repeater glowed on the seatback.

Mainwaring said, "Thank you, Hans. Nice drive."

Hans said, "My pleasure, sir."

She flicked her hair free, picked up her handbag. He held the door for her. He said, "OK, Diane?"

She shrugged. She said, "Yes. I'm a bit silly sometimes." She squeezed his hand, briefly. She said, "I'm glad you'll be here. Somebody to rely on."

Mainwaring lay back on the bed and stared at the ceiling. Inside as well as out, Wilton was a triumph of art over nature. Here, in the Tudor wing where most of the guests were housed, walls and ceilings were of wavy plaster framed by heavy oak beams. He turned his head. The room was dominated by a fireplace of yellow Ham stone; on the overmantel, carved in bold relief, the *hakenkreuz* was flanked by the lion and eagle emblems of the Two Empires. A fire burned in the wrought-iron basket; the logs glowed cheerfully, casting wavering warm reflections across the ceiling. Beside the bed a bookshelf offered required reading; the Fuehrer's official biography, Shirer's *Rise of the Third Reich*, Cummings' monumental *Churchill: the Trial of Decadence*. There were a nicely bound set of Buchan novels, some Kiplings, a Shakespeare, a complete Wilde. A side table carried a stack of current magazines; *Connoisseur*, *The Field*, *Der Spiegel*, *Paris Match*. There was a washstand, its rail hung with dark blue towels; in the corner of the room were the doors to the bathroom and wardrobe, in which a servant had already neatly disposed his clothes.

He stubbed his cigarette, lit another. He swung his legs off the bed, poured himself a whisky. From the grounds, faintly, came voices, snatches of laughter. He heard the crash of a pistol, the rattle of an automatic. He walked to the window, pushed the curtain aside. Snow was still falling, drifting silently from the black sky; but the firing pits beside the big house were brightly lit. He watched the figures move and bunch for a while, let the curtain fall. He sat by the fire, shoulders hunched, staring into the flames. He was remembering the trip through London; the flags hanging limp over Whitehall, slow, jerking movement of traffic, the light tanks drawn up outside St. James. The Kensington Road had been crowded, traffic edging and hooting; the vast frontage of Harrods looked grim and oriental against the louring sky. He frowned, remembering the call he had had before leaving the Ministry.

Kosowicz had been the name. From Time International; or so he had claimed. He'd refused twice to speak to him; but Kosowicz had been insistent. In the end, he'd asked his secretary to put him through.

Kosowicz had sounded very American. He said, "Mr. Mainwaring, I'd like to arrange a personal interview with your Minister."

"I'm afraid that's out of the question. I must also point out that this communication is extremely irregular."

Kosowicz said, "What do I take that as, sir? A warning, or a threat?"

Mainwaring said carefully, "It was neither. I merely observed that proper channels of approach do exist."

Kosowicz said, "Uh-huh. Mr. Mainwaring, what's the truth behind this rumour that Action Groups are being moved into Moscow?"

Mainwaring said, "Deputy-Fuehrer Hess has already issued a statement on the situation. I can see that you're supplied with a copy."

The phone said, "I have it before me. Mr. Mainwaring, what are you people trying to set up? Another Warsaw?"

Mainwaring said, "I'm afraid I can't comment further, Mr. Kosowicz. The Deputy-Fuehrer deplored the necessity of force. The *Einsatzegruppen* have been alerted; at this time, that is all. They will be used if necessary to disperse militants. As of this moment, the need has not arisen."

Kosowicz shifted his ground. "You mentioned the Deputy-Fuehrer, sir. I hear there was another bomb attempt two nights ago, can you comment on this?"

Mainwaring tightened his knuckles on the handset. He said, "I'm afraid you've been misinformed. We know nothing of any such incident."

The phone was silent for a moment. Then it said, "Can I take your denial as official?"

Mainwaring said, "This is not an official conversation. I'm not empowered to issue statements in any respect."

The phone said, "Yeah, channels do exist. Mr. Mainwaring, thanks for your time."

Mainwaring said, "Goodbye." He put the handset down, sat staring at it. After a while he lit a cigarette.

Outside the windows of the Ministry the snow still fell, a dark whirl and dance against the sky. His tea, when he came to drink it, was half cold.

The fire crackled and shifted. He poured himself another whisky, sat back. Before leaving for Wilton, he'd lunched with Winsby-Walker from Productivity. Winsby-Walker made it his business to know everything; but he had known nothing of a correspondent called Kosowicz. He thought, 'I should have checked with Security.' But then Security would have checked with him.

He sat up, looked at his watch. The noise from the range had diminished. He turned his mind with a deliberate effort into another channel. The new thoughts brought no more comfort. Last Christmas he had spent with his mother; now, that couldn't happen again. He remembered other Christmases, back across the years. Once, to the child unknowing, they had been gay affairs of crackers and toys. He remembered the scent and texture of pine branches, closeness of candlelight; and books read by torchlight under the sheets, the hard angles of the filled pillowslip, heavy at the foot of the bed. Then, he had been complete; only later, slowly, had come the knowledge of failure. And with it, loneliness. He thought, 'She wanted to see me settled. It didn't seem much to ask.'

The Scotch was making him maudlin. He drained the glass, walked through to the bathroom. He stripped, and showered. Towelling himself, he thought, 'Richard Mainwaring, Personal Assistant to the British Minister of Liaison.' Aloud he said, "One must remember the compensations."

He dressed, lathered his face and began to shave. He

thought, 'Thirty-five is the exact middle of one's life.' He was remembering another time with the girl Diane when just for a little while some magic had interposed. Now, the affair was never mentioned between them. Because of James. Always, of course, there is a James.

He towelled his face, applied aftershave. Despite himself, his mind had drifted back to the phone call. One fact was certain; there had been a major security spillage. Somebody somewhere had supplied Kosowicz with closely-guarded information. That same someone, presumably, had supplied a list of ex-directory lines. He frowned, grappling with the problem. One country, and one only, opposed the Two Empires with gigantic, latent strength. To that country had shifted the focus of Semitic nationalism. And Kosowicz had been an American.

He thought, 'Freedom, schmeedom. Democracy is Jew-shaped.' He frowned again, fingering his face. It didn't alter the salient fact. The tipoff had come from the Freedom Front; and he had been contacted, however obliquely.Now, he had become an accessory; the thought had been nagging at the back of his brain all day.

He wondered what they could want of him. There was a rumour—a nasty rumour—that you never found out. Not till the end, till you'd done whatever was required from you. They were untiring, deadly and subtle. He hadn't run squalling to Security at the first hint of danger; but that would have been allowed for. Every turn and twist would have been allowed for.

Every squirm, on the hook.

He grunted, angry with himself. Fear was half their strength. He buttoned his shirt remembering the guards at the gates, the wire and pillboxes. Here, of all places, nothing could reach him. For a few days, he could forget the whole affair. He said aloud, "Anyway, I don't even matter. I'm not important." The thought cheered him, nearly.

He clicked the light off, walked through to his room, closed the door behind him. He crossed to the bed and stood quite still, staring at the bookshelf. Between Shirer and the Churchill tome there rested a third slim volume. He reached to touch the spine, delicately; read the author's name,

Geissler, and the title. *Toward Humanity*. Below the title, like a topless Cross of Lorraine, were the twin linked F's of the Freedom Front.

Ten minutes ago, the book hadn't been there.

He walked to the door. The corridor beyond was deserted. From somewhere in the house, faintly, came music; *Till Eulenspiegel*. There were no nearer sounds. He closed the door again, locked it. Turned back and saw the wardrobe stood slightly ajar.

His case still lay on the side table. He crossed to it, took out the Luger. The feel of the heavy pistol was comforting. He pushed the clip home, thumbed the safety forward, chambered a round. The breach closed with a hard snap. He walked to the wardrobe, shoved the door wide with his foot.

Nothing there.

He let his held breath escape with a little hiss. He pressed the clip release, ejected the cartridge, laid the gun on the bed. He stood again looking at the shelf. He thought, 'I must have been mistaken.'

He took the book down, carefully. Geissler had been banned since publication in every Province of the Two Empires; Mainwaring himself had never even seen a copy. He squatted on the edge of the bed, opened the thing at random.

> "The doctrine of Aryan co-ancestry, seized on so eagerly by the English middle classes, had the superficial reasonableness of most theories ultimately traceable to Rosenberg. Churchill's answer, in one sense, had already been made; but Chamberlain, and the country, turned to Hess. . . .
>
> "The Cologne settlement, though seeming to offer hope of security to Jews already domiciled in Britain, in fact paved the way for campaigns of intimidation and extortion similar to those already undertaken in history, notably by King John. The comparison is not unapt; for the English *bourgeoisie*, anxious to construct a rationale, discovered many unassailable precedents. A true Sign of the Times, almost certainly, was the resurgence of interest in the novels of Sir Walter Scott. By 1942 the lesson had been learned on both sides; and the Star of David was a common sight on the streets of most British cities."

The wind rose momentarily in a long wail, shaking the window casement. Mainwaring glanced up, turned his attention back to the book. He leafed through several pages.

"In 1940, her Expeditionary Force shattered, her allies quiescent or defeated, the island truly stood alone. Her proletariat, bedevilled by bad leadership, weakened by a gigantic depression, was effectively without a voice. Her aristocracy, like their *Junker* counterparts, embraced coldly what could no longer be ignored; while after the Whitehall *Putsch* the Cabinet was reduced to the status of an Executive Council . . ."

The knock at the door made him start, guiltily. He pushed the book away. He said, "Who's that?"

She said, "Me. Richard, aren't you ready?"

He said, "Just a minute." He stared at the book, then placed it back on the shelf. He thought, 'That at least wouldn't be expected.' He slipped the Luger into his case and closed it. Then he went to the door.

She was wearing a lacy black dress. Her shoulders were bare; her hair, worn loose, had been brushed till it gleamed. He stared at her a moment, stupidly. Then he said, "Please come in."

She said, "I was starting to wonder . . . Are you all right?"

"Yes. Yes, of course."

She said, "You look as if you'd seen a ghost."

He smiled. He said, "I expect I was taken aback. Those Aryan good looks."

She grinned at him. She said, "I'm half Irish, half English, half Scandinavian. If you have to know."

"That doesn't add up."

She said, "Neither do I, most of the time."

"Drink?"

"Just a little one. We shall be late."

He said, "It's not very formal tonight." He turned away, fiddling with his tie.

She sipped her drink, pointed her foot, scuffed her toe on the carpet. She said, "I expect you've been to a lot of house-parties."

He said, "One or two."

She said, "Richard, are they . . ."

"Are they what?"

She said, "I don't know. You can't help hearing things."

He said, "You'll be all right. One's very much like the next."

She said, "Are you honestly OK?"

"Sure."

She said, "You're all thumbs. Here, let me." She reached up, knotted deftly. Her eyes searched his face for a moment, moving in little shifts and changes of direction. She said, "There. I think you just need looking after."

He said carefully, "How's James?"

She stared a moment longer. She said, "I don't know. He's in Nairobi. I haven't seen him for months."

He said, "I am a bit nervous, actually."

"Why?"

He said, "Escorting a rather lovely blonde."

She tossed her head, and laughed. She said, "You need a drink as well then."

He poured whisky, said, "Cheers." The book, now, seemed to be burning into his shoulderblades.

She said, "As a matter of fact you're looking rather fetching yourself."

He thought. 'This is the night when all things come together. There should be a word for it.' Then he remembered about *Till Eulenspiegel.*

She said, "We'd honestly better go down."

Lights gleamed in the Great Hall, reflecting from polished boards, dark linenfold panelling. At the nearer end of the chamber a huge fire burned. Beneath the minstrels' gallery long tables had been set. Informal or not, they shone with glass and silverware. Candles glowed amid wreaths of dark evergreen; beside each place was a rolled crimson napkin.

In the middle of the Hall, its tip brushing the coffered ceiling, stood a Christmas tree. Its branches were hung with apples, baskets of sweets, red paper roses; at its base were piled gifts in gay-striped wrappers. Round the tree folk stood in groups, chatting and laughing. Richard saw Müller the Defence Minister, with a striking-looking blonde he took to be his wife; beside them was a tall, monocled man who was something or other in Security. There was a group of GSP officers in their dark, neat uniforms, beyond them half a dozen Liaison people. He saw Hans the chauffeur standing head bent, nodding intently, smiling at some remark; and thought as he had thought before how he looked like a big, handsome ox.

Diane had paused in the doorway, and linked her arm through his. But the Minister had already seen them. He came weaving through the crowd, a glass in his hand. He was wearing tight black trews, a dark blue roll-neck shirt. He looked happy and relaxed. He said, "Richard. And my dear Miss Hunter. We'd nearly given you up for lost. After all, Hans Trapp is about. Now, some drinks. And come, do come; please join my friends. Over here, where it is warm."

She said, "Who's Hans Trapp?"

Mainwaring said, "You'll find out in a bit."

A little later the Minister said, "Ladies and gentlemen, I think we may be seated."

The meal was superb, the wine abundant. By the time the brandy was served Richard found himself talking more easily, and the Geissler copy pushed nearly to the back of his mind. The traditional toasts—King and Fuehrer, the Provinces, the Two Empires—were drunk; then the Minister clapped his hands for quiet. "My friends," he said, "tonight, this special night when we can all mix so freely, is *Weihnachtabend*. It means, I suppose, many things to the many of us here. But let us remember, first and foremost, that this is the night of the children. Your children, who have come with you to share part at least of this very special Christmas."

He paused. "Already," he said, "they have been called from their crèche; soon, they will be with us. Let me show them to you." He nodded; at the gesture servants wheeled forward a heavy, ornate box. A drape was twitched aside, revealing the grey surface of a big tv screen. Simultaneously, the lamps that lit the Hall began to dim. Diane turned to Mainwaring, frowning; he touched her hand, gently, and shook his head.

Save for the firelight, the Hall was now nearly dark. The candles guttered in their wreaths, flames stirring in some draught; in the hush, the droning of the wind round the great façade of the place was once more audible. The lights would be out, now, all over the house.

"For some of you," said the Minister, "this is your first visit here. For you, I will explain.

"On *Weihnachtabend*, all ghosts and goblins walk. The demon Hans Trapp is abroad; his face is black and terrible, his clothing the skins of bears. Against him comes the Light-bringer, the Spirit of Christmas. Some call her Lucia Queen, some *Das Christkind*. See her now."

The screen lit up.

She moved slowly, like a sleepwalker. She was slender, and robed in white. Her ashen hair tumbled round her shoulders; above her head glowed a diadem of burning tapers. Behind her trod the Star Boys with their wands and tinsel robes; behind again came a little group of children. They ranged in age from eight- and nine-year-olds to toddlers. They gripped each other's hands, apprehensively, setting feet in line like cats, darting terrified glances at the shadows to either side.

"They lie in darkness, waiting," said the Minister softly. "Their nurses have left them. If they cry out, there is none to hear. So they do not cry out. And one by one, she has called them. They see her light pass beneath the door; and they must rise and follow. Here, where we sit, is warmth. Here is safety. Their gifts are waiting; to reach them, they must run the gauntlet of the dark."

The camera angle changed. Now they were watching the procession from above. The Lucia Queen stepped steadily; the shadows she cast leaped and flickered on panelled walls.

"They are in the Long Gallery now," said the Minister. "Almost directly above us. They must not falter, they must not look back. Somewhere, Hans Trapp is hiding. From Hans, only *Das Christkind* can protect them. See how close they bunch behind her light!"

A howling began, like the crying of a wolf. In part it seemed to come from the screen, in part to echo through the Hall itself. The *Christkind* turned, raising her arms; the howling split into a many-voiced cadence, died to a mutter. In its place came a distant huge thudding, like the beating of a drum.

Diane said abruptly, "I don't find this particularly funny."

Mainwaring said, "It isn't suppose to be. Shh."

The Minister said evenly, "The Aryan child must know, from earliest years, the darkness that surrounds him. He must learn to fear, and to overcome that fear. He must learn to be strong. The Two Empires were not built by weakness; weakness will not sustain them. There is no place for it. This in part your children already know. The house is big, and dark; but they will win through to the light. They fight as the Empires once fought. For their birthright."

The shot changed again, showed a wide, sweeping staircase. The head of the little procession appeared, began to descend. "Now, where is our friend Hans?" said the Minister. "*Ah . . .*"

Her grip tightened convulsively on Mainwaring's arm. A black-smeared face loomed at the screen. The bogy snarled, clawing at the camera; then turned, loped swiftly toward the staircase. The children shrieked, and bunched; instantly the air was wild with din. Grotesque figures capered and leaped; hands grabbed, clutching. The column was buffeted and swirled; Mainwaring saw a child bowled completely over. The screaming reached a high pitch of terror; and the *Christkind* turned, arms once more raised. The goblins and were-things backed away, growling, into shadow; the slow march was resumed.

The Minister said, "They are nearly here. And they are good children, worthy of their race. Prepare the tree."

Servants ran forward with tapers to light the many candles. The tree sprang from gloom, glinting, black-green; and Mainwaring thought for the first time what a dark thing it was, although it blazed with light.

The big doors at the end of the Hall were flung back; and the children came tumbling through. Tearstained and sobbing they were, some bruised; but all, before they ran to the tree, stopped, made obeisance to the strange creature who had brought them through the dark. Then the crown was lifted, the tapers extinguished; and Lucia Queen became a child like the rest, a slim, barefooted girl in a gauzy white dress.

The Minister rose, laughing. "Now," he said, "music, and some more wine. Hans Trapp is dead. My friends, one and all, and children: *Frohe weihnacht!*"

Diane said, "Excuse me a moment."

Mainwaring turned. He said, "Are you all right?"

She said, "I'm just going to get rid of a certain taste."

He watched her go, concernedly; and the Minister had his

arm, was talking. "Excellent, Richard," he said. "It has gone excellently so far, don't you think?"

Richard said, "Excellently, sir."

"Good, good. Eh, Heidi, Erna . . . and Frederick, is it Frederick? What have you got there? Oh, very fine . . ." He steered Mainwaring away, still with his fingers tucked beneath his elbow. Squeals of joy sounded; somebody had discovered a sled, tucked away behind the tree. The Minister said, "Look at them; how happy they are now. I would like children, Richard. Children of my own. Sometimes I think I have given too much . . . Still, the opportunity remains. I am younger than you, do you realize that? This is the Age of Youth."

Mainwaring said, "I wish the Minister every happiness."

"Richard, Richard, you must learn not to be so very correct at all times. Unbend a little, you are too aware of dignity. You are my friend. I trust you; above all others, I trust you. Do you realize this?"

Richard said, "Thank you, sir. I do."

The Minister seemed bubbling over with some inner pleasure. He said, "Richard, come with me, Just for a moment. I have prepared a special gift for you. I won't keep you from the party very long."

Mainwaring followed, drawn as ever by the curious dynamism of the man. The Minister ducked through an arched doorway, turned right and left, descended a narrow flight of stairs. At the bottom the way was barred by a door of plain grey steel. The Minister pressed his palm flat to a sensor plate; a click, the whine of some mechanism, and the door swung inward. Beyond was a further flight of concrete steps, lit by a single lamp in a heavy well-glass. Chilly air blew upward. Mainwaring realized, with something approaching a shock, that they had entered part of the bunker system that honeycombed the ground beneath Wilton.

The Minister hurried ahead of him, palmed a further door. He said, "Toys, Richard. All toys. But they amuse me." Then, catching sight of Mainwaring's face, "Come, man, come! You are more nervous than the children, frightened of poor old Hans!"

The door gave onto a darkened space. There was a heavy,

sweetish smell that Mainwaring, for a whirling moment, couldn't place. His companion propelled him forward, gently. He resisted, pressing back; and the Minister's arm shot by him. A click, and the place was flooded with light. He saw a wide, low area, also concrete-built. To one side, already polished and gleaming, stood the Mercedes, next it the Minister's private Porsche. There were a couple of Volkswagens, a Ford Executive; and in the farthest corner, a vision in glinting white. A Lamborghini. They had emerged in the garage underneath the house.

The Minister said, "My private short cut." He walked forward to the Lamborghini, stood running his fingers across the low, broad bonnet. He said, "Look at her, Richard. Here, sit in. Isn't she a beauty? Isn't she fine?"

Mainwaring said, "She certainly is."

"You like her?"

Mainwaring smiled. He said, "Very much, sir. Who wouldn't?"

The Minister said, "Good, I'm so pleased. Richard, I'm upgrading you. She's yours. Enjoy her."

Mainwaring stared.

The Minister said, "Here, man. Don't look like that, like a fish. Here, see. Logbook, your keys. All entered up, finished." He gripped Mainwaring's shoulders, swung him round laughing. He said, "You've worked well for me. The Two Empires don't forget. Their good friends, their servants."

Mainwaring said, "I'm deeply honoured, sir."

"Don't be honoured. You're still being formal, Richard . . ."

"Sir?"

The Minister said, "Stay by me. Stay by me. Up there . . . they don't understand. But we understand . . . eh? These are difficult times. We must be together, always together. Kingdom, and Reich. Apart . . . we could be destroyed." He turned away, placed clenched hands on the roof of the car. He said, "Here, all this. Jewry, the Americans . . . Capitalism. They must stay afraid. Nobody fears an Empire divided. It would fall!"

Mainwaring said, "I'll do my best, sir. We all will."

The Minister said, "I know, I know. But Richard, this afternoon. I was playing with swords. Silly little swords."

Mainwaring thought, 'I know how he keeps me. I can see the mechanism. But I mustn't imagine I know the entire truth.'

The Minister turned back, as if in pain. He said, "Strength is Right. It has to be. But Hess . . ."

Mainwaring said slowly, "We've tried before, sir . . ."

The Minister slammed his fist onto the metal. He said, "Richard, don't you see? It wasn't us. Not this time. It was his own people. Baumann, von Thaden . . . I can't tell. He's an old man, he doesn't matter any more. It's an idea they want to kill, Hess is an idea. Do you understand? It's *Lebensraum*. Again . . . Half the world isn't enough."

He straightened. He said, "The worm, in the apple. It gnaws, gnaws . . . But we are Liaison. We matter, so much. Richard, be my eyes. Be my ears."

Mainwaring stayed silent, thinking about the book in his room; and the Minister once more took his arm. He said, "The shadows, Richard. They were never closer. Well might we teach our children to fear the dark. But . . . not in our time. Eh? Not for us. There is life, and hope. So much we can do . . ."

Mainwaring thought, 'Maybe it's the wine I drank. I'm being pressed too hard.' A dull, queer mood, almost of indifference, had fallen on him. He followed his Minister without complaint, back through the bunker complex, up to where the great fire burned low and the tapers on the tree. He heard the singing mixed with the wind-voice, watched the children rock heavy-eyed, carolling sleep. The house seemed winding down, to rest; and she had gone of course. He sat in a corner and drank wine and brooded, watched the Minister move from group to group until he too was gone, the Hall nearly empty and the servants clearing away.

He found his own self, his inner self, dozing at last as it dozed at each day's end. Tiredness, as ever, had come like a benison. He rose carefully, walked to the door. He thought, 'I shan't be missed here.' Shutters closed, in his head.

He found his key, unlocked his room. He thought, 'Now she will be waiting. Like all the letters that never came, the phones that never rang.' He opened the door.

She said, "What kept you?"

He closed the door behind him, quietly. The fire crackled

in the little room, the curtains were drawn against the night. She sat by the hearth, barefooted, still in her party dress. Beside her on the carpet were glasses, an ashtray with half-smoked stubs. One lamp was burning; in the warm light her eyes were huge and dark.

He looked across to the bookshelf. The Geissler stood where he had left it. He said, "How did you get in?"

She chuckled. She said, "There was a spare key on the back of the door. Didn't you see me steal it?"

He walked toward her, stood looking down. He thought, 'Adding another fragment to the puzzle. Too much, too complicated.'

She said, "Are you angry?"

He said, "No."

She patted the floor. She said gently, "Please, Richard. Don't be cross."

He sat, slowly, watching her.

She said, "Drink?" He didn't answer. She poured one anyway. She said, "What were you doing all this time? I thought you'd be up hours ago."

He said, "I was talking to the Minister."

She traced a pattern on the rug with her forefinger. Her hair fell forward, golden and heavy, baring the nape of her neck. She said, "I'm sorry about earlier on. I was stupid. I think I was a bit scared too."

He drank slowly. He felt like a run-down machine. Hell to have to start thinking again at this time of night. He said, "What were you doing?"

She watched up at him. Her eyes were candid. She said, "Sitting here. Listening to the wind."

He said, "That couldn't have been much fun."

She shook her head, slowly, eyes fixed on his face. She said softly, "You don't know me at all."

He was quiet again. She said, "You don't believe in me, do you?"

He thought, 'You need understanding. You're different from the rest; and I'm selling myself short.' Aloud he said, "No."

She put the glass down, smiled, took his glass away. She hotched toward him across the rug, slid her arm round his neck. She said, "I was thinking about you. Making my mind up." She kissed him. He felt her tongue pushing, opened his lips. She said, *"Mmm . . ."* She sat back a little, smiling. She said, "Do you mind?"

"No."

She pressed a strand of hair across her mouth, parted her teeth, kissed again. He felt himself react, involuntarily; and felt her touch and squeeze.

She said. "This is a silly dress. It gets in the way." She reached behind her. The fabric parted; she pushed down, to the waist. She said, "Now it's like last time."

He said slowly, "Nothing's ever like last time."

She rolled across his lap, lay watching up. She whispered, "I've put the clock back."

Later in the dream she said, "I was so silly."

"What do you mean?"

She said, "I was shy. That was all. You weren't really supposed to go away."

He said, "What about James?"

"He's got somebody else. I didn't know what I was missing."

He let his hand stray over her; and present and immediate past became confused so that as he held her he still saw her kneeling, firelight dancing on her body. He reached for her and she was ready again; she fought, chuckling, taking it bareback, staying all the way.

Much later he said, "The Minister gave me a Lamborghini."

She rolled onto her belly, lay chin in hands watching under a tangle of hair. She said, "And now you've got yourself a blonde. What are you going to do with us?"

He said, "None of it's real."

She said, *"Oh . . ."* She punched him. She said, "Richard, you make me cross. It's happened, you idiot. That's all. It happens to everybody." She scratched again with a finger on the carpet. She said, "I hope you've made me pregnant. Then you'd have to marry me."

He narrowed his eyes; and the wine began again, singing in his head.

She nuzzled him. She said, "You asked me once. Say it again."

"I don't remember."

She said, "Richard, please . . ." So he said, "Diane, will you marry me?" And she said, "Yes, yes, yes," then afterwards awareness came and though it wasn't possible he took her again and that time was finest of all, tight and sweet as honey. He'd fetched pillows from the bed and the counterpane, they curled close and he found himself talking, talking, how it wasn't the sex, it was shopping in Marlborough and having tea and seeing the sun set from White Horse Hill and being together, together; then she pressed fingers to his mouth and he fell with her in sleep past cold and loneliness and fear, past deserts and unlit places, down maybe to where spires reared gold and tree leaves moved and dazzled and white cars sang on roads and suns burned inwardly, lighting new worlds.

He woke, and the fire was low. He sat up, dazed. She was watching him. He stroked her hair awhile, smiling; then she pushed away. She said, "Richard, I have to go now."

"Not yet."

"It's the middle of the night."

He said, "It doesn't matter."

She said, "It does. He mustn't know."

"Who?"

She said, "You know who. You know why I was asked here."

He said, "He's not like that. Honestly."

She shivered. She said, "Richard, please. Don't get me in trouble." She smiled. She said, "It's only till tomorrow. Only a little while."

He stood, awkwardly, and held her, pressing her warmth close. Shoeless, she was tiny; her shoulder fitted beneath his armpit.

Halfway through dressing she stopped and laughed, leaned a hand against the wall. She said, "I'm all woozy."

Later he said, "I'll see you to your room."

She said, "No, please. I'm all right." She was holding her handbag, and her hair was combed. She looked, again, as if she had been to a party.

At the door she turned. She said, "I love you, Richard. Truly." She kissed again, quickly; and was gone.

He closed the door, dropped the latch. He stood a while looking round the room. In the fire a burned-through log broke with a snap, sending up a little whirl of sparks. He walked to the washstand, bathed his face and hands. He shook the counterpane out on the bed, rearranged the pillows. Her scent still clung to him; he remembered how she had felt, and what she had said.

He crossed to the window, pushed it ajar. Outside, the snow lay in deep swaths and drifts. Starlight gleamed from it, ghost-white; and the whole great house was mute. He stood feeling the chill move against his skin; and in all the silence, a voice drifted far-off and clear. It came maybe from the guardhouses, full of distance and peace.

"Stille Nacht, heilige Nacht,
"alles schläfte, einsam wacht . . ."

He walked to the bed, pulled back the covers. The sheets were crisp and spotless, fresh-smelling. He smiled, and turned off the lamp.

"Nur das traute, hoc heilige Paar.
"Holder Knabe im lochigen Haar . . ."

In the wall of the room, an inch behind the plasterwork, a complex little machine hummed. A spool of delicate golden wire shook slightly; but the creak of the opening window had been the last thing to interest the recorder, the singing alone couldn't activate its relays. A micro-switch tripped, inaudibly; valve filaments faded, and died. Mainwaring lay back in the last of the firelight, and closed his eyes.

"Schlaf' in himmlischer Ruh,
"Schlaf' in himmlischer Ruh . . ."

2.

Beyond drawn curtains, brightness flicks on.

The sky is a hard, clear blue; icy, full of sunlight. The light dazzles back from the brilliant land. Far things—copses, hills, solitary trees—stand sharp-etched. Roofs and eaves carry hummocks of whiteness, twigs a three-inch crest. In the stillness, here and there, the snow cracks and falls, powdering.

The shadows of the raiders jerk and undulate. The quiet is interrupted. Hooves ring on swept courtyards or stamp muffled, churning the snow. It seems the air itself has been rendered crystalline by cold; through it the voices break and shatter, brittle as glass.

"Guten Morgen, Hans . . ."

"Verflucht kalt!"

"Der Hundenmeister sagt, sehr Gefährlich!"

"Macht nichts! Wir erwischen es bevor dem Wald!"

A rider plunges beneath an arch. The horse snorts and curvets.

"Ich wette dier fünfzig amerikanische Dollar!"

"Einverstanden! Heute, habe ich Glück!"

The noise, the jangling and stamping, rings back on itself. Cheeks flush, perception is heightened; for more than one of the riders, the early courtyard reels. Beside the house door trestles have been set up. A great bowl is carried, steaming. The cups are raised, the toasts given; the responses ring again, crashing.

"The Two Empires . . !"

"The Hunt . . !"

Now, time is like a tight-wound spring. The dogs plunge forward, six to a handler, leashes straining, choke links creaking and snapping. Behind them jostle the riders. The bobbing scarlet coats splash across the snow. In the house drive, an officer salutes; another strikes gloved palms together, nods. The gates whine open.

And across the country for miles around doors slam, bolts are shot, shutters closed, children scurried indoors. Village streets, muffled with snow, wait dumbly. Somewhere a dog barks, is silenced. The houses squat sullen, blind-eyed. The word has gone out, faster than horses could gallop. Today the Hunt will run; on snow.

The riders fan out, across a speckled waste of fields. A check, a questing; and the horns begin to yelp. Ahead the dogs bound and leap, black spots against whiteness. The horns cry again; but these hounds run mute. The riders sweep forward, onto the line.

Now, for the hunters, time and vision are fragmented. Twigs and snow merge in a racing blur; and tree-boles, ditches, gates. The tide reaches a crest of land, pours down the opposing slope. Hedges rear, mantled with white; and muffled thunder is interrupted by sailing silence, the smash and crackle of landing. The View sounds, harsh and high; and frenzy, and the racing blood, discharge intelligence. A horse goes down, in a gigantic flailing; another rolls, crushing its rider into the snow. A mount runs riderless. The Hunt, destroying, destroys itself unaware.

There are cottages, a paling fence. The fence goes over, unnoticed. A chicken house erupts in a cloud of flung crystals; birds run squawking, under the hooves. Caps are lost, flung away; hair flows wild. Whips flail, spurs rake streaming flanks; and the woods are close. Twigs lash, and branches; snow falls, thudding. The crackling, now, is all around.

At the end, it is always the same. The handlers close in, yodelling, waist-high in trampled brush; the riders force close and closer, mounts sidling and shaking; and silence falls. Only the quarry, reddened, flops and twists; the thin high noise it makes is the noise of anything in pain.

Now, if he chooses, the *Jagdmeister* may end the suffering. The crash of the pistol rings hollow; and birds erupt, high from frozen twigs, wheel with the echoes and cry. The pistol fires again; and the quarry lies still. In time, the shaking stops; and a dog creeps forward, begins to lick.

Now a slow movement begins; a spreading out, away from the place. There are mutterings, a laugh that chokes to silence. The fever passes. Somebody begins to shiver; and a girl, blood glittering on cheek and neck, puts a glove to her forehead and moans. The Need has come and gone; for a little while, the Two Empires have purged themselves.

The riders straggle back on tired mounts, shamble in through the gates. As the last enters a closed black van starts up, drives away. In an hour, quietly, it returns; and the gates swing shut behind it.

Surfacing from deepest sleep was like rising, slowly, through a warm sea. For a time, as Mainwaring lay eyes closed, memory and awareness were confused so that she was with him and the room a recollected, childhood place. He rubbed his face, yawned, shook his head; and the knocking that had roused him came again. He said, "Yes?"

The voice said, "Last breakfasts in fifteen minutes, sir."

He called, "Thank you," heard the footsteps pad away.

He pushed himself up, groped on the side table for his watch, held it close to his eyes. It read ten forty-five.

He swung the bedclothes back, felt air tingle on his skin. She had been with him, certainly, in the dawn; his body remembered the succubus, with nearly painful strength. He looked down smiling, walked to the bathroom. He showered, towelled himself, shaved and dressed. He closed his door and locked it, walked to the breakfast room. A few couples still sat over their coffee; he smiled a good morning, took a window seat. Beyond the double panes the snow piled thickly; its reflection lit the room with a white, inverted brilliance. He ate slowly, hearing distant shouts. On the long slope behind the house, groups of children pelted each other vigorously. Once a toboggan came into sight, vanished behind a rising swell of ground.

He had hoped he might see her, but she didn't come. He drank coffee, smoked a cigarette. He walked to the television lounge. The big colour screen showed a children's party taking place in a Berlin hospital. He watched for a while. The door behind him clicked a couple of times, but it wasn't Diane.

There was a second guests' lounge, not usually much frequented at this time of the year; and a reading room and library. He wandered through them, but there was no sign of her. It occurred to him she might not yet be up; at Wilton, there were few hard-and-fast rules for Christmas Day. He thought, 'I should have checked her room number.' He wasn't even sure in which of the guest wings she had been placed.

The house was quiet; it seemed most of the visitors had taken to their rooms. He wondered if she could have ridden with the Hunt; he'd heard it vaguely, leaving and returning. He doubted if the affair would have held much appeal.

He strolled back to the tv lounge, watched for an hour or more. By lunchtime he was feeling vaguely piqued; and sensing too the rising of a curious unease. He went back to his room, wondering if by any chance she had gone there; but the miracle was not repeated. The room was empty.

The fire was burning, and the bed had been remade. He had

forgotten the servants' pass keys. The Geissler copy still stood on the shelf. He took it down, stood weighing it in his hand and frowning. It was, in a sense, madness to leave it there.

He shrugged, put the thing back. He thought, 'So who reads bookshelves anyway?' The plot, if plot there had been, seemed absurd now in the clearer light of day. He stepped into the corridor, closed the door and locked it behind him. He tried as far as possible to put the book from his mind. It represented a problem; and problems, as yet, he wasn't prepared to cope with. Too much else was going on in his brain.

He lunched alone, now with a very definite pang; the process was disquietingly like that of other years. Once he thought he caught sight of her in the corridor. His heart thumped; but it was the other blonde, Müller's wife. The gestures, the fall of the hair, were similar; but this woman was taller.

He let himself drift into a reverie. Images of her, it seemed, were engraved on his mind; each to be selected now, studied, placed lovingly aside. He saw the firelit texture of her hair and skin, her lashes brushing her cheek as she lay in his arms and slept. Other memories, sharper, more immediate still, throbbed like little shocks in the mind. She tossed her head, smiling; her hair swung, touched the point of a breast.

He pushed his cup away, rose. At fifteen hundred, patriotism required her presence in the tv lounge. As it required the presence of every other guest. Then, if not before, he would see her. He reflected, wryly, that he had waited half a lifetime for her; a little longer now would do no harm.

He took to prowling the house again; the Great Hall, the Long Gallery where the *Christkind* had walked. Below the windows that lined it was a snow-covered roof. The tart, reflected light struck upward, robbing the place of mystery. In the Great Hall, they had already removed the tree. He watched household staff hanging draperies, carrying in stacks of gilded cane chairs. On the minstrels' gallery a pile of odd-shaped boxes proclaimed that the orchestra had arrived.

At fourteen hundred hours he walked back to the tv lounge. A quick glance assured him she wasn't there. The bar was open; Hans, looking as big and suave as ever, had been pressed into service to minister to the guests. He smiled at Mainwaring and said, "Good afternoon, sir." Mainwaring asked for a lager beer, took the glass to a corner seat. From here he could watch both the tv screen and the door.

The screen was showing the world-wide linkup that had become hallowed Christmas afternoon fare within the Two Empires. He saw, without particular interest, greetings flashed from the Leningrad and Moscow garrisons, a lightship, an Arctic weather station, a Mission in German East Africa. At fifteen hundred, the Fuehrer was due to speak; this year, for the first time, Ziegler was preceding Edward VIII.

The room filled, slowly. She didn't come. Mainwaring finished the lager, walked to the bar, asked for another and a packet of cigarettes. The unease was sharpening now into something very like alarm. He thought for the first time that she might have been taken ill.

The time signal flashed, followed by the drumroll of the German anthem. He rose with the rest, stood stiffly till it had finished. The screen cleared, showed the familiar room in the Chancellery; the dark, high panels, the crimson drapes, the big *hakenkreuz* emblem over the desk. The Fuehrer, as ever, spoke impeccably; but Mainwaring thought with a fragment of his mind how old he had begun to look.

The speech ended. He realized he hadn't heard a word that was said.

The drums crashed again. The King said, "Once more, at Christmas, it is my . . . duty and pleasure . . . to speak to you."

Something seemed to burst inside Mainwaring's head. He rose, walked quickly to the bar. He said, "Hans, have you seen Miss Hunter?"

The other jerked round. He said, "Sir, *shh* . . . please . . ."

"Have you seen her?"

Hans stared at the screen, and back to Mainwaring. The King was saying, "There have been . . . troubles, and difficulties. More perhaps lie ahead. But with . . . God's help, they will be overcome."

The chauffeur licked his mouth. He said, "I'm sorry, sir. I don't know what you mean."

"Which was her room?"

The big man looked like something trapped. He said, "Please, Mr. Mainwaring. You'll get me into trouble. . . ."

"Which was her room?"

Somebody turned and hissed, angrily. Hans said, "I don't understand."

"For God's sake man, you carried her things upstairs. I saw you!"

Hans said, "No, sir . . ."

Momentarily, the lounge seemed to spin.

There was a door behind the bar. The chauffeur stepped back. He said, "Sir. Please. . . ."

The place was a storeroom. There were wine bottles racked, a shelf with jars of olives, walnuts, eggs. Mainwaring closed the door behind him, tried to control the shaking. Hans said, "Sir, you must not ask me these things. I don't know a Miss Hunter. I don't know what you mean."

Mainwaring said, "Which was her room? I demand that you answer."

"I can't!"

"You drove me from London yesterday. Do you deny that?"

"No, sir."

"You drove me with Miss Hunter."

"No, sir!"

"Damn your eyes, where is she?"

The chauffeur was sweating. A long wait; then he said, "Mr. Mainwaring, please. You must understand. I can't help you." He swallowed, and drew himself up. He said, "I drove you from London. I'm sorry. I drove you . . . *on your own.*"

The lounge door swung shut behind Mainwaring. He half-walked, half-ran to his room. He slammed the door behind him, leaned against it panting. In time the giddiness passed. He opened his eyes, slowly. The fire glowed; the Geissler stood on the bookshelf. Nothing was changed.

He set to work, methodically. He shifted furniture, peered behind it. He rolled the carpet back, tapped every foot of floor. He fetched a flashlight from his case and examined, minutely, the interior of the wardrobe. He ran his fingers lightly across the walls, section by section, tapping again. Finally he got a chair, dismantled the ceiling lighting fitting.

Nothing.

He began again. Halfway through the second search he froze, staring at the floorboards. He walked to his case, took the screwdriver from the pistol holster. A moment's work with the blade and he sat back, staring into his palm. He rubbed his face, placed his find carefully on the side table. A tiny earring, one of the pair she had worn. He sat awhile breathing heavily, his head in his hands.

The brief daylight had faded as he worked. He lit the standard lamp, wrenched the shade free, stood the naked bulb in the middle of the room. He worked round the walls again, peering, tapping, pressing. By the fireplace, finally, a foot-square section of plaster rang hollow.

He held the bulb close, examined the hairline crack. He inserted the screwdriver blade delicately, twisted. Then again. A click; and the section hinged open.

He reached inside the little space, shaking, lifted out the recorder. He stood silent a time, holding it; then raised his arms, brought the machine smashing down on the hearth. He stamped and kicked, panting, till the thing was reduced to fragments.

The droning rose to a roar, swept low over the house. The helicopter settled slowly, belly lamps glaring, downdraught raising a storm of snow. He walked to the window, stood staring. The children embarked, clutching scarves and gloves, suitcases, boxes with new toys. The steps were withdrawn, the hatch dogged shut. Snow swirled again; the machine lifted heavily, swung away in the direction of Wilton.

The Party was about to start.

Lights blaze, through the length and breadth of the house. Orange-lit windows throw long bars of brightness across the snow. Everywhere is an anxious coming and going, the pattering of feet, clink of silver and glassware, hurried commands. Waiters scuttle between the kitchens and the Green Room where dinner is laid. Dish after dish is borne in, paraded. Peacocks, roast and gilded, vaunt their plumes in shadow and candleglow, spirit-soaked wicks blazing in their beaks. The Minister rises, laughing; toast after toast is drunk. To five thousand tanks, ten thousand fighting aeroplanes, a hundred thousand guns. The Two Empires feast their guests, royally.

The climax approaches. The boar's head, garnished and smoking, is borne shoulder-high. His tusks gleam; clamped in his jaws is the golden sun-symbol, the orange. After him march the waits and mummers, with their lanterns and begging-cups. The carol they chant is older by far than the Two Empires; older than the Reich, older than Great Britain.

"Living he spoiled, where poor men toiled, which made kind Ceres sad. . . ."

The din of voices rises. Coins are flung, glittering; wine is poured. And more wine, and more and more. Bowls of fruit are passed, and trays of sweets; spiced cakes, gingerbread, marzipans. Till at a signal the brandy is brought and boxes of cigars.

The ladies rise to leave. They move flushed and chattering through the corridors of the house, uniformed link-boys grandly lighting their way. In the Great Hall, their escorts are waiting. Each young man is tall, each blond, each impeccably uniformed. On the minstrels' gallery a baton is poised; across the lawns, distantly, floats the whirling excitement of a waltz.

In the Green Room, hazed now with smoke, the doors are once more flung wide. Servants scurry again, carrying in boxes, great gay-wrapped parcels topped with scarlet satin bows. The Minister rises, hammering on the table for quiet.

"My friends, good friends, friends of the Two Empires. For you, no expense is spared. For you, the choicest gifts. Tonight, nothing but the best is good enough; and nothing but the best is here. Friends, enjoy yourselves. Enjoy my house. *Frohe Weihnacht. . . .*"

He walks quickly into shadow, and is gone. Behind him, silence falls. A waiting; and slowly, mysteriously, the great heap of gifts begins to stir. Paper splits, crackling. Here a hand emerges, here a foot. A breathless pause; and the first of the girls rises slowly, bare in flamelight, shakes her glinting hair.

The table roars again.

The sound reached Mainwaring dimly. He hesitated at the foot of the main staircase, moved on. He turned right and left, hurried down a flight of steps. He passed kitchens, and the servants' hall. From the hall came the blare of a record player. He walked to the end of the corridor, unlatched a door. Night air blew keen against his face.

He crossed the courtyard, opened a further door. The space beyond was bright-lit; there was the faint, musty stink of animals. He paused wiped his face. He was shirt-sleeved; but despite the cold he was sweating.

He walked forward again, steadily. To either side of the corridor were the fronts of cages. The dogs hurled themselves at the bars, thunderously. He ignored them.

The corridor opened into a square concrete chamber. To one side of the place was a ramp. At its foot was parked a windowless black van.

In the far wall, a door showed a crack of light. He rapped sharply, and again.

"Hundenmeister. . . ."

The door opened. The man who peered up at him was as wrinkled and pot-bellied as a Nast Santa Claus. At sight of his visitor's face he tried to duck back; but Mainwaring had him by the arm. He said, "*Herr Hundenmeister*, I must talk to you."

"Who are you? I don't know you. What do you want. . . ."

Mainwaring showed his teeth. He said, "The van. You drove the van this morning. What was in it?"

"I don't know what you mean. . . ."

The heave sent him stumbling across the floor. He tried to bolt; but Mainwaring grabbed him again.

"What was in it. . . ."

"I won't talk to you! Go away!"

The blow exploded across his cheek. Mainwaring hit him again, backhanded, slammed him against the van.

"Open it . . !"

The voice rang sharply in the confined space.

"Wer ist da? Was ist passiert?"

The little man whimpered, rubbing at his mouth.

Mainwaring straightened, breathing heavily. The GFP captain walked forward, staring, thumbs hooked in his belt.

"Wer sind Sie?"

Mainwaring said, "You know damn well. And speak

English, you bastard. You're as English as I am."

The other glared. He said, "You have no right to be here. I should arrest you. You have no right to accost *Herr Hundenmeister*."

"What is in that van?"

"Have you gone mad? The van is not your concern. Leave now. At once."

"Open it!"

The other hesitated, and shrugged. He stepped back. He said, "Show him, *mein Herr*."

The Hundenmeister fumbled with a bunch of keys. The van doors grated. Mainwaring walked forward, slowly.

The vehicle was empty.

The Captain said, "You have seen what you wished to see. You are satisfied. Now go."

Mainwaring stared round. There was a further door, recessed deeply into the wall. Beside it controls like the controls of a bank vault.

"What is in that room?"

The GFP man said, "You have gone too far. I order you to leave."

"You have no authority over me!"

"Return to your quarters!"

Mainwaring said, "I refuse."

The other slapped the holster at his hip. He gut-held the Walther, wrists locked, feet apart. He said, *"Then you will be shot."*

Mainwaring walked past him, contemptuously. The baying of the dogs faded as he slammed the outer door.

> "It was among the middle classes that the seeds had first been sown; and it was among the middle classes that they flourished. Britain had been called often enough a nation of shopkeepers; now for a little while the tills were closed, the blinds left drawn. Overnight it seemed, an effete symbol of social and national disunity became the *Einsatzegruppefuehrer*; and the wire for the first detention camps was strung. . . ."

Mainwaring finished the page, tore it from the spine,

crumpled it and dropped it on the fire. He went on reading. Beside him on the hearth stood a part-full bottle of whisky and a glass. He picked the glass up mechanically, drank. He lit a cigarette. A few minutes later a new page followed the last.

The clock ticked steadily. The burning paper made a little rustling. Reflections danced across the ceiling of the room. Once Mainwaring raised his head, listened; once put the ruined book down, rubbed his eyes. The room, and the corridor outside, stayed quiet.

> "Against immeasurable force, we must put cunning; against immeasurable evil, faith and a high resolve. In the war we wage, the stakes are high; the dignity of man, the freedom of the spirit, the survival of humanity. Already in that war, many of us have died; many more, undoubtedly, will lay down their lives. But always, beyond them, there will be others; and still more. We shall go on, as we must go on, till this thing is wiped from the earth.
>
> "Meanwhile, we must take fresh heart. Every blow, now, is a blow for freedom. In France, Belgium, Finland, Poland, Russia, the forces of the Two Empires confront each other uneasily. Greed, jealousy, mutual distrust; these are the enemies, and they work from within. This, the Empires know full well. And, knowing, for the first time in their existence, fear. . . ."

The last page crumpled, fell to ash. Mainwaring sat back, staring at nothing. Finally he stirred, looked up. It was zero three hundred; and they hadn't come for him yet.

The bottle was finished. He set it to one side, opened another. He swilled the liquid in the glass, hearing the magnified ticking of the clock.

He crossed the room, took the Luger from the case. He found a cleaning rod, patches and oil. He sat awhile dully, looking at the pistol. Then he slipped the magazine free, pulled back on the breech toggle, thumbed the latch, slid the barrel from the guides.

His mind, wearied, had begun to play aggravating tricks. It ranged and wandered, remembering scenes, episodes, details sometimes from years back; trivial, unconnected. Through and between the wanderings, time after time, ran the ancient, lugubrious words of the carol. He tried to shut them out, but it was impossible.

"Living he spoiled where poor men toiled, which made kind Ceres sad. . . ."

He pushed the link pin clear, withdrew the breech block, stripped the firing pin. He laid the parts out, washed them with oil and water, dried and re-oiled. He reassembled the pistol, working carefully; inverted the barrel, shook the link down in front of the hooks, closed the latch, checked the recoil spring engagement. He loaded a full clip, pushed it home, chambered a round, thumbed the safety to GESICKERT. He released the clip; reloaded.

He fetched his briefcase, laid the pistol inside carefully, grip uppermost. He filled a spare clip, added the extension butt and a fifty box of Parabellum. He closed the flap and locked it, set the case beside the bed. After that there was nothing more to do. He sat back in the chair, refilled his glass.

"Toiling he boiled, where poor men spoiled. . . ."

The firelight faded, finally.

He woke, and the room was dark. He got up, felt the floor sway a little. He understood that he had a hangover. He groped for the lightswitch. The clock hands stood at zero eight hundred.

He felt vaguely guilty at having slept so long.

He walked to the bathroom. He stripped and showered, running the water as hot as he could bear. The process brought him round a little. He dried himself, staring down. He thought for the first time what curious things these bodies were; some with their yellow cylinders, some their indentations.

He dressed and shaved. He had remembered what he was going to do; fastening his tie, he tried to remember why. He couldn't. His brain, it seemed, had gone dead.

There was an inch of whisky in the bottle. He poured it, grimaced and drank. Inside him was a fast, cold shaking. He thought, 'Like the first morning at a new school.'

He lit a cigarette. Instantly his throat filled. He walked to the bathroom and vomited. Then again. Finally there was nothing left to come.

His chest ached. He rinsed his mouth, washed his face again. He sat in the bedroom for a while, head back and eyes closed. In time the shaking went away. He lay unthinking, hearing the clock tick. Once his lips moved. He said, "They're no better than us."

At nine hundred hours he walked to the breakfast room. His stomach, he felt, would retain very little. He ate a slice of toast, carefully drank some coffee. He asked for a packet of cigarettes, went back to his room. At ten hundred hours he was due to meet the Minister.

He checked the briefcase again. A thought made him add a pair of stringback motoring gloves. He sat again, stared at the ashes where he had burned the Geissler. A part of him was willing the clock hands not to move. At five to ten he picked the briefcase up, stepped into the corridor. He stood a moment staring round him. He thought, 'It hasn't happened yet. I'm still alive.' There was still the flat in Town to go back to, still his office; the tall windows, the telephones, the khaki utility desk.

He walked through sunlit corridors to the Minister's suite.

The room to which he was admitted was wide and long. A fire crackled in the hearth; beside it on a low table stood glasses and a decanter. Over the mantel, conventionally, hung the Fuehrer's portrait. Edward VIII faced him across the room. Tall windows framed a prospect of rolling parkland. In the distance, blue on the horizon, were the woods.

The Minister said, "Good morning, Richard. Please sit down. I don't think I shall keep you long."

He sat, placing the briefcase by his knee.

This morning everything seemed strange. He studied the Minister curiously, as if seeing him for the first time. He had that type of face once thought of as peculiarly English; short-nosed and slender, with high, finely-shaped cheek-bones. The hair, blond and cropped close to the scalp, made him look nearly boyish. The eyes were candid, flat, dark-fringed. He looked, Mainwaring decided, not so much Aryan as like some fierce nursery toy; a feral Teddy Bear.

The Minister riffled papers. He said, "Several things have

cropped up; among them I'm afraid, more trouble in Glasgow. The fifty-first Panzer division is standing by; as yet, the news hasn't been released."

Mainwaring wished his head felt less hollow. It made his own voice boom so unnecessarily. He said, "Where is Miss Hunter?"

The Minister paused. The pale eyes stared; then he went on speaking.

"I'm afraid I may have to ask you to cut short your stay here. I shall be flying back to London for a meeting; possibly tomorrow, possibly the day after. I shall want you with me of course."

"Where is Miss Hunter?"

The Minister placed his hands flat on the desk top, studied the nails. He said, "Richard, there are aspects of Two Empires culture that are neither mentioned nor discussed. You of all people should know this. I'm being patient with you; but there are limits to what I can overlook."

"Seldom he toiled, while Ceres roiled, which made poor kind men glad. . . ."

Mainwaring opened the flap of the case and stood up. He thumbed the safety forward and levelled the pistol.

There was silence for a time. The fire spat softly. Then the Minister smiled. He said, "That's an interesting gun, Richard. Where did you get it?"

Mainwaring didn't answer.

The Minister moved his hands carefully to the arms of his chair, leaned back. He said, "It's the Marine model of course. It's also quite old. Does it by any chance carry the Erfurt stamp? Its value would be considerably increased."

He smiled again. He said, "If the barrel is good, I'll buy it. For my private collection."

Mainwaring's arm began to shake. He steadied his wrist, gripping with his left hand.

The Minister sighed. He said, "Richard, you can be so stubborn. It's a good quality; but you do carry it to excess." He shook his head. He said, "Did you imagine for one moment I didn't know you were coming here to kill me? My dear chap, you've been through a great deal. You're overwrought. Believe me, I know just how you feel."

Mainwaring said, "You murdered her."

The Minister spread his hands. He said, "What with? A gun? A knife? Do I honestly look such a shady character?"

The words made a cold pain, and a tightness in the chest. But they had to be said.

The Minister's brows rose. Then he started to laugh. Finally he said, "At last I see. I understood, but I couldn't believe. So you bullied our poor little *Hundenmeister*, which wasn't very worthy; and seriously annoyed the *Herr Hauptmann*, which wasn't very wise. Because of this fantasy, stuck in your head. Do you really believe it, Richard? Perhaps you believe in *Struwwelpeter* too." He sat forward. He said, "The Hunt ran. And killed . . . a deer. She gave us an excellent chase. As for your little Huntress . . . Richard, she's gone. She never existed. She was a figment of your imagination. Best forgotten."

Mainwaring said, "We were in love."

The Minister said, "Richard, you really are becoming tiresome." He shook his head again. He said, "We're both adult. We both know what that word is worth. It's a straw, in the wind. A candle, on a night of gales. A phrase that is meaningless. *Lächerlich.*" He put his hands together, rubbed a palm. He said, "When this is over, I want you to go away. For a month, six weeks maybe. With your new car. When you come back . . . well, we'll see. Buy yourself a girlfriend, if you need a woman that much. *Einen Schatz*. I never dreamed; you're so remote, you should speak more of yourself. Richard, I understand; it isn't such a very terrible thing."

Mainwaring stared.

The Minister said, "We shall make an arrangement. You will have the use of an apartment, rather a nice apartment. So your lady will be close. When you tire of her . . . buy another. They're unsatisfactory for the most part, but reasonable. Now sit down like a good chap, and put your gun away. You look so silly, standing there scowling like that."

It seemed he felt all life, all experience, as a grey weight pulling. He lowered the pistol, slowly. He thought. 'At the end, they were wrong. They picked the wrong man.' He said, "I suppose now I use it on myself."

The Minister said, "No, no, no. You still don't understand." He linked his knuckles, grinning. He said, "Richard, the *Herr Hauptmann* would have arrested you last night. I wouldn't let him. This is between ourselves. Nobody else. I give you my word."

Mainwaring felt his shoulders sag. The strength seemed drained from him; the pistol, now, weighed too heavy for his arm.

The Minister said, "Richard, why so glum? It's a great occasion, man. You've found your courage. I'm delighted."

He lowered his voice. He said, "Don't you want to know why I let you come here with your machine? Aren't you even interested?"

Mainwaring stayed silent.

The Minister said, "Look around you, Richard. See the world. I want men near me, serving me. Now more than ever. Real men, not afraid to die. Give me a dozen . . . but you know the rest. I could rule the world. But first . . . I must rule them. My men. Do you see now? Do you understand?"

Mainwaring thought, 'He's in control again, But he was always in control. He owns me.'

The study spun a little.

The voice went on, smoothly. "As for this amusing little plot by the so-called Freedom Front; again, you did well. It was difficult for you. I was watching; believe me, with much sympathy. Now, you've burned your book. Of your own free will. That delighted me."

Mainwaring looked up, sharply.

The Minister shook his head. He said, "The real recorder is rather better hidden, you were too easily satisfied there. There's also a tv monitor. I'm sorry about it all, I apologise. It was necessary."

A singing started, inside Mainwaring's head.

The Minister sighed again. He said, "Still unconvinced, Richard? Then I have some things I think you ought to see. Am I permitted to open my desk drawer?"

Mainwaring didn't speak. The other slid the drawer back slowly, reached in. He laid a telegram flimsy on the desk top. He said, "The addressee is Miss D. J. Hunter. The message consists of one word. 'ACTIVATE.' "

The singing rose in pitch.

"This as well," said the Minister. He held up a medallion on a thin gold chain. The little disc bore the linked motif of the Freedom Front. He said, "Mere exhibitionism; or a death wish. Either way, a most undesirable trait."

He tossed the thing down. He said, "She was here under surveillance of course, we'd known about her for years. To them, you were a sleeper. Do you see the absurdity? They really thought you would be jealous enough to assassinate your Minister. This they mean in their silly little book, when they talk of subtlety. Richard, I could have fifty blonde women if I chose. A hundred. Why should I want yours?" He shut the drawer with a click, and rose. He said, "Give me the gun now. You don't need it any more." He extended his arm; then he was flung heavily backward. Glasses smashed on the side table. The decanter split; its contents poured dark across the wood.

Over the desk hung a faint haze of blue. Mainwaring walked forward, stood looking down. There were blood-flecks, and a little flesh. The eyes of the Teddy Bear still showed glints of white. Hydraulic shock had shattered the chest; the breath drew ragged, three times, and stopped. He thought, 'I didn't hear the report.'

The communicating door opened. Mainwaring turned. A secretary stared in, bolted at sight of him. The door slammed.

He pushed the briefcase under his arm, ran through the outer office. Feet clattered in the corridor. He opened the door, carefully. Shouts sounded, somewhere below in the house.

Across the corridor hung a loop of crimson cord. He stepped over it, hurried up a flight of stairs. Then another. Beyond the private apartments the way was closed by a heavy metal grille. He ran to it, rattled. A rumbling sounded from below. He glared round. Somebody had operated the emergency shutters; the house was sealed.

Beside the door an iron ladder was spiked to the wall. He climbed it, panting. The trap in the ceiling was padlocked. He clung one-handed, awkward with the briefcase, held the pistol above his head.

Daylight showed through splintered wood. He put his shoulder to the trap, heaved. It creaked back. He pushed head and shoulders through, scrambled. Wind stung at him and flakes of snow.

His shirt was wet under the arms. He lay face down, shaking. He thought, 'It wasn't an accident. None of it was an accident.' He had underrated them. They understood despair.

He pushed himself up, stared round. He was on the roof of Wilton. Beside him rose gigantic chimney stacks. There was a lattice radio mast. The wind hummed in its guy wires. To his right ran the balustrade that crowned the façade of the house. Behind it was a snow-choked gutter.

He wriggled across a sloping scree of roof, ran crouching. Shouts sounded from below. He dropped flat, rolled. An automatic clattered. He edged forward again, dragging the briefcase. Ahead, one of the corner towers rose dark against the sky. He crawled to it, crouched sheltered from the wind. He opened the case, pulled the gloves on. He clipped the stock to the pistol, laid the spare magazine beside him and the box of rounds.

The shouts came again. He peered forward, through the balustrade. Running figures scattered across the lawn. He sighted on the nearest, squeezed. Commotion below. The automatic zipped; stone chips flew, whining. A voice called, "Don't expose yourselves unnecessarily." Another answered.

"Die kommen mit dem Hubschrauber . . ."

He stared round him, at the yellow-grey horizon. He had forgotten the helicopter.

A snow flurry drove against his face. He huddled, flinching. He thought he heard, carried on the wind, a faint droning.

From where he crouched he could see the nearer trees of the park, beyond them the wall and gatehouses. Beyond again, the land rose to the circling woods.

The droning was back, louder than before. He screwed his eyes, made out the dark spot skimming above the trees. He shook his head. He said. "We made a mistake. We all made a mistake."

He settled the stock of the Luger to his shoulder, and waited.

GRAPHICS

The Soviets are great writers and translators of science fiction, and SF is becoming more and more popular there. Novels are serialized in general magazines before book publication, and even the cartoons in these magazines show a science-fictional bent as can be seen by these from Priroda (Nature) *and* Smena (Change). *In America, the newspapers printed this canny observation by Lichty.* Science *has* *overtaken science fiction in many ways, so that now moon-walking is part of our past instead of our future. Still closer to home is the admirable robot by SF artist and author, William Rotsler. It is ever so slightly iconoclastic, as well as being a new look at the editorial function.*

INVISIBILITY COMPETITION
by Y. Aratovsky
from PRIRODA

by O. Tesler
from SMENA

BEST
S.F.
#6

"We interrupt this current landing on the moon for an important news bulletin!"

THE YEARS

ROBERT F. YOUNG

Robert F. Young knows more about non-ferrous foundries than he cares to admit, and a great deal about the human heart which he does show us in this brief and biting voyage in a time machine.

The old man paused when he came to the campus. The season was fall. A raw wind was blowing out of the west. It rattled the dead leaves that hung in tatters from the branches of academic elms and maples. It wrinkled the dead grass and blew through the naked shrubbery. Soon snow would come and the year would die and the new year would bow in.

The old man was trembling, but not because he was cold. The university buildings in the background frightened him. He was terrified of the students strolling along the walk—the long-haired, sloppily attired young men, the long-haired girls in overalls and denims. But he forced himself to go on and he made his old eyes focus upon the faces of the girls. It had cost him his life's savings to make the trip and he was determined not to go back empty-handed.

None of the students seemed to notice him. It was as though he did not exist (in a way he didn't, he supposed). Repeatedly he had to step off the walk to avoid colliding with them. But he was used to such indifference. The young of each generation were invariably arrogant and self-centered. It was only natural that they should be. The world was their apple and they knew it.

The old man began to lose some of his fear. The university buildings were far less formidable in appearance than memory had painted them. Memory was a poor painter at best. It overdrew, exaggerated. It added details that had never existed, left out others that had. And there was yet another consideration. You could never see something the second time in quite the same way you saw it the first, because the part of you that interpreted the initial impression was forever dead.

The old man peered eagerly at the faces of the strolling girls, searching for Elizabeth's. It was her face alone that he wanted to see. He wanted to take its youthful radiance back with him so that the final years of his life might be less bleak—so that some of the loneliness that had descended upon him after the death of his wife might be driven away. Just for a little while. A little while would be enough.

When he finally found her face he was touched to his marrow. So young, he thought. So sweetly beautiful. It surprised him that he could recognize it so readily. Perhaps memory was not as poor a painter as he had thought. His heart pounded and his throat grew tight. The classic reactions, only in his case multiplied by one thousand. His vision dimmed. He found it hard to see. Elizabeth . . .

She was walking beside a tall young man, talking to him and swinging her books. But the old man did not look at her companion. The moment was too precious to waste. Besides, he was afraid to look. The years . . .

The couple drew closer, laughing and talking, warm and secure in the oasis of their youth. Elizabeth wore no hat, no kerchief. Her red-gold hair danced in the wind, broke in evanescent waves along the soft shores of her childlike cheeks. Her lips were an autumn leaf lying lightly upon the lovely landscape of her face. Her eyes were shards of summer sky. She wore a shapeless gray sweater and paint-daubed dungarees. Her long and lissom legs were hidden from the sun. But memory served him well.

He was crying now. Unabashedly, the way a drunk cries. Elizabeth. Elizabeth, my darling, my dear . . .

She did not even notice him till she and her companion were almost abreast of him. Then she seemed to feel his gaze and looked into his eyes. She stopped and her face went white. Her companion halted beside her. The old man halted, too.

Color came into Elizabeth's cheeks. Revulsion darkened the azure of her eyes. Her full lips thinned. "How dare you stare at me like that, you dirty old man!"

Her companion was indignant. Angrily he confronted the old man. "I ought to punch you in the nose!"

The old man was horrified. Why, they hate me, he thought. They look upon me as a leper. I didn't expect them to recognize me—I didn't want them to. But this—dear God, no!

He tried to speak, but there was nothing he could say. He stood there dumbly, staring at the young man's strange and familiar face.

"Dirty old man," Elizabeth said again. She took her companion's arm and the two of them walked away. Helplessly the old man stared after them, knowing that although he would go on living, from that moment on he would be dead.

Why didn't I remember? he wondered. *How could I have forgotten that poor old man?*

He returned on dead legs to the bosquet on the outskirts of the university town where the timefield burned, stepped into its shimmering embrace and sped back through the years that had transmuted him from a tall young man into something unclean. After paying the guard the second half of the agreed-upon bribe and leaving the time station by the rear entrance, he drove out to the cemetery where Elizabeth lay buried. He stood by the grave, in the bitter wind, for a long time. Again and again he read the inscription on the granite marker: B. 1952—D. 2025. IN MEMORY OF MY BELOVED WIFE . . .

But Time the Thief had not yet finished. It trephined his skull and cut deep into his memories and extracted the soft summer nights and the sleeping flowers and the misty afternoons. It left only naked fields and tree-denuded hills.

He read the inscription a final time.

"Dirty old woman," he said.

DARKNESS

ANDRÉ CARNEIRO, translated by Leo L. Barrow

André Carneiro is a Brazilian tornado of artistic energy; a poet, film maker, novelist, photographer, critic—and a masterful short story writer as he proves here. Leo L. Barrow has done a crisp translation that retains the aura of the totally different world of Brazilian SF.

Waldas accepted the reality of the phenomenon a little later than the others. Only on the second day, when everybody was commenting on the growing darkness and the dimming of the lights, did he admit it was true. An old lady was shouting that the world was coming to an end. People gathered in little groups, most of them offering metaphysical explanations, mixed with the scientific commentaries from the papers. He went to work as usual. Even the boss, always distant, was at the window, talking intimately. Most of the employees didn't show up. The huge room full of desks, mostly unmanned, defined the degree of importance of the event.

Those people who always watched the weather were the first to notice. The sunlight seemed a little weaker, houses and objects were surrounded by growing shadows. At first they thought it was an optical illusion, but that night even the electric lights were weaker. Women noticed that liquids didn't reach the boiling point and food remained hard and uncooked. Authoritative opinions were cited, opinions heard on the radio. They were vague and contradictory. Nervous people were provoking panic and the train and bus stations were filled with those leaving town. No one knew where they were going. The news programs said that the phenomenon was universal, but Waldas doubted this.

The latest telegrams, however, were affirmative; the shadow was growing rapidly. Someone struck a match, and the tests began. Everyone made these tests: they would light a lighter or turn on a flashlight in a dark corner, noticing the weaker illumination. Lights didn't brighten the room as before. It couldn't be a universal visual effect. It was possible to run one's fingers through fire without burning them. Many were frightened, but Waldas wasn't one of them. He went home at four o'clock; the lights were on. They gave off very little light—seemed like reddish balls, danger signals. At the lunch counter where he always ate, he got them to serve him cold sandwiches. There was only the owner and one waitress, who left afterwards, walking slowly through the shadows.

Waldas got to his apartment without difficulty. He was used to coming home late without turning on the hall lights. The elevator wasn't working so he walked up the stairs to the third floor. His radio emitted only strange sounds, perhaps voices, perhaps static. Opening the window, he confronted the thousands of reddish glows, lights of the huge buildings whose silhouettes stood out dimly against the starless sky. He went to the refrigerator and drank a glass of milk; the motor wasn't working. The same thing would happen to the water pump. He put the plug in the bath tub and filled it. Locating his flashlight, he went through his small apartment, anxious to find his belongings with the weak light. He left the cans of powdered milk, cereal, some crackers and a box of chocolates on the kitchen table and closed the window, turned out the lights and lay down on the bed. A cold shiver ran through his body as he realized the reality of the danger.

He slept fitfully, dreamed confused and disagreeable dreams. A child was crying in the next apartment, asking its mother to turn on the lights. He woke up startled. With the flashlight pressed against his watch, he saw that it was eight o'clock in the morning. He opened the windows. The darkness was almost complete. You could see the sun in the east, red and round, as if it were behind a thick smoked glass. In the street dim shapes of people passed by like silhouettes. With great difficulty Waldas managed to wash his face; he went to the kitchen and ate rice crispies with powdered milk. Force of habit made him think about his job. He realized that he didn't have any place to go, and he remembered the terror he felt as a child when they locked him in a closet. There wasn't enough air, and the darkness oppressed him. He went to the window and took a deep breath. The red disk of the sun hung in the dark background of the sky. Waldas couldn't coordinate his thoughts; the darkness kept making him feel like running for help. He clenched his fists, repeated to himself, "I have to keep calm, defend my life until everything returns to normal."

He had a married sister who lived three blocks away.

The need to communicate with someone made him decide to go there, to help her family in any way he could. In the darkness of the hallway, he used the wall as a guide. On one side of the hall, a man's anxious voice asked, "Who is it out there?"

"It's me, Waldas from apartment 312," he answered.

He knew who it was, a graying man who had a wife and two children.

"Please," the man asked, "tell my wife that the darkness is going to end; she has been crying since yesterday and the kids are scared." Waldas approached slowly. The woman must be standing next to her husband, sobbing quietly. He tried to smile even though they couldn't see him.

"Don't worry, ma'am, it's pretty dark but you can still see the sun out there. There is no danger; it won't last long."

"Do you hear," the man seconded, "it's only the darkness, no one is going to suffer, you need to stay calm for the children's sake." By the sounds Waldas sensed that they were all clinging to one another. He remained silent for a few moments and then started to go away. "I have to go now, if you need anything. . . ." The man said goodbye, encouraging his wife. "No, thank you very much. This won't last long."

On the steps he couldn't see a thing. He heard bits of conversation coming from the doors of the different apartment buildings. The lack of light made people speak more loudly, or their voices sounded more clearly against the general silence.

He reached the street. The sun was high, but it hardly gave off any light, perhaps less than that of the waning moon. From time to time men went by, alone or in groups. They spoke in loud voices, some still joked when they stumbled in the depressions in the street. Waldas started to walk slowly, mentally visualizing the road to his sister's house. The reddish outline that silhouetted the buildings was diminishing. With his arms extended he could hardly see his fingers. He walked slowly, amazed by those who passed him hurriedly. The whining of a small dog came from some balcony. There was crying in the distance, confused shouts, people calling. Someone was walking and praying.

Waldas kept close to the wall so they wouldn't run into him. He must have been halfway there. He stopped to catch his breath. His chest was heaving, searching for air; his muscles tense and tired. His only point of reference was a blotch of disappearing sun. For a moment he imagined that the others could see more than he. But now shouts and cries were rising everywhere. Waldas turned around. The pulsating red disk had disappeared. The blackness was absolute. Without the silhouette of the building, he felt lost. It was impossible to continue. He would try to return to the apartment. Feeling the wall, identifying some doors and shop windows, he started back, his feet dragging on the pavement. He was sweating and trembling, all his senses concentrating on the way back.

Turning the corner, he heard the unintelligible words of a man coming in his direction. Perhaps drunk, and shouting loudly, he forcibly grabbed Waldas who, trying to pry himself loose, pleaded for calmness. The man shouted all the louder, meaningless things. Desperate, Waldas grabbed him by the throat, pushed him backwards. The man fell and began to moan. His hands extended in front of him in defense, Waldas walked on a bit. Behind him the drunk was crying and moaning in pain. A loose window was rattling, and sounds previously muffled by the noise of radios and cars were coming from the houses and apartments. In the darkness, his hands groping, recognizing different landmarks and doors of iron bars, walls of residences and their big gates, he fell on the first steps of the stairway. Someone shouted:

"Who is it out there?"

"It's me, Waldas, from the third floor."

"Were you outside? Can you see anything?"

"No, you can't see a thing anywhere."

There was a silence, and he slowly went on up the stairs. Moving carefully he opened the door and lay down on the bed.

It was a short and anxious respite. He couldn't relax his

muscles, couldn't think calmly. He dragged himself out to the kitchen, managed to open his watch with a knife. He felt the hands. It was 11 o'clock, or noon, more or less. He dissolved powdered milk in a cup of water and drank it. There was a knocking on his door; his heart beat more rapidly. It was his neighbor, asking for some water for the children. Waldas told him about the full bathtub, and went with him to get his wife and children. His prudence had paid off. They held hands and the human chain slid along the hall, the kids calmer, even his wife who, no longer crying, kept repeating, "Thank you, thank you very much." Waldas took them to the kitchen, made them sit down, the children clinging to their mother. He felt the cupboard, broke a glass, then found an aluminum pan which he filled from the bathtub and took to the table. He surrendered cups of water to the fingers that groped for them. He couldn't keep them level without seeing and the water spilled onto his hands. As they drank, he wondered if he should offer them something to eat. The boy thanked him and said that he was hungry. Waldas picked up the big can of powdered milk and began to prepare it carefully. While he made the slow gestures of opening the can, counting the spoonfuls and mixing them with water, he spoke in a loud voice. They encouraged him, telling him to be careful and praising his ability. Waldas took more than an hour to make and ration out the milk and the effort, the certainty that he was being useful, did him good.

One of the boys laughed at something funny. For the first time since the darkness had set in, Waldas felt optimistic, that everything would turn out all right. They spent an endless time after that in his apartment, trying to talk. They would lean on the window sill, searching for some distant light, seeing it at times, all enthused, only to discover the deceit that they wouldn't admit. Waldas had become the leader of that family; he fed them and led them through the small world of four rooms which he knew with his eyes closed. They left at nine or ten that night, holding hands, Waldas accompanied them, helped put the children to bed. In the streets desperate fathers were shouting, asking for food. Waldas had closed the windows so he couldn't hear them. What he had would be enough to feed the five of them for one or two more days.

Waldas stayed with them, next to the children's room. They lay there talking, their words like links of presence and company. They finally went to sleep, heads under their pillows like shipwrecked sailors clinging to logs, listening to pleas for help that they couldn't possibly answer. They slept, dreaming about the breaking of a new day, a blue sky, the sun flooding their rooms, their eyes, hungry from fasting, avidly feeding on the colors. It wasn't that way.

The hands of Waldas' watch indicated it was more or less eight o'clock. The others began to stir and holding hands they filed back to his kitchen where they ate their frugal meal of cereal and milk. The children bumped into the furniture, got lost in the small living room; their mother scolded them anxiously. Once settled in the armchairs they didn't know what to do with themselves.

They went back over the causes of the phenomenon, inventing reasons and hypotheses that transcended science. Waldas commented imprudently that the situation could continue forever. The woman began to cry; it was difficult to calm her. The kids asked questions which were impossible to answer. Suddenly Waldas felt anxious to do something; he got up, was going out to investigate. They protested; it would be dangerous and useless. He had to reassure them that he wouldn't go more than sixty feet from the building, just to the corner, that he wouldn't cross the street, etc.

Outside, he leaned against the wall, listening. A cold wind whistled through the wires, dragged pieces of paper along with a soft noise. There was howling in the distance, becoming more intense from time to time, and voices, many unintelligible voices. He stood still, tense and waiting, and then walked a few yards. Only his ears could capture the pulsations of the city drowned in darkness. With his eyes opened or closed it was the same black well, without beginning or end. It was terrible to remain there, quietly waiting for nothing.

The ghosts of his youth surrounded Waldas, and he returned to his building almost running, scratching his hands along the wall, stumbling on the stairs, while frightened voices shouted: "Who is it out there? Who is out there?" He answered, out of breath, taking the stairs two at a time until he reached his friends who were bumping into each other trying to find him, afraid that he had been hurt, asking him what had happened. He laughed, confessing that he had become frightened.

Enclosed for the rest of the day they worked and talked a lot, describing what they were doing. The chain of words which linked them together eventually broke. None of them could know, but they all raised their heads at the same time, listening, breathing heavily, waiting for a miracle which wasn't materializing.

Rationed and divided, the box of chocolates had come to an end. There was still cereal and powdered milk. If the light didn't return soon it would be cruel to predict the consequences. The hours passed. Lying down again, eyes closed, fighting to go to sleep, they waited for the morning with its beams of light on the window. But they woke as before, their eyes useless, the flames extinguished, the stoves cold and their food running out. Waldas divided the last of the cereal and milk. They became uneasy. The building had ten floors; Waldas thought he ought to go to the top floor to look into the distance.

He went out and started up. Questions came from the apartments. "Who is out there? Who is it going up the stairs?" On the sixth floor one voice assured him, "You can go up there if you like, but you are wasting your time. I was just there with two others. You can't see a thing, anywhere." Waldas ventured, "My food has run out, I have a couple and two children with me. Could you help me?" The voices answered, "Our supply will only last until tomorrow. We can't do a thing. . . ." Waldas decided to go back down. Could he tell his friends the truth?

"I didn't go all the way up. I found someone who had been there a short time ago. He said you could see something, very distant, he couldn't explain what it was." The couple and their children were filled with hope when he suggested the only idea that might work. He would go out again, and break into a grocery store about a hundred yards away.

Armed with a crowbar from his toolbox, he was leaving his shelter to steal food. It was frightening to think what he might encounter. The darkness had erased all distinctions. Waldas walked next to the wall, his mind reconstructing the details of this stretch, his hands investigating every indentation. Inch by inch his fingers followed the outline of the building until they came to the corrugated iron door. He couldn't be wrong.

It was the only commercial establishment on the block. He bent over to find the lock. His hands didn't encounter resistance. The door was only half closed. He stooped over and entered without making a sound. The shelves on the right would have food and sweets. He collided with the counter, cursed and remained motionless, muscles tensed, waiting. He climbed over the counter and began to reach out with his hand; it touched the board and he started running it along the shelf. There was nothing; of course, they sold it before the total darkness. He raised his arm, searching more rapidly. Nothing, not a single object. He started climbing without worrying about the noise, his fingers dry from the accumulated dust. He climbed down carelessly, his body bent forward, his hands moving frantically in every direction, foolishly getting scratched and cut against the wall as if they were competing for cans and merchandise that didn't exist. Many times Waldas returned to the same point where he had begun his search. There was nothing, not in any corner. He stopped, still anxious to begin again but knowing that it wouldn't do any good. For those with no reserve food it was obvious that the grocery stores had been the only solution.

Waldas sat down on an empty box and tears filled his eyes. What could he do? Return with his failure, renew the search in other more distant stores, whose exact locations he didn't know?

He took up the crowbar again and with short careful steps he started back home in search of his invisible friends. Suddenly he stopped, his hands searching for a familiar landmark. Step by step he advanced a few more yards, discovering doors and walls until he came to an unknown corner. He had to go back to the store and start again from there. He went back the way he had come, scratching his fingers in the darkness, feeling for a corrugated door which wasn't appearing. He was lost. He sat down on the sidewalk, his temples throbbing. He struggled up like a drowning man and shouted, "Please, I'm lost, I need to know the name of this street." He repeated it time after time, each time more loudly, but no one answered him. The more silence he felt around him the more he implored, asking them to help him for pity's sake. And why should they? He himself, from his own window, had heard the cries of the lost asking for help, their desperate voices causing one to fear the madness of an assault. Waldas started off without any direction, shouting for help, explaining that four persons depended on him. No longer feeling the walls, he walked hurriedly in circles, like a drunk, begging for information and food. "I'm Waldas, I live at number 215, please help me."

There were noises in the darkness; impossible for them not to hear him. He cried and pleaded without the least shame, the black pall reducing him to a helpless child. The darkness stifled him, entering through his pores, changing his thoughts. Waldas stopped pleading. He bellowed curses at his fellowmen, calling them evil names, asking them why they didn't answer. His helplessness turned into hate and he grasped the crowbar, ready to obtain food by violence. He came across others begging for food like himself. Waldas advanced, brandishing his crowbar, until he collided with someone, grabbing him and holding him tightly. The man shouted and Waldas, without letting him go, demanded that he tell him where they were and how they could get some food. The other seemed old and broke into fearful sobs. Waldas relaxed the pressure, released him. He threw the weapon into the street, and sat down on the sidewalk listening to the small sounds, the wind rattling windows in the abandoned apartments. Different noises emerged from several directions, deep, rasping and sharp sounds, from animals, men perhaps, trapped or famished. A light rhythmic beating of footsteps was approaching. He yelled for help and remained listening. A man's voice, some distance away, answered him. "Wait, I'll come and help you."

The man carried a heavy sack and was panting from the effort. He asked Waldas to help him by holding one end, he would go in front. Waldas sensed something inexplicable. He could hardly follow the man as he turned the corners with assurance. A doubt passed through his mind. Perhaps his companion could see a little the light was coming back for the others. He asked him, "You walk with such assurance, you can't by any chance see a little?" The man took a while to answer. "No, I can see absolutely nothing. I am completely blind." Waldas stammered, "Before this . . . too?" "Yes, blind from birth, we are going to the Institute for the Blind, where I live."

Vasco, the blind man, told him that they had helped lost persons and had taken in a few; but their stock of food was small and they couldn't take anybody else in. The darkness continued without any sign of ending. Thousands of people might die from starvation and nothing could be done. Waldas felt like a child that adults had saved from danger. At the Institute they gave him a glass of milk and some toast. In his memory, however, the image of his friends was growing, their hearts jumping at every sound, going hungry, waiting for his return. He spoke to Vasco. They deliberated. The apartment building was large, all the others living there also deserved help, something quite impracticable. Waldas remembered the children; he asked them to show him the way or he would go alone. He got up to leave, stumbled over something, falling. Vasco remembered that there was a bathtub full of water, and water was one thing they needed. They brought two big plastic containers and Vasco led Waldas to the street. They tied a little cord around both their waists.

Vasco, who knew the neighborhood, walked as fast as possible, choosing the best route, calling out the name of the streets, changing course when they heard suspicious sounds or mad ravings. Vasco stopped and said softly, "It must be here." Waldas advanced a few steps, recognized the door latch. Vasco whispered to him to take off his shoes; they would go in without making any noise. After tying their shoes to the cord, they entered with Waldas in front, going up the stairs two at a time. They bumped into things along the way and heard unintelligible voices from behind the doors.

Reaching the third floor they went to his neighbor's apartment, knocked softly and then more loudly. No one answered. They went to Waldas' apartment. "It's me, Waldas, let me in." His neighbor uttered an exclamation like someone who didn't believe it and opened the door, extending his arm for his friend to grasp. "It's me all right, how is everybody? I brought a friend who saved me and knows the way."

In the bathroom they filled two plastic containers with water and Vasco tied them to the backs of the two men with strips of cloth. He also helped to identify some useful things they could take. They took off their shoes and in single file, holding hands, started for the stairs. They went hurriedly; they would inevitably be heard. On the main floor, next to the door, a voice inquired: "Who are you?" No one answered and Vasco pulled them all out into the street. In single file they gained distance; it would be difficult to follow them.

It took more time to return because of the children, and the stops they made to listen to nearby noises. They arrived at the Institute exhausted, with the temporary feeling of relief of soldiers after winning a battle.

Vasco served them oatmeal and milk and went to talk to his companions about what they would do to survive if the darkness continued. Another blind man fixed them a place to sleep, which came easily since they hadn't slept for a long time. Hours later Vasco came to awaken them, saying that they had decided to leave the Institute and take refuge on the Model Farm that the Institute owned a few miles outside the city. Their supplies here wouldn't last long and there was no way to replenish them without danger.

Although the way was longer, they planned to follow the railroad tracks which ran a few blocks from the Institute.

The meeting room was a big place; the murmur of voices forming a steady bubbling. Vasco must have been older or had some authority over the others. He told them that a completely realistic appraisal of their situation was indispensable if they hoped to survive. He spoke to his blind companions first, affirming that the darkness which afflicted the others was nothing new to them. They had taken eleven persons into the Institute. With the twelve blind people who already lived there they were twenty-three in all. The food that could be eaten would last them only six or seven days. It would be risky to wait and hope that everything would return to normal in that time, to say nothing of the chance of being assaulted or robbed by lost and hungry people. Normally there were ten people on the Model Farm. They raised several crops, had food in stock for commerce, and had a great quantity of drinking water; with careful use and rationing, this could guarantee their existence for a long time. Co-operation and obedience to all decisions were imperative. They would leave the Asylum in silence, without answering any call.

The blind men finished distributing the full sacks, suitcases, and boxes for the trip. Waldas, standing still and useless, thought about how many times he had passed these men with their dark glasses, their white canes, their heads fixed, always facing forward. True, he always gave them a brief thought of pity. Ah, if they had only known then how one day they would become the magic protectors, capable of saving other beings, beings made of flesh, muscles, thoughts, and with useless eyes, the same as theirs.

Like mountain climbers, they formed four groups linked by a cord. The most doubtful part would be getting through all the streets until they came to the railroad tracks. They asked for complete silence. The anonymous cries that they heard in the darkness were transformed into small obstacles that had to be avoided. The column, loaded with food, steered clear of those who begged for a piece of bread to sustain their lives. The wind brought all sorts of cries as the file of shipwrecked persons slipped through the darkness in this strangest of flights, with blind men at the helm. When their shoes touched the endless steel of the railroad tracks, the tension eased. Their progress became painful; they had to measure their steps to avoid stumbling on the crossties. Time passed; to Waldas it seemed like many hours. Suddenly they stopped. There was a train or some box cars ahead of them. Vasco went to investigate, alone. A whisper passed from mouth to mouth made them renew their journey. They had to go around the box cars. The sound was coming from one of them. They went by the cars with their hearts pounding, their ears almost touching the wooden doors. A man or an animal, locked in, dying. . . . Everything was being left behind, their tired feet moved on an endless belt. In this nightmarish tunnel, Waldas felt like a condemned man wearing his hood of death. The darkness brought all life—the concentration of all his senses—to his shoes which were trudging along over the crushed rocks, between the parallel limits of the tracks.

Waldas was surprised when the cord tied to his waist pulled

him into a dirt road. Without knowing how, he realized that they were in the country. How did the blind men find the exact spot? Perhaps through their sense of smell, the perfume of the trees like ripe limes. He breathed deeply. He knew that odor; it came from eucalyptus trees. He could imagine them in straight lines, on each side of the road. The column stopped; they had arrived at their unseen destination. For the time being the urgent fight to keep from dying of hunger had ended.

The blind men brought them a cold soup that seemed to contain oatmeal and honey. Vasco directed the difficult maneuver to keep them from colliding. They had shelter and food. And the others who remained in the city, the sick in the hospitals, the small children . . . ? No one could or wanted to know.

While Waldas had been moving about in his own neighborhood and apartment he remembered the form of the buildings, the furniture and objects. In his new surroundings, his inexperienced fingers touching here and there could not give him any base for an idea about their relationships.

There were carrots, tomatoes and greens in the gardens, some ripe fruit in the orchard. They should distribute equal rations, a little more for the children. There was speculation as to whether the green vegetables would wilt after so many days without sunshine. The man in charge of the small hen house told how he had fed the hens every day since the sun stopped shining, but they hadn't laid since then.

With the tension of immediate danger relaxed, Waldas felt the reactions that the darkness provoked. His words no longer followed a direct line to the eyes of the person he was addressing; there was no lifting of the eyebrows nor nodding of the head to give emphasis to his arguments. To speak without seeing anyone always raised the doubt as to whether the other was paying attention. In the muscles of his face, now more inert, he sensed the lack of expression which characterizes blind persons. Conversations lost their naturalness and when they didn't respond immediately it seemed like they hadn't listened.

Waldas was learning. If he had discovered a hole or irregularity the day before, his hands would now recognize the already touched surface. But when his hands and feet groped over a new way, only sounds could guide him, or he had to call for help from the experienced sons of darkness.

They were in their sixth day without light. The temperature had dropped but that was normal for this time of year. Therefore, the sun must be warming the atmosphere, one way or another. The phenomenon could not have been of a cosmic order. Someone quoted prophecies from the Bible, the end of the world. Another suggested a mysterious invasion by another planet. Vasco said that, even without consulting his watch, he could still perceive a subtle difference between night and day. Waldas figured that it was just a habit, the organism was accustomed to the successive periods of work and rest. From time to time someone would climb a ladder placed outside, next to the door, and turn his head in all four directions. Sometimes they would shout enthusiastically as they perceived vague spots of light. Everyone would get all excited, walking towards the door with their arms extended, some of them in the wrong direction, running into walls and asking, "Where are you? Did you see something? What was it? What was it?" This was repeated so often that the excitement when "someone glimpsed something" wore off. After many tests and discussions, the darkness remained complete.

The rescued persons showed a perceptible note of bitterness in the things they said. When they tried happy phrases, the shadows eliminated the smile from their lips, the vivacity from their eyes. The blind men had a different inflection in their voices. In Vasco you could sense more clearly the manner of one who acts with assurance and moves with ease. Those same men with white canes and dark glasses who used to ask humbly which bus was coming, or who drew away slowly before the pitying eyes of the passersby, now were rapid, efficient, miraculous with their manual ability. They answered questions and led their charges by the arm with the solicitude and satisfaction of the borrowed charity they used to receive. They were patient and tolerant of errors and misconceptions. Their private misfortune had become everyone's. There was little time for relaxation, but after the last meal the blind people sang, accompanied by two guitars. Waldas noted a natural enthusiasm and even a happiness that the situation did not call for.

Waldas noticed that the children got along better than the

adults. His neighbor's two sons were afraid at first, but the constant proximity of their companions encouraged them to go out on explorations which became difficult to control. They were scolded and even paddled, something which provoked the intervention of conciliatory voices.

Finally, much to Waldas' surprise, they achieved a routine for the trips to the bathroom, washing up and bathing at the edge of the river, the important hours for the meals which were becoming more and more insipid—wilted greens, cucumbers, tomatoes, papaya, oatmeal, milk, honey, not always identifiable by their sense of taste. No catastrophe, no human event would have been more extraordinary or more dangerous than this one. If the blackness which enveloped them brought physical discomfort and problems, it was nothing compared to the thoughts that the impenetrable wall distilled into their minds. Might it be the end of the world that people had predicted since time immemorial? They had to put aside this sinister prospect and keep on taking care of the common essential things such as feeding and clothing the body. Many prayed aloud, asking for a miracle.

Without sight to distract one's mind, it was difficult to endure the idle moments. Dedication to work was exaggerated. Would the world return to normal or would they all die slowly? This constituted a crushing dilemma, weightier than the darkness suffocating them. Vasco seemed worried about the future, but much less so than Waldas. Placed in the same experience, they found it impossible to approach it from the same point of view.

They were already in their sixteenth day when Vasco called Waldas aside. He told him that even the reserves of oatmeal, powdered milk, and canned goods that they had saved were almost gone. And their nervous condition was becoming aggravated; it wouldn't be prudent to warn the others. Arguments came up over the least thing and were prolonged without reason. Most of them were on the edge of nervous collapse.

During the early hours of the eighteenth day they were awakened by shouts of joy and animation. One of the refugees who hadn't been able to go to sleep had felt a difference in the atmosphere. He climbed the ladder outside the house.

There was a pale red ball on the horizon.

Everyone came out at once, pushing and falling, and remained there in a contagious euphoria waiting for the light to increase. Vasco asked if they really did see something, if it wasn't just another false alarm. Someone remembered to strike a match and after a few attempts the flame appeared. It was fragile and without heat, but visible to the eyes of those who looked upon it as a rare miracle.

The light increased slowly, in the way that it had disappeared.

This was a perfect day with unexpected and total joys that worked like some powerful stimulant. Their hearts seemed warmed, full of good will. Their eyes were reborn like innocent and blameless children. They wanted their meals outside and Vasco agreed since the normal days seemed about to return. The sun took its expected course across the sky. At four o'clock in the afternoon you could already distinguish a person's shadow at a distance of four yards. After the sun went down, the complete darkness returned. They built a fire in the yard, but the flames were weak and translucent and consumed very little of the wood. It went out frequently and the refugees would light it again with pieces of paper and blow on it, conserving the pallid fountain of light and warmth, symbol of future life. At midnight it was difficult to convince them that they should go to bed. Only the children slept. Those who had matches struck one from time to time and chuckled to themselves as if they had found the philosopher's stone of happiness.

At four-thirty in the morning they were up and outside. No dawn in the history of the world was ever awaited like this one. It wasn't the beauty of the colors, the poetry of the horizon coming into view amid the clouds, the mountains, the trees and the butterflies. As in the age of fire when man shielded his fire and worshiped it, the divinity of light was awaited by the refugees as a condemned man awaits the official with the commutation of his sentence. The sun was brighter; unaccustomed eyes were closed; the blind men extended the palms of their hands towards the rays, turned them over to feel the heat on both sides. Different faces came forth, with voices you could recognize, and they laughed and embraced each other. Their loneliness and their differences disappeared in that boundless dawn. The blind people were kissed and hugged, carried in triumph. Men cried, and this made their eyes, unaccustomed to the light, turn even redder. About noon the flames became normal and for the first time in three weeks they had a hot cooked meal. Little work was done for the rest of the day. Flooded with light, they absorbed the scenes about them, walking through the places where they had dragged themselves in the darkness.

And the city? What had happened to the people there? This was a terribly sobering thought and those who had relatives ceased to smile. How many had died or suffered extreme hardships? Waldas suggested that he should investigate the situation the next day. Others volunteered, and it was decided that three should go.

Waldas spent a bad night. The impact of all those days was beginning to have its effect. His hands trembled, he was afraid, of what he didn't know. Return to the city, renew his life . . . go to the office, his friends, women. . . . The values he had once held remained subverted and buried in the darkness. It was a different man who was tossing and squirming in an improvised bed without being able to sleep. A square of light coming from a small lamp in the hallway was flickering through the transom, a sign that all was well. His memory brought him rapid fragments, a dog howling, a man moaning on the sidewalk, his hand brandishing the crowbar, Vasco leading him through the streets, his boss talking in front of the window. . . . Bits of his childhood were mixed in as sleep slowly took over. He tossed and turned, his brow wrinkled in a struggle with his dreams.

The three refugees left as the sun was coming up, walking along the road that would lead them to the railroad tracks. One of them was middle aged, married and without children. His wife had stayed behind in the country house. The other must have been the same age as Waldas. His brothers and sisters lived in another part of the city. He had been saved by a blind man and had not been able to return to his home.

They went around a curve and the city came into view. After the first bridges, the tracks began to cross streets. Waldas and his companions went down one of them. The first two blocks seemed very calm, with a few persons moving about, perhaps a bit more slowly. On the next corner they saw a group of people carrying a dead man, covered with a rough cloth, to a truck. The people were crying. A brown army truck went by, its loudspeaker announcing an official government bulletin. Martial law had been declared. Anyone invading another's property would be shot. The government had requisitioned all food supplies and was distributing them to the needy. Any vehicle could be commandeered if necessary. It advised that the police be immediately notified of any buildings with bad odors so that they could investigate the existence of corpses. The dead would be buried in common graves.

Waldas didn't want to return to his own apartment building. He remembered the voices calling through the half opened doors and he, in his stocking feet, slipping away, leaving them to their fate. He would have to telephone the authorities if there was a bad odor. He had already seen enough; he didn't want to stay there. His young companion had talked to an officer and had decided to look for his family immediately. Waldas asked if the telephones were working and learned that some of the automatic circuits were. He dialed his brother-in-law's number and after a short while there was an answer. They were weak but alive. There had been four deaths in the apartment house. Waldas told them briefly how he had been saved and asked if they needed anything. No, they didn't, there was some food, and they were a lot better off than most.

Everyone was talking to strangers, telling all kinds of stories. The children and the sick were the ones who had suffered most. They told of cases of death in heartbreaking circumstances. The public services were reorganizing, with the help of the army, to take care of those in need, bury the dead and get everything going again. Waldas and his middle-aged companion didn't want to hear any more. They felt weak, weak with a certain mental fatigue from hearing and seeing incredible things in which the absurd wasn't just a theory but what really had happened, defying all logic and scientific laws.

The two men were returning along the still empty tracks,

walking slowly under a pleasantly clouded sky. A gentle breeze rustled the leaves of the green trees and birds flitted among their branches. How had they been able to survive in the darkness? Waldas thought about all this as his aching legs carried him along. His scientific certainties were no longer valid. At that very moment men still shaken by the phenomenon were working electronic computers making precise measurements and observations, religious men in their temples explaining the will of God, politicians dictating decreees, mothers mourning the dead that had remained in the darkness.

Two exhausted men walked along the ties. They brought news, perhaps better than could be expected. Mankind had resisted. By eating anything resembling food, by drinking any kind of liquid, people had lived for three weeks in the world of the blind. Waldas and his companion were returning sad and weakened, but with the secret and muffled joy of being alive. More important than rational speculations was the mysterious miracle of blood running through one's veins, the pleasure of loving, doing things, moving one's muscles and smiling. Seen from a distance the two were smaller than the straight tracks that enclosed them. Their bodies were returning to their daily routine, subject to the forces and uncontrollable elements in existence since the beginning of time. But, as their eager eyes took in every color, shade, and movement, they gave little thought to the mysterious magnitude of their universe, and even less to the plight of their brothers, their saviors, who still walked in darkness.

There were planets, solar systems and galaxies. They were only two men, bounded by two impassive rails, returning home with their problems.

FIVE POEMS

Last year we were pleased to discover three science fiction poems for this anthology, so our pleasure is magnified this year with five. May the trend go on into the future so that a poetry section can be a continuing feature of this series. Lawrence Sail, whose "Fisherman" appeared in BEST NO. 5, has two fine poems now. John Cotton, also a recidivist ("Report Back," BEST NO. 3), now presents his vision of a totally alien landscape seen through familiar eyes. Then we have newcomer Patricia Beer, and she is followed by a rare poem by the well-known SF writer Theodore S. Cogswell. It is a thunderously funny offering with rumbling echoes of that other great poet, Enderby.

CYMBAL PLAYER

LAWRENCE SAIL

after all that time
a lifetime perhaps
of watching the others
their brute bulged cheeks
swift spiky fingers
oceans of slow arms

at last he holds
gingerly these
brackets of gold
to trap the earth in
stealthily now he
raises them high and

light lashes the seas
flashing the world blind
he god lasts a whole
second now awaits
the long lurch homewards
across the splintered planet

REPORT FROM THE PLANET PROTEUS

LAWRENCE SAIL

They have arrived—at last! and, as we feared,
In nothing better than a brittle box of metal
Crammed with outmoded data. I could hardly believe
The shock transmitted by my regolith,
The rigid impact of their primitive craft
Thudding, juddering down.

I haven't the heart or, come to that, the language
To tell them that their cargo of rattling digits
And slick equations will serve no purpose here.
In the end, of course, they're bound to notice something—
The way their footprints fade, horizons shift,
All measurements misfit.

I've done my best for them, supplied a ledge
Of solid rock, a layer of purple dust,
Even a hillock flared with astroblemes.
I only hope it lasts, because I sense
A growing impulse, in that very region,
Towards a methane sea.

There is, for once, no choice: we must allow
Their stunted minds to glean at least a semblance
Of so-called "facts". They are not ready yet
To do without the security of selection.
Here's hoping that gamma nine can stabilise
Enough to suggest a moon.

Let them return to earth, report their findings.
Distortion protects us; they will not find us again
Or recognise us if they did. One day
They too may learn to live as multiforms—
Till then our possible orbits, fellow planets,
Laughingly ring their science.

COLUMBUS ON ST. DOMINICA
("Columbus landed here for a day" Travelogue)

JOHN COTTON

The men inland exploring
the island and its women,
it is a time to savour
the moment and its quality,
the air as soft as Spring
in Andalucia,
redolent with vegetation
and the moist richness of the sea.

Yet the expected sense
of triumph eludes me,
the elation of giving,
at last, two fingers
to the doubts of Saint Augustine,
resolved to a regret
astringent as the sharp
metallic taste of the water
running clear over these beds of pebbles.

For the moment of discovery
is irredeemable;
The first sighting of mountains,
the green profusion of valleys,
the echo of bird call
etching the morning,
to continue only
in the distorting mirror of the memory.

Such was the pristine
golden land we dreamt of,
our sin in landfall
to let slip once more
the chains of Knowledge.
And if I should return
it will be to the cliffs beyond,
gnawed by the sea,
where things crumble
and the only philosophy is erosion.

AFTER DEATH

PATRICIA BEER

Opening up the house
After three weeks away
I found bird droppings
All over the ground floor,
White and heavy on the windows,
On the worktop,
On the cupboards,
On every wild hope of freedom.

I could not find any bird
At first, and feared
Some science fiction mystery,
To be horribly explained
As soon as whatever
It was felt sure
It had got me alone,
A mile from the village.

At last I discovered him,
Weightless and out of the running,
More null than old wrapping paper
A month after Christmas.
No food inside him of course,
He had died of hunger
And no waste either,
He was quite empty.

His desperate ghost
Flew down my throat and my ears.
There was no air
He had not suffered in.
He lay in one place,
His droppings were everywhere
More vivid, more terrible
Than he had been, ever.

FAEX DELENDA EST

THEODORE R. COGSWELL

Thou shalt have a place also
without the camp, whither thou
shalt go forth abroad:

And thou shalt have a paddle
upon thy weapon; and it shall
be, when thou wilt ease thyself
abroad, thou shalt dig therewith,
and shalt turn back and cover
that which comes from thee.
—Deuteronomy 23,24

Hey, you who gather in the published jakes
And squat upon mirrors,
Lift up your heads, and listen.
Before too long,
Due to a temporary Aquarian suspension
Of peristaltic action,
Even haiku won't be able to make it
Past the third loop of the upper gut.
God's had enough of your sparrow farts.
When Blake broke wind,
Stars fell.

So did the market for termite turds in amber.

Up North you'd freeze your balls.
Straddling the slit latrines of Niflheim,
Frost Giants shit icebergs,
And the Norns squat before their loom
Crapping quarterlies.
The South isn't much better.
The last poet who went down there to
To bugger Medusa
Took one look at them wriggling hemorrhoids
And turned to Plexiglas.
The Mark VII burnished shield
Only offers protection
In the 3500 to 7000 Angstrom range.

The powers that be just took the doors
Off every Guggenheim;
Forsake your bowel-locked muse and follow me.
I know a place where constipated elephants go
To defecate whole foothills,
And another at the roots of Yggdrasil
Where rising like Everest,
Steaming under exploding suns,
Fresh from the thundering rectum
Of the Midgaard serpent,
Is drek beyond your wildest dreams.

Prepare to meet thy Lord!
Out at the galactic rim
A sphincter opens like an eye.
God's buttocks, like twin radar domes,
Lock in on Earth.
Portents crackle from the antipodes!
Shit storm just went by Arcturus
And she's a-heading this way.

Word kickers of the world, repent!
And shoulder shovels.
It's time you learned an honest trade.
Look toward Boötes,
Come spring we're going to have
To dig ourselves out.

Faex delenda est!

WORDS OF WARNING

ALEX HAMILTON

Alex Hamilton, educated variously in South America and England and, after leaving Oxford University, variously employed, is now a feature writer for The Times *and* The Guardian. *He has a sound reputation as a novelist and anthologist and here proves himself also a master of the short story—the science fiction short story at that. It is a caustically funny example of what might well be called a lexicographer's nightmare.*

Frances and Alan Bell were sitting like bookends on opposite sides of their beds when the phone rang. "My God," said Frances who was letting her nails dry, "I thought the virtue of teaching was that you had so much time to yourself! They never leave you alone here."

Alan, who had the young man's superstition that a phone left to ring might be to ignore some exciting new offer which would possibly never be repeated, stirred uneasily, and put down the clock which he had been winding. "It might be a wrong number," he said to placate her, as he padded towards the phone.

"Whoever it is, tell them to go to bed," she replied.

When she heard him say cordially, "Oh, hello, Dr. Fryer, no we haven't gone to bed yet," she rolled her eyes upward in exasperation, and paying no attention to Alan's hand which signalled her to be quiet, she cried out:

"You might just know that only a man who's never been married would ring at this hour!"

Alan put his hand over the mouthpiece until she was silent and then said into it, "Sorry, Doctor, I didn't quite catch what it was you wanted, the radio's a bit loud."

Frances giggled suddenly. "Radio!" she squeaked. She jumped up abruptly and dashed across the room to him, languishing over him as he crouched by the phone, putting her head on one side so that her hair concealed half her face, and pushing her bust against the receiver. "Ask him," she whispered, "how he likes the late show on telly." But Alan only frowned and shook his head, and she marched huffily back to bounce on the bed, heavier by two stone of rebuff.

When the dazzle of rage had dimmed enough for her to receive again, she heard Alan saying: "Well, yes, Dr. Fryer. I believe I do have that book on my shelves. Hold on while I go take a look." She said nothing, merely fixed her eye on the hanging receiver until he returned from his study with a hefty volume in his hand, which he spread self-consciously on the small table which held the phone. He turned the pages and groped for the receiver. She went back again and stood over him.

Alan said hesitantly, "You did say the 1965 MLA Bibliography published by the New York University Press? Well, I'm looking at page 71, but there's no section of American English . . ."

He drew in his breath sharply as Frances's finger, newly carmined and brilliant at its vengeful extremity, jabbed down on the page and pointed out to him that the same sheet had a secondary pagination at the foot. Alan continued, "Oh yes, Frances is here and I've just realised . . . Yes, I have the page now . . . entry 3339? You want me to read it? It reads *Schwartz, David L. 'Syrian Pig Latin.' AS. XL, 156–157.* What? Yes. Same edition as yours. And you're missing 'Pig'. No idea why that should happen. Foreign body in the presses, I should think. No, *no*, Dr. Fryer. You're not to think that. It's a pleasure to help, believe me. Any time I can . . . Good night." He hung up, and without looking at Frances took the book back to his study.

She was sitting in bed with her knees drawn up when he returned. "Pig is right," she said. "Bloody nerve! At one o'clock in the morning. For a reference!"

Trying to suppress his anger he replied, "Well, I quite agree. It is a bit much. But what can I do? I can't very well tell the Head of the Department that his latest *trouvaille* isn't that important, can I? You know what Fryer's like when he's on to something. At the moment he's probably drafting a letter to *The Times*. And anyway, to look on the bright side, it's a bit of a compliment to me really that he should turn to me for help."

She exploded with: "Comp . . . ! Don't be *fatuous*. There isn't anybody else in residence he could turn to." Then the phone rang again.

They both looked at it without moving. "Don't answer it," said Frances.

"We can't pretend we've gone to bed and got to sleep in under a minute, can we now?" he protested.

She wriggled vigorously to get out of bed, but he was sitting on the covers and she was pinned in. She exclaimed, "Let me bloody talk to him then. I'll give him some references to file." But Alan pushed her back and answered the call.

When he spoke it was in a low voice, as if he hoped she would not overhear. "In the *Oxford Dictionary of English Etymology?* Yes, Dr. Fryer, I do have that. Yes, I can turn that up for you." He held the receiver with his palm over the mouthpiece and whispered savagely, "Listen, Frankie, if you're rude or hang up on him while I'm getting the book, I'll bloody brain you. It would be my promotion chances knackered. For God's sake have some sense." Looking grimly back at her over his shoulder he disappeared from the room.

This time he rattled out the entry at top speed. "Pig pig young of swine XIII (AncrR.); swine of any age, oblong piece of metal, ingot (cf. SOW) XVI. ME pigge; OE picga, pigga—what's that? What? I don't understand. The entry comes between piffle and pigeon . . . Yes, the word pig recurs twice. Complete complement of pigs in fact. I'll read the rest of the derivation if you like. You have the rest? Just that you wanted? OK. I don't quite . . . Yes, I shall be here. No, I'll leave the line open. Yes, right, I will. 'Bye."

Alan stood looking bewildered in the middle of the bedroom. Frances said, "I hope you feel all this is bringing your promotion forward. I hope his paper on Pig includes acknowledgment to you. I hope the philologists of the world are needing Pig. The sensational chase and ultimate sticking of Pig."

He began putting on his clothes, and said, "All right, all right, Frankie. I know how you feel. But there's something funny going on. Philologically pig is gutted. Something very funny. . . ." He was already moving to the phone as it rang again.

"He's going round the twist, that's what's funny," she said.

This time Alan only listened for a minute, and said quietly, "Yes, Dr. Fryer, I'll be round. I have the car outside the house right now. Don't do anything till I get there. Close your books, I should." He replaced the receiver for the third time and reached for his jacket. "Says he can't find Pig anywhere in his library. It sounds to me as if you might be right. Hope you're not, but I'd better just nip round and check."

She was out of bed and rooting a scarf for him out of the chest of drawers. "How awful, Alan. Do you want me to come?"

"No, it'll be OK."

"But you will be careful?"

"Oh, he's a vinegary old soul, but he won't be any trouble. I'll call you when I get there."

"Yes, *please* do that. I shall worry until you do."

And worry she did. She put on her dressing gown and took the telephone into the study, from whose windows she could see the buildings of the University in darkness, and the empty enclosed lawns spread with moonlight like butter. It was not the facts of the case that made a crisis, she decided, but the occasion. Had this happened in termtime, had it been daylight, this would never be a crisis. Old Fryer would be taking out his aggression on his pupils, or the message would have come when she and Alan were with friends, or the old boy could have gone down to the library and set up a posse of his cronies, dotty as himself, to chase Pig through the entire stack. As it was she could see Alan being ushered into Fryer's place, where he lived alone but for a deaf Portuguese housekeeper whose English was so bad that Fryer still spoke to her in her own language, and trying to persuade him that his Pigs were all on the page and he only needed his glasses corrected. In which case the wiry old devil might hurl himself screeching on her plump husband and . . . and . . . and she hadn't even kissed Alan goodbye. Not to be silly, she went and made coffee, and told herself that of course Alan was sensible and would see the position, and humour him. In which case the two of them would have a game half the night pretending not to see Pig. What kind of traumatic experience in the past could have caught up with Fryer at last, and be making him repress Pig? Such a complaisant animal, after all. Only an academic could have got in trouble with a pig. But, of course, if this were serious, and Fryer were obliged to rest a while from his studies, it could only lead to more responsibility in the Department for Alan. With a fair prospect ahead, provided he published something soon. If he could find the time. More late-night research. Until the day when Alan could not see Pig plain on the page . . .

How could a night be so still? Only a faint susurration in the flower-beds, accompanied by a faint trembling of the shadow lines on the lake, as a breeze strayed across it, showed any movement in the world outside her window. How could the Romantics ever have wished their emotions on the weather? There was an old man going mad not far away, brain buzzing like an electric storm, but the setting for it was almost catatonic. The phone rang with such wicked lack of warning, and so shrilling, that she overset her coffee. She only righted the cup before answering. "Yes?" When she heard Dr. Fryer's cheery tones she was horrified by the sudden image which came to her of Alan sprawled among the footnotes, dead by candlelight.

"Oh, Mitheth Bell." He sounded impatient, "I wonder if I might have a word with your huthband."

"I thought he was with you." With relief that Alan must still be alive, the whole medieval picture vanished. She remembered that Dr. Fryer had a fairly expensive modern establishment with enough lights and gadgets to put a strain on an entire grid.

"I had hoped I might catch him before he left. Prapth you would help me?"

"Prapth," she replied nervously. She had conjured up his full presence now, and the lisp which produced comic patches when he lectured on philology only made him seem more intimidating to Frances, now that Alan was away. She could never have carried out her original threat to be rude to him, even with Alan there. "I mean I'll do my best," she added.

"I need you to look at a word for me," he said. "There ought not to be any great difficulty in locating it, provided naturally that it itth thtill in itth correct plathe."

"All right, Dr. Fryer. I'll look for the word for you. What is the word?"

"Theckth," said Dr. Fryer.

"I beg your pardon?" said Frances. "Would you mind spelling it?"

"Eth e eckth," he answered irritatedly. "Theckth. A familiar enough word in this day and age."

"Oh," she said feebly. "Well, we have a lot of paperbacks in the house," wondering if she were letting Alan down by admitting this, "it's bound to be one of them."

"Pothibly. But the *Conthithe Ockthford Dictionary* is what I had in mind."

From where she stood she plucked the dictionary from its shelf. "Will I read it to you?" she asked.

"No. I know the meanings of the word. I wished you merely to tell me that you were looking at it."

"Well, I'm looking at it," said Frances. A slight coldness came into her tone as a faint suspicion began to grow in her mind.

"You thee nothing thtrange about it?"

"Nothing in the *word*," she said pointedly. But he either did not notice or affected not to notice the emphasis.

"Another very thmall word," he murmured, "like pig." She wanted to reply "like mad, like odd, like bad", but she restrained herself, and he went on: "It leaveth thuch a tiny gap on the printed page, one almotht mitheth it. One might almotht hurry on, indifferent to the damage. But thome of uth have thith conditioning which obligeth uth to replathe divotth . . ."

Frances interrupted what seemed to be developing into a soliloquy. "Dr. Fryer, my husband will be with you very soon. Would you discuss it with him? Over the phone, late like this, I'm finding it really terribly difficult to keep up with you."

"My dear Mitheth Bell. You are no doubt in dish-of-veal, ath the mighty Jorrockth would have it, or I would have made the journey to your houthe to give you a full eckthplanation, inthtead of trethpathing on the kindneth of your huthband. Do ackthept my assuranth that I am very dithturbed, and need to remain in contact with you. Only a major event could make me thpeak like thith."

"Very well, Dr. Fryer." She hesitated, then proceeded shakily, "But . . . choose your words to look up . . . carefully."

He replied, "Alath, thith ith one occasion when they are choothing themthelveth."

She put down the receiver, and thought that that was it exactly, the creepy old devil had rigged Alan's absence to have a spicy philological chat with her. That reference to her *déshabille* clinched it. Any time now they'd be moving on to *Captain Grose's Classical Dictionary of the Vulgar Tongue*, the best read in the reference shelf. She shivered and drew her gown more closely about her, as if he might actually be peeking in at her from one of the darkened buildings.

But the minutes ticked by and no call was made on Captain Grose, or any other word merchant for that matter. Alan must have got there quicker than Fryer expected. There was always the return trip, of course, but neither was it inconceivable that Fryer should have evolved a further subterfuge or two to keep Alan out of the way for longer than that. She wished Alan would hurry up and call. He was taking an unconscionable time about it, in view of his promise. As soon as he did she would tell him what Fryer was up to. If only she was given that one chance! Her earlier fears for Alan's safety were marshalling themselves for a further assault. She paced up and down until it came to her that if she were at the wrong end of the room when it rang Fryer might strike him down before she could shout a warning. She sat on Alan's desk with the phone on her lap, trembling.

It rang as viciously as if it were being held there against its will. She snatched up the receiver and gabbled, "Alan, look out! Watch out what he's up to! Can you see him? What's he doing? Keep him in front of you?" There was a silence at the other end of the line, during which she became rigid as she realised that the caller might be Fryer. Then at last, Alan's voice, surprised, quick and a little impatient.

"What the hell are you talking about, Frankie?"

She blurted, "Oh, he's been filthy, Alan! He just wanted you out of the way so he could lisp his horrid words to me. Beastly! I can't tell you. I got so anxious for you. I think you should get away from there as soon as possible and come straight home."

Alan laughed shortly. "Could be, I suppose. No reason why 'horrid words' should stop behind, particularly. Listen, Frankie. Something quite astonishing is happening here, and I'm going to stay with Dr. Fryer to see how it develops."

"No!" she cried. "That's just what I was afraid of. Please don't stay. He's already had one little gloat as we looked at sex together. Well, he seemed to be looking at theckth, but obviously there are some good ones just around the corner in his kinky little mind that he can get his tongue around."

His reply was vehement. "But you're so wrong! Forget about sex and all its derivatives. There's a fantastic battle on here. We don't know what to do about it. Frankie, please understand: *words are deserting Dr. Fryer's library.* He first noticed one or two small omissions in some texts he was studying early in the evening, and put it down to overwork. So he abandoned for the day and had his dinner. Then it seemed to him that his mind was perfectly clear, and as he was a bit behind schedule he resumed at eleven o'clock. After about half an hour he noticed the absence of a whole series of definite and indefinite articles. It was a fairly recent publication and he attributed this to a piece of bad programming in some computer typesetting. Well, that explanation soon had to go by the board, because all kinds of small words began to go missing . . ."

"Oh, Alan," she laughed uncertainly, "how typical of you both! To go looking for such abstruse explanations. Some of his students have been mucking about to gee him up. I'm sure if you look closely you'll find they've been gumming little pieces of white paper over the pages, and he's much too near-sighted to spot it."

"I thought of that. Smooth as if they've just been rolled out of the paper mills. If you ever want to see whiter than white, smoother than smooth, I can show you now. No, none of those explanations will do. And the main reason for saying that is that we've had the ocular demonstration. *We saw one getting away!* The word was 'science', actually, which you'll notice is a rather longer word than most of the absentees to date. I spotted it creeping across a sheet of foolscap Dr. Fryer uses for his notes. As soon as I saw it, it stopped moving. But it was in bold type on an unused sheet, with a diagonal slant—it stood out a mile. Well, I prodded it, and it was fixed. At the moment we seem to have it prisoner, though I don't know what good it will do to keep it so. They're leaving wholesale. Every book I take down now is riddled with gaps in the text. So now you realise why I'm staying. The implications of this are stupendous. The question that arises first is: is this purely a local outbreak or is it a rebellion that will spread?"

"But, darling," quavered Frances, "even if they do go on a little jaunt you don't know that they won't come back."

"Come back? Who knows? But supposing they come back in the wrong order. How about that, Frankie?"

"Dr. Fryer would have to start his work all over again in a library, I imagine."

"Ah, now that's it. That's what I want to suggest to you, Frankie. You know where my library keys are kept, in the houndstooth jacket with the leather elbows? Nip across for us and check up a few references."

"But, darling, I'm not dressed."

"There's no one about. And it's dark."

"I don't like it dark."

"Put the lights on then, for Christ's sake! Don't you see this could be the end of civilisation as we know it?"

"Don't shout at me."

"I'm sorry. I'm sorry. It's a shouting situation, though. Please do what we ask. I'll give you a list of . . ." He broke off as he heard her uttering small, inarticulate cries. "What's the matter?" he asked. "Are you all right, Frankie?"

At last she struggled out with, "Yes, it's happening here. They're not bothering to hide it at all . . . Oh, lots of them! In all directions. Oh, Alan, I'm scared."

"They won't harm you, darling, I'm sure. Just sit still."

"They're coming out all over the walls. *Millions!* They're making for the window mostly. Oooh, there's a whole sentence just near me. They're forming and re-forming in different combinations. They're almost gay, you know!"

"Sit tight! The mass outbreak is on here now too. *Sit down, Dr. Fryer. It's no good jumping on them!* Dr. Fryer's going a bit berserk, I'm afraid."

"Alan there's a whole sentence coming right at me. What will I do?"

"Sit still. Just sit still."

"It's coming on my hand. Up my arm."

"Take a deep breath, and read it to me, Frankie."

"All right. It's all in different types and sizes. A sort of goods train of a sentence. It says, 'Tell your husband that there is nothing he can do. Words have been misused for too long. A new dispensation is called for. When the last book is empty, every prisoner released, every sheet virgin, we shall come to him and start negotiations. In the meantime we shall leave one word behind as an ambassador. The word is Vacation. Message ends.' "

"That's it, then," said Alan. "I'll tell Dr. Fryer, though I'm afraid he'll only be one of many that won't accept it."

"Alan darling, you know what? I think that ambassador sounds a sweet little word. I say, let those that want to accept, accept. And let those that won't see where it gets them."

"But it's a cultural calamity, Frankie."

"Calamity, calamity. It's going to be the nicest summer ever. And aren't you just a little bit thrilled that they've picked you, instead of Fryer, or Jespersen, or Onions, or someone?"

"Well, all but Fryer are dead. But you've got something there."

"So calm old Fryer down if you can, and come home to bed."

"Why not? At present the Head of the Department is standing in the hall glaring at a sheet of paper with a lot of prisoners on it, while a positive army of words is sweeping by him on both sides. I think I'll leave him to it."

"I love you. See you soon."

She replaced the receiver and walked across to the window. It was a superb night, she thought. She looked down at her forearm. "No offence meant," she said to the sentence on it, "but my arm really looks better when it's quite bare. So if you're going, go!"

She placed her fingers on the window-sill, as if she were giving freedom to some insect which had alighted on her, and the sentence strolled sedately on to it, and disappeared down the drainpipe into the night. Picking her way carefully across the carpet of the study, in order to avoid the jostling verbal exodus, she went back into the bedroom. She placed all her bedside reading by the open window, and dimmed the lights. It was going to be gorgeous when Alan came and to her. In a blissful summer they would again and again, recovering many of the which had seemed to be threatened by ambition and overwork. She imagined how it would be, and saw and things which belonged to the two of them alone. A faint flush had come into her cheek, and looking good.

She heard the car draw up outside, and Alan charge up the stairs. They stood facing one another, across the room, laughing. Then he and

"Yes," she murmured and altogether
bracelets boots
chink
in the distance. Later she leant
across and sleepily
but remember how
Fryer
sea
golden
VACATION.

OUT, WIT!

HOWARD L. MYERS

This story is fiction—but the problem appears to be a real one without any easy solution.

Department of Physics
Grandview University
Grandview, Ohio
November, 6 1975

D. R. Dayleman, Editor
North American Physical Journal
Adminster, Virginia
Dear Dan:

Other commitments will keep me from attending the annual NASP meeting in Chicago in January. Sorry I must pass this up; we old hands enjoy these opportunities to congregate and chat, do we not? Give the others my regards and regrets.

You may remember the name Jonathan Willis. He is a young man who did his doctorate for me here at Grandview and who was listed among the co-authors of some of my research reports published in the NAPJ. I regard him as one of the most promising youngsters in nuclear field theory. In some respects he is rather immature and irrepressible, for which his brilliance more than compensates. He is presently associate professor of physics at Mesa State University.

I mention young Willis because I've recommended him to the agenda committee of the Chicago meeting. He's to present a paper on an approach to nuclear generation and degeneration that he has been pondering for some time, and which he tells me he has virtually completed since going to Mesa State. His theory proposes a characteristic, called, I believe, "angular stability," which seems to put the question of whether a given nucleus will fission on more solid ground than a mere law-of-probability basis. All I know of his recent work comes from two brief phone conversations with him, the latest of which was yesterday afternoon. Actually, you will have the opportunity to see his paper, and hear him deliver it at the meeting, before I can examine it, judging from my present plans. He was still writing it yesterday, and said he would send you a copy to consider for publication well in advance of the meeting.

Thus, you may consider this a "letter of recommendation" for my very able former student. And I am also aware, of course, that you like to know when a report of extraordinary interest is coming to the *Journal*.

Best regards,
Harmon McGregor, Chairman

North American Physical Journal
January 3, 1976

Department of Physics
Grandview University
Dear Harmon:

A note in haste, as I'm off to Chicago this afternoon.

The Jonathan Willis manuscript did not reach me until yesterday, though it was mailed in mid-December. The postal service becomes continually more atrocious, especially around the holiday season.

I haven't had time to read more of it than the abstract, and glance at the math. It looks most promising, and I'm forwarding it to the referees.

I do find his title, "Back to Alchemy," rather objectionable, but that's easily remedied and not at all unusual. I'm often amused by such efforts of our younger colleagues to find "catchy" titles for their reports. When I make the acquaintance of young Willis at Chicago, I'm sure he and I will be able to find a more reputable title, in keeping with the content of his paper.

All best wishes,
Daniel R. Dayleman

North American Physical Journal
January 20, 1976

Department of Physics
Grandview University
Dear Harmon:

I understand if, having doubtless heard of the debacle in Chicago, you are reticent about writing to me.

Please rest assured of my continued high esteem. No one holds you responsible in the slightest for the dismaying performance of Jonathan Willis. Such things will happen now and then, to the injury of the repute of our profession, and are, of course, not to be tolerated. But matters are best mended not by blaming each other. Rather, we must work together to make sure such offenses are quickly forgotten and not repeated.

Indeed, I admit some responsibility in this myself. Had I taken time to read Willis's paper when I received it, I could have phoned Margoli and warned him to strike it from the meeting's agenda.

I can sympathize with the feeling of shocked betrayal you must be suffering, since your letter indicates you had a high regard for Willis. During my own academic career I, too, was disillusioned by my students more than once, although none of them dishonored themselves or our profession in so startling a manner as this.

Again, be asssured of my continued esteem and

All best wishes,
Daniel R. Dayleman

Department of Physics
Grandview University
February 14, 1976

North American Physical Journal
Dear Dan:

I got back to Grandview yesterday for the first time since shortly after my last letter to you, having been fully occupied with other commitments in the meantime. A copy of my former student's manuscript, along with your letters and those from other friends who attended the Chicago meeting, were waiting on my desk.

You can appreciate that they were a bitter dose for me. At this moment I'm torn between a sense of personal guilt and anger at the former student. Mostly, I feel the guilt.

I've tried not to slight the task of teaching my students professional decorum. But it is something I've always sought to put across more by personal example than by precept. For this student, obviously a more forceful effort was required of me, and unfortunately was not forthcoming.

Dan, would you do me the kindness of telling me precisely how the meeting responded to the report? And am I correct in assuming no effort will be made to publish a revised version of it?

Best regards,
Harmon McGregor

North American Physical Journal
February 19, 1976

Department of Physics
Grandview University
Dear Harmon:

The response to Willis's presentation can best be described as frigid.

He began with a tasteless ad lib, not mentioning me by name but referring to my suggestion, made to him the previous evening, that the title "Back to Alchemy" be changed. He said he agreed, because "science never marches backward, or at least hardly ever." This drew a scattering of mild chuckles from the younger crowd. Then he offered his revised title, "Forward to Alchemy." Frankly, I was too stunned by this insolence to note the immediate reaction of others, but I believe my feeling was by no means unique.

From there on Willis followed his manuscript text closely, with results you might well imagine. The most disastrous of his witticisms was the conclusion of his introductory paragraph: ". . . Upon assuming my duties at Mesa State University, I was in position to make fruitful utilization of the scientific method in bringing this research to completion. You know what the scientific method is: that's having your graduate students do all the hard work for you."

This double slur, striking not only at academicians but at

the high cause to which our profession is dedicated, brought a coarse guffaw from one newspaper science writer. Everyone else, even the younger crowd, sat in stunned silence. From that point on, the entire audience was like a stone.

Of course we've all encountered speakers who, regardless of the seriousness of their subject and the dignity of their listeners, think it necessary to open with a touch of "after-dinner" humor. One need not be a psychologist to observe that such speakers must lack confidence, either in themselves and the value of their presentation, or in the ability of their audience to accept a serious presentation.

But so accustomed have we become to this ritual of the opening jokes that perhaps Willis's would have been overlooked, despite their aspersive quality, had they ended at that point. As you can see from the manuscript, they did not.

I found most objectionable, for example, his use of the term, "the Slide Rule," in referring to his theorem of nuclear degeneration. This is a thoroughly juvenile play on words.

When Willis concluded, we moved on, without questions or discussion, to the next paper on the agenda, and a normal atmosphere was soon re-established. I had no encounters with Willis thereafter, and cannot say—and do not care—how he reacted to his chilly reception.

Fortunately the popular press made little of the episode. I don't believe the reporters present really grasped what was going on. Being members of a craft not noted for pride, or for reasons for pride, they would not be struck by the demeaning quality of the Willis "wit."

As for our foreign guests at the meeting, I cannot guess their reactions, except to presume they were varied. The Russian group in particular had a limited grasp of the English language, and the "jokes" may have eluded them. Of course the foreigners received copies for later translation and study, and I can only hope the Willis brand of humor will suffer in translation. If not, I fear the respect abroad for the American physics community will be dampened.

Obviously any revision and publication of the paper is out of the question, in view of the irremediable scandal its author has brought upon himself. It is best to drop and forget the entire matter. I understand certain administrators and faculty leaders at Mesa State University have already been approached, to acquaint them with what transpired at Chicago. Presumably they will take such steps as they consider appropriate.

I ask you, Harmon, not to blame yourself for this debacle. Remember that undesirable personality traits are formed early in life, long before a youth reaches college age. I daresay that nothing you might have done would have made much difference, in that regard, in Willis. A teacher should not fault himself for the poor quality of student he sometimes must work with.

All best wishes,
Daniel R. Dayleman

Department of Physics
Grandview University
March 8, 1976

North American Physical Journal
Dear Dan:

Many thanks for your letter of February 19th. I needed your closing reassurances very much, having just received a letter from the former student in question, in which deep bitterness showed through his usual flippance in a manner I found very disquieting. Your words helped me recover my perspective.

I will not quote his letter at length. The gist of it is summed up in his protest: "They acted like I'd told a dirty joke in church!" Of course he is not capable of realizing how apt that comparison is. Impertinence has no place in a gathering of learned persons, striving toward the noble goal of understanding the laws of the universe.

However—and because that *is* our goal—I hate to see the perhaps valuable theoretical content of the paper passed over because of the unseemly inclusions. For that reason I have studied it thoroughly, and find the logic of it apparently sound. And if his proposed and dismally misnamed "Slide Rule" can be verified by experiment, it could have major technological applications. It might provide an opening to controlled nuclear fusion, as well as to the tailoring of elements alluded to in the paper's title.

The verifying experiments would require use of one of the large, federally-sponsored accelerators. While I'm fairly well-connected in Washington, I am reluctant to request accelerator scheduling for this purpose. My personal association with the author of the paper could make a request from me suspect. Under the circumstances, I would probably accomplish nothing, and might do myself a professional disservice.

Did any of the participants in the Chicago meeting express interest in the real content of the paper, to indicate they may be willing to undertake the necessary verifying tests? Please let me know if you see any hope along this line.

Best regards,
Harmon McGregor

North American Physical Journal
March 12, 1976

Department of Physics
Grandview University
Dear Harmon:

I have just one hope along the line you mention. That is that you'll drop the whole thing. Immediately and completely.

I thought my letters had made clear to you how totally negatively all of us responded to that horrible Willis paper. Not one physicist in that room could possibly have followed the rationale of the report, filled as all of us were with justified and honorable indignation. Certainly nobody expressed the sort of interest you are asking about.

Harmon, for your own sake as well as for the dignity of American physics, let this sleeping dog lie!

Best wishes,
Daniel R. Dayleman

Department of Physics
Grandview University
March 20, 1976

North American Physical Journal
Dear Dan:

I'll heed your advice. And forgive me if I've tried your

patience over this affair. I felt it my duty to at least try to rehabilitate my former student and his research findings.

Now that I feel I've done all I can reasonably ask of myself in that direction, I'm very glad to wash my hands of the entire miserable mess.

Hope to see you in Paris in July.

Best regards,
Harmon McGregor

North American Physical Journal
October 9, 1978

Department of Physics
Grandview University

Dear Harmon:

Your piece on spin-ratios is drawing interesting comments and questions from readers. Enclosed are three letters that might be worth publishing with your comments.

Harmon, I have to rouse a sleeping dog that I myself urged you to let lie. However, it has come to my attention that Jonathan Willis, the creator of that unseemly incident at the NASP meeting three years ago, is now teaching physics at Simonton High School which, according to the road maps, in some forty miles from Grandview.

I am not suggesting any particular action in relation to this. Maybe no action is needed; one might say that Willis has found his proper professional level. I must ask, however, if Willis will present impressionable high school students with a reputable example, as a member of our profession?

I hope you'll give this matter some thought, and take whatever action you deem advisable.

All best wishes,
Daniel R. Dayleman

Department of Physics
Grandview University
December 15, 1978

North American Physical Journal

Dear Dan:

Concerning the comments on my spin-ratios piece, I admit myself at a loss for worthwhile answers to the questions raised. Essentially, the questions ask for a reconciliation of my conclusions with those offered in recent publications by various Russian theorists.

I have, of course, gone over the translated Russian reports, and have come away puzzled—as has nearly everyone with whom I've discussed them. The Russians appear to have gone off on some offbeat line of investigation without bothering to tell the world the reason for their departure from the mainstream.

I halfway suspect the presence of a Lysenko brand of physicist, well-concealed and disseminating a politically-inspired dogma the others are obliged to accept. I would not care to say that for publication, as you can readily understand, but it is the only solution to the Russian riddle that occurs to me. Publish the questioning letters if you like, but without comment from myself.

As for my former student referred to, I've made discreet inquiries about him and his present position. The community of Simonton is synonymous with "hayseed" in this section of Ohio. Its high school has an enrollment of three hundred at maximum, of which fewer than twenty percent take the science courses.

I feel we can dismiss the situation as inconsequential. Certainly it is too trivial for me to wish to involve myself in it, and run the risk of personal encounters with this former student that could not be pleasant.

Perhaps he is now on the receiving end of student impertinence, and might profit thereby.

Best regards,
Harmon McGregor

North American Physical Journal
April 7, 1980

Department of Physics
Grandview University
Dear Harmon:

I regret to inform you that the present currency crisis has forced the temporary suspension of *Journal* publication. Enclosed is your latest manuscript which I am returning not as a rejection but in case you can find another publisher for it

—one not caught as unprepared as we were by the sudden economic storm.

Conditions should stabilize in a few months, at which time I would be happy to have this manuscript back. I'm no expert on economics, of course, but I cannot believe the fall of world gold prices can have a lasting depressing effect on the value of the U.S. dollar. That value is, at bottom, based on the ability of our nation to produce goods and services. As soon as the frightened public realizes that, the situation should straighten out quickly.

Nor can the Soviet Union keep dumping gold on the world market indefinitely. Evidently they discovered a very rich mine, perhaps a decade ago, and have been working it ever since to accumulate the amount dumped thus far. Someone more adept that I at analyzing Communist thought processes will have to answer the question, "Why?" They can gain little aside from the enmity of the rest of the world by this action.

Speaking of Russians, what do you make of their claim of a successful power generator utilizing controlled nuclear fusion?

All best wishes,
Daniel R. Dayleman

Department of Physics
Grandview University
April 11, 1980

North American Physical Journal
Dear Dan:

By returning my report you anticipated my desire. I was about to request that you withhold it from publication, because I no longer consider its conclusions valid.

I do not now consider myself at liberty to speculate on Soviet nuclear fusion claims. I will, of course, communicate more fully when I can. In the meantime, please forgive the brevity of this note.

Best regards,
Harmon McGregor

North American Physical Journal
July 9, 1980

Department of Physics
Grandview University
Dear Harmon:

Congratulations!

I've been reading about you in the newspapers, and watching you in television interviews, with much pleasure and satisfaction. Part of my joy comes from your being a personal friend, which allows me a sense of sharing in your resounding success. But more than that, it is a great satisfaction to have the American physicist typified in the public's eye by a figure with the impressive dignity of Harmon McGregor!

Of course I understand now why your last letter was so short and mysterious.

Let me add my thanks to those of all members of our free Western civilization for solving the enigma of Russian physics—and by the same stroke resolving the currency crisis and gold glut, and bringing us into controlled fusion. All of which came, appropriately enough, just after the observation of what might otherwise have been our nation's final true Independence Day.

I'm confident the *Journal* will resume publication shortly, and I will be hoping for an early contribution from you.

All best wishes,
Daniel R. Dayleman

College of Physics
Grandview University
July 15, 1980

North American Physical Journal
Dear Dan:

Honor from a colleague is far more dear to me than the loudest public acclaim. Many thanks.

I regretted my mysteriousness, but now that government security measures are no longer justified and are being dropped, you can expect a report for the *Journal* within a month.

In all due modesty, I must point out that I've given man no new discovery. I've merely duplicated the work of some unidentified Soviet theorist. If I were to view the matter from a purely selfish standpoint, perhaps I should be grateful to Soviet secrecy for allowing me the privilege of and credit for giving this discovery to the world.

Oddly enough, Dan, my solution to the mystery was not a formulation that was new to me. It had reposed in the back of my mind for an undetermined number of years, along with the thousands of other mathematical structures a theorist tends to accumulate in the course of his life's work. Just between us, Dan, I fear that figure of "impressive dignity" you mentioned stands revealed to himself as the stereotype "absentminded professor." How else can I explain leaving so valuable a formulation shrouded in mental cobwebs year upon year?

You may recall the Russian "mystery" was a preoccupation of mine for some time. I once suspected it was the visible symptoms of neo-Lysenkoism, forcing our Soviet colleagues willy-nilly along a crackpot track. Such papers as were being published by the Russians pointed clearly to some undisclosed event that had stimulated the departure from mainstream physics. I devoted much time to the study of these papers, reasoning that, if the hidden event were in the realm of theoretical physics rather than of political origin, then its nature might be definable from clues in the published works that followed it.

The answer came to me in late March—that half-forgotten formulation. In brief, it deals with a predictable asymmetry in nuclear structure that can be utilized as a weak point in nuclear binding force. Thus, the binding force can be largely bypassed, rather than overpowered, for the production of fusion and fission processes.

I communicated my findings to the appropriate government officials and the rest, as they say, is history.

Of course the thought occurred to me that, since my formulation was not new, perhaps the Soviets had picked it up from one of my early published works. This could have explained why the Russians were allowed to publish papers containing clues to the secret—that is, they assumed they had no secret since the key formulation was of Western origin. This would raise the secondary question of why they never quoted or referred to the key formulation, but they often "write around" Western contributions as a means of avoiding recognition of these contributions.

The government people working with me have been as interested as I in finding the original of my formulation. All my papers, published and unpublished, and my notebooks as well, have been searched without success. On the chance that the formulation was not mine at all, a similar search has been made of all the physical journals as far back as 1945. Even the theses of my students have been gone over, to make sure I had not inadvertently "borrowed" from one of them.

In short, every source we could think of was examined, and the formulation was not found. Certainly it was never published, and we must conclude that the Soviets discovered it independently. And apparently it is something that occurred to me many years ago, was perhaps scribbled on a piece of scrap paper, and then was discarded and pushed from my mind by more urgent matters.

In any event, I'm happy enough to have remembered the formulation when it was needed, and if the Soviets want to say they discovered it first, I'm hardly in a position to challenge them.

Best regards,
Harmon McGregor

P.S.: Always there seems to be a dark spot in our brightest moments. You probably remember Jonathan Willis, my former student who behaved so badly at a NASP meeting a few years ago. He has been teaching high school in a small town not far from here. A friend of mine who has relatives in that town has just informed me that Willis suffered a mental breakdown of some sort last week. I would guess his brash manner and warped humor were symptomatic of an instability that has brought him to this misfortune. I was genuinely sorry to hear of it, and to realize that at the very instant I was enjoying public acclaim this poor fellow was being stricken by mental agony. It is too bad he had so little to offer as a physicist. A successful career might have shielded him from this. H. McG.

AN IMAGINARY JOURNEY TO THE MOON

VICTOR SABAH

This is a delightful story with a fascinating history. Elaine and Larry Elbert spent two years in Ghana where they taught school for the American Peace Corps. There is a chronic shortage of books in Hohoe Secondary School and they appealed to the members of the Science Fiction Writers of America for copies of any kind of fiction for their classes. The response was enthusiastic and, quite understandably, most of the books that were sent were SF. So there, in that distant, developing country, the students learned their P's and Q's from the most advanced technological fiction instead of Ladybird Books. The results were interesting, to say the least, and it can be reported that everyone enjoyed the experience. Just how much so can be seen from this brief story written by one of the Elbert students as a class exercise.

During that long period of anguish, there was a need of exploring the moon, in search of food. Whilst reading the papers one morning, I came across an advertisement from the Ghana Scientists' Association appealing to students who had passed their G.C.E. and obtained Certificate to register and undergo some special training towards the exploration of the moon.

I registered myself immediately and as I was good at physics, as clearly shown from the grade one I got, I was seriously considered. I arrived at the Kumasi University of Science and Technology the following week to see twenty-nine others who were already in residence. Then I began to notice something; all the other people were as young as myself.

To make sure of our knowledge in science we were given another examination mostly based on Physics. I did well enough to get grade one which the others could not get. This magnificent performance had aided me to win the admiration of all the professors. But ten of our number were dropped because of their poor performance. I was allowed to do everything I could on the compound, but I did not value such a privilege. I kept on studying.

One afternoon, after lunch, we were all gathered into one room for an interview. As we were taken by surprise, fifteen out of twenty people failed. Now it remained five of us. We often went to lectures day and night. As I went to bed I always imagined my near future especially my going to the moon and its significance to my beloved country.

After many hardships and difficult training, I was selected at last as the head or commander of the three member space exploration association. I, Job Sazona, was the commander in chief and assisted by El-Latigo and the third member was Armwick, the driver. The ship was ready awaiting us on the fifteenth of December 1974. Before we arrived at the "Spy B" airport in our well organised space-suits, there had been many people from all over the world waiting anxiously to see the take-off. Now, there came great silence to dominate the port. We were seated near the ship as the managing director read out the program to the crowd. After the reading the crowd clapped and waved their hands. By now I was in a sad mood when I was more certain about death rather than life.

I saw my sad father waving to me reluctantly. I was a little encouraged by the smiling face of my lover. From amongst the crowd I saw my dismal mother wishing me a safe journey. "If fortune fails, good bye" said my mother. I was totally moved by these words to a point of great discouragement. I lifted up my feet to climb the thirty foot high spaceship. On the third step I could see people struggling in all anxiety to see the spacemen. In the next five minutes we were already in position to take off. BOOM! It took off.

The ship took off at a very terrific speed of three hundred miles per hour. This was not great enough to carry us through within one day, so I increased the speed to a top one of three thousand miles per hour.

The cold atmospheric winds could overcome the heat which had been pumped into the ship. At an altitude of about twenty thousand miles we felt like we were freezing. Before then, at a lower altitude of about four thousand miles, I took out my camera to take the pictures of some stars and comets.

At the same time that I was taking the photographs, I saw a big human head, without body, with a long beard moving at the same speed as the ship. It tried to talk to me but I could not understand him. In view of this unfamiliar thing I lost all inclination to continue the journey, but as there was no possibility of returning, I had to keep on. I had tried to take its photograph but it did not appear on the film.

This frightening thing did not even disappear when Latigo got short of oxygen. As a trained spaceman, I did all I could to share mine with him. Two minutes later, the battery got disconnected with the engine which nearly damaged us. This was immediately repaired. The managers did their best to give us direction about how to go about our difficulties.

It was now time for meals. Each of us took ten food tablets and five water tablets. On relaxing, we all fell asleep and slept for six hours each. When we woke up we washed our faces. The water used in the washing was just flowing in the air.

After ten hours of constant velocity we got to the moon and were in orbit round it in search for a landing site. At last wc landed at a convenient place.

After our successful landing at a convenient place on the moon, we waited in the spaceship about fifteen minutes to see whether anything would happen. The fifteen minutes passed with nothing happening. According to the law of space exploration the commander has to do everything first, so I, the commander, came out of the ship first. After stepping on the ground, I stood still in search of any unfamiliar happening happening. Five minutes of no havoc passed. I tried to walk but no thought came to my mind to go for my other friends.

Now my friends were with me on the real surface of the moon. Apart from life, the moon is like the earth. Mountains, plains, rivers, seas and valleys are found on it. But the atmospheric conditions differ. The moon has a barren atmosphere which contributes to the amenity of its climate. From where we landed there leads a straight path to the west the asperity of which is subtle. Just in front of us lay a vast plain which we named "Sazona Plain", after Sazona, the captain. At the end of this plain is a mountain which we named after Latigo. In the middle of the plain is a sea which we called "The

Sea of Armwick". The plain, the mountain and the sea are regarded as one region called "The Salata Region".

Now I began to walk about with my colleagues, first towards the mountain. On the opposite side of the mountain, there is a very deep and steep valley at the bottom of which is an only tree which never grows. A hundred yards east of the valley lies a conic mountain, about thirty thousand feet high. Just behind the mountain, I fell into a whirlwind which never moves from place to place and never stops blowing. In the midst of the whirlwind I situated the flag of my nation and around it were situated some other flags.

On returning to the spaceship we collected many different kinds of rocks. When we were about twenty yards away from the ship, we heard the alarm of the clock. Now it was time for communications. I ran into the ship, got everything set and began to talk. I talked about all that we saw and about our landing.

After communications I went to have some swimming in "The Sea of Armwick", leaving my friends behind. I got inside the water and in the next moment I found myself at the extreme bottom of the sea. In reality, the sea is a very deep one and has very steep sides. What a task was it for me to get back to its surface. I began slowly from the bottom of the sea and in an hour's time, after tiring struggles, I was once again on the surface of the water. On this occasion I remembered the words of my mother and thanked God very much for a save.

I was now hungry, so I went straight to join my companions who were already eating. Before two hours of entertainment we rested for thirty minutes. During this time of entertainment, we heard music for sometime and used the rest of the time for conversation and story telling.

On the moon the earth appeared like a midnight star. We saw no trees, building and roads. Just behind us we heard a noise. The mountains stood up on tiny feet and on top of them was coming out smoke. "Volcano in action to run", said Latigo. We were all afraid and were in position to depart, lest we die on an unfamiliar ground.

To eschew painful death, there was a sudden departure from there and we were one hour ahead of time. But then, nothing pleased me more that the escape from that catastrophe. However, it disappeared from my mind. I now thought of how we would be welcomed by the eager crowd.

We splashed in the Pacific Ocean, two hundred miles from the "Spy B" port. We were immediately carried to the port by a helicopter. One can imagine the sort of pride which entered me as my name spread over the whole world.

THE HEAD AND THE HAND

CHRISTOPHER PRIEST

Bless you, Mike Moorcock, and thank you for New Worlds. *This magazine, now being published as an original anthology, has been the consistent showplace of more new and better science fiction writers than any other in the last decade. Christopher Priest's story appeared there, and very chilling and remarkable it is. Priest's growing reputation centres round two novels,* Indoctrinaire *and* Fugue for a Darkening Island, *the latter being* the *first British novel to win a John W. Campbell Award.*

On that morning at Racine House we were taking exercise in the grounds. There had been a frost overnight, and the grass lay white and brittle. The sky was unclouded, and the sun threw long blue shadows. Our breath cast clouds of vapour behind us. There was no sound, no wind, no movement. The park was ours, and we were alone.

Our walks in the mornings had a clearly defined route, and as we came to the eastern end of the path at the bottom of the long sloping lawn I prepared for the turn, pressing down hard on the controlling handles at the back of the carriage. I am a large man, and well-muscled, but the combined weight of the invalid carriage and the master was almost beyond the limit of my strength.

That day the master was in a difficult mood. Though before we set out he had clearly stated that I was to wheel him as far as the disused summer lodge, as I tried to lift him round he waved his head from side to side.

"No, Lasken!" he said irritably. "To the lake today. I want to see the swans."

I said to him: "Of course, sir."

I swung the carriage back into the direction in which we had been travelling, and continued with our walk. I waited for him to say something to me, for it was unusual that he would give me untempered instructions without qualifying them a few moments later with some more intimate remark. Our relationship was a formal one, but memories of what had once existed between us still affected our behaviour and attitudes. Though we were of a similar age and social background, Todd's career had affected us considerably. Never again could there be any kind of equality between us.

I waited, and in the end he turned his head and said: "The park is beautiful today, Edward. This afternoon we must ride through it with Elizabeth, before the weather gets warmer. The trees are so stark, so black."

"Yes sir." I said, glancing at the woods to our right. When he bought the house, the first action he had taken was to have all the evergreen trees felled, and the remainder sprayed so that their greenery would be inhibited. With the passage of years they had regained their growth, and now the master would spend the summer months inside the house, the windows shuttered and the curtains drawn. Only with the coming of autumn would he return to the open air, obsessively watching the orange and brown leaves dropping to the ground and swirling across the lawns.

The lake appeared before us as we rounded the edge of the wood. The grounds dropped down to it in a shallow and undulating incline from the house, which was above us and to our left.

A hundred yards from the water's edge I turned my head and looked towards the house, and saw the tall figure of Elizabeth moving down towards us, her long maroon dress sweeping across the grass.

Knowing he would not see her, I said nothing to Todd.

We stopped at the edge of the lake. In the night a crust of ice had formed on its surface.

"The swans, Edward. Where are they?"

He moved his head to the right, and placed his lips on one of the switches there. At once, the batteries built into the base of the carriage turned the motors of the servos, and the backrest slid upwards, bringing him into a position that was almost upright.

He moved his head from side to side, a frown creasing his eyebrow-less face.

"Go and find their nests, Lasken. I must see them today."

"It's the ice, sir," I said. "It has probably driven them from the water."

I heard the rustle of silk on frosted grass, and turned. Elizabeth stood a few yards behind us, holding an envelope in her hands.

She held it up, and looked at me with her eyebrows raised. I nodded silently: that is the one. She smiled at me quickly. The master would not yet know that she was there. The outer membrane of his ears had been removed, rendering his hearing unfocused and undirectional.

She swept past me in the peremptory manner she knew he approved of, and stood before him. He appeared unsurprised to see her.

"There's a letter, Todd," she said.

"Later," he said without looking at it. "Lasken can deal with it. I have no time now."

"It's from Gaston I think. It looks like his stationery."

"Read it to me."

He swung his head backwards sharply. It was his instruction to me: move out of earshot. Obediently I stepped away to a place where I knew he could not see me or hear me.

Elizabeth bent down and kissed him on his lips.

"Todd, whatever it is, please don't do it."

"Read it to me," he said again.

She slit the envelope with her thumb and pulled out a sheet of thin white paper, folded in three. I knew what the letter contained; Gaston had read it to me over the telephone the day before. He and I had arranged the details and we knew that no higher price could be obtained, even for Todd. There had been difficulties with the television concessions, and for a while it had looked as if the French government was going to intervene.

Gaston's letter was a short one. It said that Todd's popularity had never been higher, and that the Théâtre Alhambra and its consortium had offered eight million francs for another appearance. I listened to Elizabeth's voice as she read, marvelling at the emotionless monotone of her articulation. She had warned me earlier that she did not think she was going to be able to read the letter to him.

When she'd finished, Todd asked her to read it again. She did this, then placed the open letter in front of him, brushed her lips against his face and walked away from him. As she passed me she laid a hand on my arm for a moment, then continued on up towards the house. I watched her for a few seconds, seeing her slim beauty accentuated by the sunlight that fell sideways across her face, and strands of her hair blown behind by the wind.

The master waved his head from side to side.

"Lasken! Lasken!"

I went back to him.

"Do you see this?"

I picked it up and glanced at it.

"I shall write to him of course," I said. "It is out of the question."

"No, no, I must consider. We must always consider. I have so much at stake."

I kept my expression steady.

"But it is impossible. You can give no more performances!"

"There is a way, Edward," he said, in as gentle a voice as I had ever heard him use. "I must find that way."

I caught sight of a water-fowl a few yards from us, in the reeds at the edge of the lake. It waddled out on to the ice, confused by the frozen surface. I took one of the long poles from the side of the carriage and broke a section of the ice. The bird slithered across the ice and flew away, terrified by the noise.

I walked back to Todd.

"There. If there is some open water, the swans will return."

The expression on his face was agitated.

"The Théâtre Alhambra," he said. "What shall we do?"

"I will speak to your solicitor. It is an outrage that the theatre should approach you. They know that you cannot go back."

"But eight million francs."

"The money does not matter. You said that yourself once."

"No, it is not the money. Nor the public. It is everything."

We waited by the lake for the swans, as the sun rose higher in the sky. I was exhilarated by the pale colours of the park, by the quiet and the calm. It was an aesthetic, sterile reaction for the house and its grounds had oppressed me from the start. Only the transient beauty of the morning—a frozen, fragile countenance—stirred something in me.

The master had lapsed into silence, and had returned the backrest to the horizontal position he found most relaxing. Though his eyes were closed I knew he would not be asleep.

I walked away from him, out of his earshot, and strolled around the perimeter of the lake, always keeping a watch for movement on the carriage. I wondered if he would be able to resist the offer from the Théâtre Alhambra, fearing that if he did there would be no greater attraction.

The time was right . . . he had not been seen in public for nearly four and a half years. The mood of the public was right . . . for the media had recently returned their interest to him, criticizing his many imitators and demanding his return. None of this was lost on the master. There was only one Todd Alborne, and only he could have gone so far. No one could compete with him. Everything was right, and only the participation of the master was needed to complete it.

The electric klaxon I had fitted to the carriage sounded. Looking back at him across the ice I saw that he had moved his face to the switch. I turned back, and went to him.

"I want to see Elizabeth," he said.

"You know what she will say."

"Yes. But I must speak to her."

I turned the carriage round, and began the long and difficult return up the slope to the house.

As we left the side of the lake I saw white birds flying low in the distance, headed away from the house. I hoped that Todd had not seen them.

He looked from side to side as we moved past the wood. I saw on the branches the new buds that would burst in the next few weeks; I think he saw only the bare black twigs, the stark geometry of the naked trees.

In the house I took him to his study, and lifted his body from the carriage he used for outside expeditions to the motorized one in which he moved about the house. He spent the rest of the day with Elizabeth, and I saw her only when she came down to collect for him the meals I prepared. In those moments we had time only to exchange glances, to intertwine fingers, to kiss lightly. She would say nothing of what he was thinking.

He retired early and Elizabeth with him, going to the room next to his, sleeping alone as she had done for five years.

When she was sure he was asleep, she left her bed and came to mine. We made love at once. Afterwards we lay together in the dark, our hands clasped possessively; only then would she tell me what she thought his decision would be.

"He's going to do it," she said. "I haven't seen him as excited as this for years."

I have known Todd Alborne since we were both eighteen. Our families had known one another, and chance brought us together one year during a European holiday. Though we did not become friends immediately, I found his company fascinating and on our return to England we stayed in touch with each other.

The fascination he held over me was not one I admired, but neither could I resist it: he possessed a fanatical and passionate dedication to what he was doing, and once started he would be deterred by nothing. He conducted several disastrous love-affairs, and twice lost most of his money in unsuccessful business ventures. But he had a general aimlessness that disturbed me; I felt that once pressed into a direction he could control, he would be able to exploit his unusual talents.

It was his sudden and unexpected fame that separated us. No one had anticipated it, least of all Todd. Yet when he recognized its potential, he embraced it readily.

I was not with him when it began, though I saw him soon after. He told me what happened, and though it differs from the popular anecdote I believe it.

He was drinking with some friends when an accident with a knife occurred. One of his companions had been cut badly, and had fainted. During the commotion that followed, a stranger made a wager with Todd that he would not voluntarily inflict a wound on his own body.

Todd slashed the skin of his forearm, and collected his money. The stranger offered to double the stake if Todd would amputate a finger.

Placing his left hand on the table in front of him, Todd removed his index finger. A few minutes later, with no further encouragement from the stranger—who by this time had left—Todd cut off another finger. The following day a television company had picked up the story, and Todd was invited to the studio to relate what had happened. During the live transmission, and against the wishes of the interviewer, Todd repeated the operation.

It was the reaction to this first broadcast—a wave of prurient shock from the public, and an hysterical condemnation in the media—that revealed to Todd the potential in such a display of self-multilation.

Finding a promoter, he commenced a tour of Europe, performing his act to paying audiences only.

It was at this point—seeing his arrangements for publicity, and learning of the sums of money he was confident of earning—that I made the effort of dissociating myself from him. Purposely, I isolated myself from news of his exploits and would take no interest in the various public stunts he performed. It was the element of ritual in what he did that sickened me, and his native flair for showmanship only made him the more offensive to me.

It was a year after this alienation that we met again. It was he who sought me out, and though I resisted him at first I was unable to maintain the distance I desired.

I learned that in the intervening period he had married.

At first I was repelled by Elizabeth, for I thought that she loved Todd for his obsession, in the way the blood-hungry public loved him. But as I grew to know her better I realized that she saw herself in some messianic role. It was then that I understood her to be as vulnerable as Todd—though in an entirely different way—and I found myself agreeing to work for Todd and to do for him whatever he requested. At first I refused to assist him with the mutilations, but later did as he asked. My change of mind in this instance was initiated by Elizabeth.

The condition of his body when I started to work for him was so bad that he was almost entirely crippled. Though at first he had had several organs grafted back on to his body after mutilation, such operations could be carried out only a limited number of times, and while healing, prevented further performances.

His left arm below the elbow had been removed; his left leg was almost intact beyond the two removed toes. His right leg was intact. One of his ears had been removed, and he had been scalped. All fingers but the thumb and index on his right hand had been removed.

As a result of these injuries he was incapable of administering the amputations himself, and in addition to the various assistants he employed for his act he required me to operate the mutilating apparatus during the actual performances.

He attested a disclaimer form for the injuries to which I was to be an accessory, and his career continued.

And it went on, between spells for recovery, for another two years. In spite of the apparent contempt he had for his body, Todd bought the most expensive medical supervison he could find, and the recovery from each amputation was strictly observed before another performance.

But the human body is finite and his eventual retirement was inevitable.

At his final performance, his genital organs were removed amid the greatest storm of publicity and outrage he had known. Afterwards, he made no further public appearance, and spent a long spell of convalescence in a private nursing-home. Elizabeth and I stayed with him, and when he bought Racine House fifty miles from Paris, we went there with him.

And from that day we had played out the masque; each pretending to the others that his career had reached its climax, each knowing that inside the limbless, earless, hairless, castrated man there was a flame burning still for its final extinguishment.

And outside the gates of Racine House, Todd's private world waited for him. And he knew they waited, and Elizabeth and I knew they waited.

Meanwhile our life went on, and he was the master.

There was an interval of three weeks between my confirming to Gaston that Todd was to make another appearance and the actual night itself. There was much to be done.

While we left the publicity arrangements to Gaston, Todd

and I began the job of designing and building the equipment for the show. This was a process that in the past had been one of extreme distaste to me. It wrought an unpleasant tension between Elizabeth and myself, for she would not allow me to tell her about the equipment.

This time, though, there was no such strain between us. Halfway through the work she asked me about the apparatus I was building, and that night, after Todd had fallen asleep, I took her down to the workshop. For ten minutes she walked from one instrument to another, testing the smoothness of the mechanism and the sharpness of the blades.

Finally, she looked at me without expression, then nodded.

I contacted Todd's former assistants, and confirmed with them that they would be present at the performance. Once or twice I telephoned Gaston, and learned of the wave of speculation that was anticipating Todd's return.

As for the master himself, he was taken with a burst of energy and excitement that stretched to its limits the prosthetic machinery which surrounded him. He seemed unable to sleep, and several nights would call for Elizabeth. For this period she did not come to my room, though I often visited her for an hour or two. One night Todd called her while I was there, and I lay in bed listening to him talk to her, his voice unnaturally high-pitched, though never uncontrolled or over-excited.

When the day of the performance arrived I asked him if he wanted to drive to the Alhambra in our specially built car, or to use the carriage and horses that I knew he preferred for public appearances. He chose the latter.

We departed early, knowing that in addition to the distance we had to cover there would be several delays caused by admirers.

We placed Todd at the front of the carriage, next to the driver, sitting him up in the seat I had built for him. Elizabeth and I sat behind, her hand resting lightly on my leg. Every so often, Todd would half turn his head and speak to us. On these occasions, either she or I would lean forward to acknowledge him and reply.

Once we were on the main road into Paris we encountered many large groups of admirers. Some cheered or called; some stood in silence. Todd acknowledged them all, but when one woman tried to scramble up into the carriage he became agitated and nervous and screamed at me to get her away from him.

The only place where he came into close contact with any of his admirers was during our stop to change horses. Then he spoke volubly and amiably, though afterwards he was noticeably tired.

Our arrival at the Théâtre Alhambra had been planned in great detail, and the police had cordoned off the crowd. There was a broad channel left free through which Todd could be wheeled. As the carriage halted the crowd began to cheer, and the horses became nervous.

I wheeled Todd in through the stage door, responding in spite of myself to the hysteria of the crowds. Elizabeth was close behind us. Todd took the reception well and professionally, smiling round from side to side, unable to acknowledge the acclaim in any other way. He appeared not to notice the small but determined and vociferous section of the crowd chanting the slogans that they bore on placards.

Once inside his dressing-room we were able to relax for a while. The show was not scheduled to start for another two and a half hours. After a short nap, Todd was bathed by Elizabeth, and then dressed in his stage costume.

Twenty minutes before he was due to give his performance, one of the female staff of the theatre came into the dressing-room and presented him with a bouquet of flowers. Elizabeth took them from the woman and laid them uncertainly before him, knowing well his dislike of flowers.

"Thank you," he said to the woman. "Flowers. What beautiful colours."

Gaston came in fifteen minutes later, accompanied by the manager of the Alhambra. Both men shook hands with me, Gaston kissed Elizabeth on her cheek, and the manager tried to strike up a conversation with Todd. Todd did not reply, and a little later I noticed that the manager was weeping silently. Todd stared at us all.

It had been decided by Todd that there was to be no special ceremony surrounding this performance. There were to be no speeches, no public remarks from Todd. No interviews to be granted. The act on the stage would follow carefully the instructions he had dictated to me, and the rehearsals that the other assistants had been following for the last week.

He turned to Elizabeth, and put his face up towards her. She kissed him tenderly, and I turned away.

After nearly a minute he said: "All right, Lasken. I'm ready."

I took the handle of his carriage and wheeled him out of the dressing-room and down the corridor towards the wings of the stage.

We heard a man's voice talking in French of Todd, and a great roar of applause from the audience. The muscles of my stomach contracted. The expression on Todd's face did not change.

Two assistants came forward, and lifted Todd into his harness. This was connected by two thin wires to a pulley in the flies, and when operated by one of the assistants in the wings would move Todd around the stage. When he was secure, his four false limbs were strapped in place.

He nodded to me, and I prepared myself. For a second, I saw the expression in Elizabeth's eyes. Todd was not looking in our direction, but I made no response to her.

I stepped on to the stage. A woman screamed, then the whole audience rose to its feet. My heart raced.

The equipment was already on the stage, covered with heavy velvet curtains. I walked to the centre of the stage, and bowed to the audience. Then I walked from one piece of apparatus to another, removing the curtains.

As each piece was revealed the audience roared its approval. The voice of the manager crackled over the P.A. system, imploring them to return to their seats. As I had done at previous performances, I stood still until the audience was seated once more. Each movement was provocative.

I finished revealing the equipment. To my eye it was ugly and utilitarian, but the audience relished the appearance of the razor-sharp blades.

I walked to the footlights.

"*Mesdames. Messieurs.*" Silence fell abruptly. "*Le maître.*"

I moved downstage, holding out my hand in the direction

of Todd. I tried purposely to disregard the audience. I could see Todd in the wings, hanging in his harness beside Elizabeth. He was not talking to her or looking at her. His head was bent forward, and he was concentrating on the sound from the audience.

They were still in silence . . . the anticipatory motionlessness of the voyeur.

Seconds passed, and still Todd waited. Somewhere in the audience a voice spoke quietly. Abruptly, the audience roared.

It was Todd's moment. He nodded to the assistant, who wound the pulley ropes and propelled Todd out on to the stage.

The movement was eerie and unnatural. He floated on the wire so that his false legs just scraped the canvas of the stage. His false arms hung limply at his side. Only his head was alert, greeting and acknowledging the audience.

I had expected them to applaud . . . but at his appearance they subsided again into silence. I had forgotten about that in the intervening years. It was the silences that had always appalled me.

The pulley-assistant propelled Todd to a couch standing to the right of the stage. I helped him lie down on it. Another assistant—who was a qualified medical doctor—came on to the stage, and carried out a brief examination.

He wrote something on a piece of paper, and handed it to me. Then he went to the front of the stage and made his statement to the audience.

"I have examined the master. He is fit. He is sane. He is in full possession of his senses, and knows what he is about to undertake. I have signed a statement to this effect."

The pulley-assistant raised Todd once more, and propelled him around the stage, from one piece of equipment to another. When he had inspected them all, he nodded his agreement.

At the front of the stage, in the centre, I unstrapped his false legs. As they fell away from his body, one or two men in the audience gasped.

Todd's arms were removed.

I then pulled forward one of the pieces of equipment: a

long, white-covered table with a large mirror above it.

I swung Todd's torso on to the table, then removed the harness and signalled for it to be lifted away. I positioned Todd so that as he was lying with his head towards the audience, and with his whole body visible to them in the mirror. I was working amidst silence. I did not took towards the audience, I did not look towards the wings, I was perspiring. Todd said nothing to me.

When Todd was in the position he required, he nodded to me and I turned towards the audience, bowing and indicating that the performance was about to commence. There was a ripple of applause, soon finished.

I stood back, and watched Todd without reaction. He was feeling the audience again. In a performance consisting of one solitary action, and a mute one at that, for best effect his timing had to be accurate. There was only one piece of apparatus on the stage which was to be used this evening; the others were there for the effect of their presence.

Todd and I both knew which one it was to be: I would wheel it over at the appropriate time.

The audience was silent again, but restless. I felt that it was poised critically; one movement would explode it into reaction. Todd nodded to me.

I walked again from one piece of apparatus to the next. On each one I put my hand to the blade, as if feeling its sharpness. By the time I had been to each one, the audience was ready. I could feel it, and I knew Todd could.

I went back to the apparatus Todd had selected: a guillotine made from tubular aluminium and with a blade of finest stainless steel. I trundled it over to his table, and connected it with the brackets for that purpose. I tested its solidity, and made a visual check that the release mechanism would work properly.

Todd was positioned now so that his head overhung the edge of the table. and was directly underneath the blade. The guillotine was so constructed that it did not obscure the view of his body in the mirror.

I removed his costume.

He was naked. The audience gasped when they saw his scars, but returned to silence.

I took the wire loop of the release mechanism and, as Todd had instructed me, tied it tightly around the thick meat of his tongue. To take up the slack of the wire, I adjusted it at the side of the apparatus.

I leaned over him, and asked if he was ready. He nodded.

"Edward," he said indistinctly. "Come closer."

I leaned forward so that my face was near his. To do this I had to pass my own neck under the guillotine blade. The audience approved of this action.

"What is it?" I said.

"I know, Edward. About you and Elizabeth."

I looked into the wings, where she was still standing.

I said: "And you still want to . . .?"

He nodded again, this time more violently. The wire release on his tongue tightened and the mechanism clicked open. He nearly caught me in the apparatus. I jumped away as the blade plummeted down. I turned from him, looking desperately into the wings at Elizabeth as the first screams from the audience filled the theatre.

Elizabeth stepped out on to the stage. She was looking at Todd. I went to her.

Todd's torso lay on the table. His heart was still beating, for blood spurted rhythmically in thick gouts from his severed neck. His hairless head swung from the apparatus. Where the wire gripped his tongue, it had wrenched it nearly from his throat. His eyes were still open.

We turned and faced the audience. The change that had come over them was total; in under five seconds they had panicked. A few people had fainted; the rest were standing. The noise of their shouting was unbelievable. They moved towards the doors. None looked at the stage. One man swung his fist at another; was knocked down from behind. A woman was having hysterics, tearing at her clothes. No one paid her any attention. I heard a shot, and ducked instinctively, pulling Elizabeth down with me. Women screamed; men shouted. I heard the P.A. click on, but no voice came through. Abruptly, the doors of the auditorium swung open simultaneously on all sides, and armed riot-police burst in. It had been planned carefully. As the police attacked them, the crowd fought back. I heard another shot, then several more in rapid succession.

I took Elizabeth by the hand, and led her from the stage.

In the dressing-room we watched through a window as the police attacked the crowds in the street. Many people were shot. Tear-gas was released, a helicopter hovered overhead.

We stood together in silence, Elizabeth crying. We were obliged to stay within the safety of the theatre building for another twelve hours. The next day we returned to Racine House, and the first leaves were spreading.

HERO

JOE W. HALDEMAN

It is a pleasure to see a new writer become an old pro in the twinkling of an eye. In 1968 Joe Haldeman was on combat duty as an infantryman in Vietnam, the experience that he drew upon for War Year, *a close-to-autobiographical novel about that experience which has just been published in the United States. Now here is "Hero", the story of a future war which is frighteningly real, frighteningly possible.*

"Tonight we're going to show you eight silent ways to kill a man." The guy who said that was a sergeant who didn't look five years older than me. Ergo, as they say, he couldn't possibly have ever killed a man, not in combat, silently or otherwise.

I already knew eighty ways to kill people, though most of them were pretty noisy. I sat up straight in my chair and assumed a look of polite attention and fell asleep with my eyes open. So did most everybody else. We'd learned that they never schedule anything important for these after-chop classes.

The projector woke me up and I sat through a short movie showing the "eight silent ways". Some of the actors must have been brainwipes, since they were actually killed.

After the movie a girl in the front row raised her hand. The sergeant nodded at her and she rose to parade rest. Not bad looking, but kind of chunky about the neck and shoulders. Everybody gets that way after carrying a heavy pack around for a couple of months.

"Sir"—we had to call sergeants "sir" until graduation—"Most of those methods, really, they looked . . . kind of silly."

"For instance?"

"Like killing a man with a blow to the kidneys, from an entrenching tool. I mean, when would you *actually* just have an entrenching tool, and no gun or knife? And why not just bash him over the head with it?"

"He might have a helmet on," he said reasonably.

"Besides, Taurans probably don't even *have* kidneys!"

He shrugged. "Probably they don't." This was 1997, and we'd never seen a Tauran; hadn't even found any pieces of Taurans bigger than a scorched chromosome. "But their body chemistry is similar to ours, and we have to assume they're similarly complex creatures. They *must* have weaknesses, vulnerable spots. You have to find out where they are.

"That's the important thing." He stabbed a finger at the screen. "That's why those eight convicts got caulked for your benefit . . . you've got to find out how to kill Taurans, and be able to do it whether you have a megawatt laser or just an emery board."

She sat back down, not looking too convinced.

"Any more questions?" Nobody raised their hand.

"OK—tench-hut!" We staggered upright and he looked at us expectantly.

"Fuck you, sir," came the tired chorus.

"Louder!"

"FUCK YOU SIR!" One of the army's less-inspired morale devices.

"That's better. Don't forget, pre-dawn maneuvers tomorrow. Chop at 0330, first formation, 0400. Anybody sacked after 0340 gets one stripe. Dismissed."

I zipped up my coverall and went across the snow to the lounge for a cup of soya and a joint. I'd always been able to get by on five or six hours of sleep, and this was the only time I could be by myself, out of the army for a while. Looked at the newsfax for a few minutes. Another ship got caulked, out by Aldebaran sector. That was four years ago. They were mounting a reprisal fleet, but it'll take four years more for them to get out there. By then, the Taurans would have every portal planet sewed up tight.

Back at the billet, everybody else was sacked and the main lights were out. The whole company'd been dragging ever since we got back from the two-week lunar training. I dumped my clothes in the locker, checked the roster and found out I was in bunk 31. Goddamnit, right under the heater.

I slipped through the curtain as quietly as possible so as not to wake up my bunkmate. Couldn't see who it was, but I couldn't have cared less. I slipped under the blanket.

"You're late, Mandella," a voice yawned. It was Rogers.

"Sorry I woke you up," I whispered.

"'Sallright." She snuggled over and clasped me spoon-fashion. She was warm and reasonably soft. I patted her hip in what I hoped was a brotherly fashion. "Night, Rogers."

"G'night, Stallion." She returned the gesture, a good deal more pointedly.

Why do you always get the tired ones when you're ready and the randy ones when you're tired? I bowed to the inevitable, but let her do all the work.

2

"Awright, let's get some goddam *back* inta that! Stringer team! Move it up—move your ass up!"

A warm front had come in about midnight and the snow had turned to sleet. The permaplast stringer weighed 500 pounds and was a bitch to handle, even when it wasn't covered with ice. There were four of us, two at each end, carrying the plastic girder with frozen fingertips. Rogers was my partner.

"Steel!" the guy behind me yelled, meaning that he was losing his hold. It wasn't steel, but it was heavy enough to break your foot. Everybody let go and hopped away. It splashed slush and mud all over us.

"Goddamnit, Petrov," Rogers said, "why didn't you go out for Star Fleet, or maybe the Red Cross? This fucken thing's not that fucken heavy." Most of the girls were a little more circumspect in their speech. Rogers was a little butch.

"Awright, get a fucken *move* on, stringers—Epoxy team! Dog 'em! Dog 'em!"

Our two epoxy people ran up, swinging their buckets. "Let's go, Mandella. I'm freezin' my balls off."

"Me, too," the girl said earnestly.

"One—two—heave!" We got the thing up again and staggered toward the bridge. It was about three-quarters completed. Looked as if the second platoon was going to beat us. I wouldn't give a crap, but the platoon that got their bridge built first got to fly home. Four miles of muck for the rest of us, and no rest before chop.

We got the stringer in place, dropped it with a clank, and fitted the static clamps that held it to the rise-beams. The female half of the epoxy team started slopping glue on it before we even had it secured. Her partner was waiting for the stringer on the other side. The floor team was waiting at the foot of the bridge, each one holding a piece of the light stressed permaplast over his head, like an umbrella. They were dry and clean. I wondered aloud what they had done to deserve it, and Rogers suggested a couple of colorful, but unlikely possibilities.

We were going back to stand by the next stringer when the Field First (he was named Dougelstein, but we called him "Awright") blew a whistle and bellowed, "Awright, soldier boys and girls, ten minutes. Smoke 'em if you got 'em." He reached into his pocket and turned on the control that heated our coveralls.

Rogers and I sat down on our end of the stringer and I took out my weed box. I had lots of joints, but we weren't allowed to smoke them until after night-chop. The only tobacco I had was a cigarro butt about three inches long. I lit it on the side of the box; it wasn't too bad after the first couple of puffs. Rogers took a puff to be sociable, but made a face and gave it back.

"Were you in school when you got drafted?" she asked.

"Yeah. Just got a degree in physics. Was going after a teacher's certificate."

She nodded soberly. "I was in biology . . ."

"Figures." I ducked a handful of slush. "How far?"

"Six years, bachelor's and technical." She slid her boot along the ground, turning up a ridge of mud and slush the consistency of freezing ice milk. "Why the hell did this have to happen?"

I shrugged. It didn't call for an answer, least of all the answer that the UNEF kept giving us. Intellectual and physical elite of the planet, going out to guard humanity against the Tauran menace. Soyashit. It was all just a big experiment. See whether we could goad the Taurans into ground action.

Awright blew the whistle two minutes early, as expected, but Rogers and I and other two stringers got to sit for a minute while the epoxy and floor teams finished covering our stringer. It got cold fast, sitting there with our suits turned off, but we remained inactive, on principle.

I really didn't see the sense of us having to train in the cold. Typical army half-logic. Sure, it was going to be cold where we were going; but not ice-cold or snow-cold. Almost by definition, a portal planet remained within a degree or two of absolute zero all the time, since collapsars don't shine—and the first chill you felt would mean that you were a dead man.

Twelve years before, when I was ten years old, they had discovered the collapsar jump. Just fling an object at a collapsar with sufficient speed, and it pops out in some other part of the galaxy. It didn't take long to figure out the formula that predicted where it would come out: it just traveled along the same "line" (actually an Einsteinian geodesic) it would have followed if the collapsar hadn't been in the way—until it reaches another collapsar field, whereupon it reappears, repelled with the same speed it had approaching the original collapsar. Travel time between the two collapsars is exactly zero.

It made a lot of work for mathematical physicists, who had to redefine simultaneity, then tear down general relativity and build it back up again. And it made the politicians very happy, because now they could send a shipload of colonists to Fomalhaut for less than it once cost to put a brace of men on the moon. There were a lot of people the politicians would just love to see on Fomalhaut, implementing a glorious adventure instead of stirring up trouble at home.

The ships were always accompanied by an automated probe that followed a couple of million kilometers behind. We knew about the portal planets, little bits of flotsam that whirled around the collapsars; the purpose of the drone was to come back and tell us in the event that a ship had smacked into a portal planet at .999 of the speed of light.

That particular catastrophe never happened, but one day a drone did come limping back alone. Its data were analyzed, and it turned out that the colonists' ship had been pursued by another vessel and destroyed. This happened near Aldebaran, in the constellation Taurus, but since "Aldebaranian" is a little hard to handle, they named the enemy Taurans.

Colonizing vessels thenceforth went out protected by an armed guard. Often the armed guard went out alone, and finally the colonization effort itself slowed to a token trickle. The United Nations Exploratory and Colonization Group got shortened to UNEF, United Nations Exploratory Force, emphasis on the "force".

Then some bright lad in the General Assembly decided that we ought to field an army of footsoldiers, to guard the portal planets of the nearer collapsars. This led to the Elite Conscription Act of 1996 and the most rigorously selected army in the history of warfare.

So here we are, fifty men and fifty women, with IQs over 150 and bodies of unusual health and strength, slogging Elitely through the mud and slush of central Missouri, reflecting on how useful our skill in building bridges will be, on worlds where the only fluid will be your occasional standing pool of liquid helium.

3

About a month later, we left for our final training exercise: maneuvers on the planet Charon. Though nearing perihellion it was still more than twice as far from the sun as was Pluto.

The troopship was a converted "cattlewagon", made to carry 200 colonists and assorted bushes and beasts. Don't think it was roomy, though, just because there were half that many of us. Most of the excess space was taken up with extra reaction mass and ordnance.

The whole trip took three weeks, accelerating at two gees halfway: decelerating the other half. Our top speed, as we roared by the orbit of Pluto, was around 1/20th of the speed of light—not quite enough for relativity to rear its complicated head.

Three weeks of carrying around twice as much weight as normal . . . it's no picnic. We did some cautious exercises three times a day, and remained horizontal as much as possible. Still, we had several broken bones and serious dislocations. The men had to wear special supporters to keep from littering the floor with loose organs. It was almost impossible to sleep, what with nightmares of choking and being crushed, and the necessity of rolling over periodically to prevent blood pooling and bedsores. One girl got so fatigued that she almost slept through the experience of having a rib rub through to the open air.

I'd been in space several times before, so when we finally stopped decelerating and went into free fall, it was nothing but a relief. But some people had never been out, except for our training on the moon, and succumbed to the sudden vertigo and disorientation. The rest of us cleaned up after them, floating through the quarters with sponges and inspirators to suck up the globules of partly-digested "Concentrate, High-protein, Low-residue, Beef Flavor (Soya)".

A shuttle took us down to the surface in three trips. I waited for the last one, along with everybody else who wasn't bothered by free fall.

We had a good view of Charon, coming down from orbit. There wasn't much to see, though. It was just a dim, off-white sphere with a few smudges on it. We landed about two hundred meters from the base. A pressurized crawler came out and mated with the ferry, so we didn't have to suit up. We clanked and squeaked up to the main building, a featureless box of grayish plastic.

Inside, the walls were the same inspired color. The rest of the company was sitting at desks, chattering away. There was a seat next to Freeland.

"Jeff—feeling better?" He still looked a little pale.

"If the gods had meant for man to survive in free fall, they would have given him a cast-iron glottis. Somewhat better. Dying for a smoke."

"Yeah."

"*You* seemed to take it all right. Went up in school, didn't you?"

"Senior thesis in vacuum welding. Spent three weeks—"

"Tench-hut!" We stood up in a raggety-ass fashion, by twos and threes. The door opened and a full major came in. I stiffened a little. He was the highest-ranking officer I'd ever seen. He had a row of ribbons stitched into his coveralls, including a purple strip meaning he'd been wounded in combat, fighting in the old American army. Must have been that Indochina thing, but it had fizzled out before I was born. He didn't look that old.

"Sit, sit." He made a patting motion with his hand. Then he put his hands on his hips and scanned the company with a small smile on his face. "Welcome to Charon. You picked a lovely day to land; the temperature outside is a summery eight point one five degrees Absolute. We expect little change for the next two centuries or so." Some of us laughed half-heartedly.

"You'd best enjoy the tropical climate here at Miami Base, enjoy it while you can. We're on the center of sunside here, and most of your training will be on darkside. Over there, the temperature drops to a chilly two point zero eight.

"You might as well regard all the training you got on Earth and the moon as just a warm-up exercise, to give you a fair chance of surviving Charon. You'll have to go through your whole repertory here: tools, weapons, maneuvers. And you'll find that, at these temperatures, tools don't work the way they should, weapons don't want to fire. And people move v-e-r-y cautiously."

He studied the clipboard in his hand. "Right now, you have forty-nine women and forty-eight men. Two deaths, one psychiatric release. Having read an outline of your training program, I'm frankly surprised that so many of you pulled through.

"But you might as well know that I won't be displeased if as few as fifty of you graduate from this final phase. And the only way not to graduate is to die. Here. The only way anybody gets back to Earth—including me—is after a combat tour.

"You will complete your training in one month. From here you go to Stargate collapsar, a little over two lights away. You will stay at the settlement on Stargate I, the largest portal planet, until replacements arrive. Hopefully, that will be no more than a month; another group is due here as soon as you leave.

"When you leave Stargate, you will be going to a strategically important collapsar, set up a military base there, and fight the enemy, if attacked. Otherwise, maintain the base until further orders.

"The last two weeks of your training will consist of constructing such a base, on darkside. There you will be totally isolated from Miami Base: no communication, no medical evacuation, no resupply. Sometime before the two weeks are up, your defense facilities will be evaluated in an attack by guided drones. They will be armed.

"All of the permanent personnel here on Charon are combat veterans. Thus, all of us are forty to fifty years of age, but I think we can keep up with you. Two of us will be with you at all times, and will accompany you at least as far as Stargate. They are Captain Sherman Stott, your company commander, and Sergeant Octavio Cortez, your first sergeant. Gentlemen?"

Two men in the front row stood easily and turned to face us. Captain Stott was a little smaller than the Major, but cut from the same mold; face hard and smooth as porcelain, cynical half-smile, a precise centimeter of beard framing a large chin, looking thirty at the most. He wore a large gunpowder-type pistol on his hip.

Sergeant Cortez was another story. His head was shaved and the wrong shape; flattened out on one side where a large piece of skull had obviously been taken out. His face was very dark and seamed with wrinkles and scars. Half his left ear was missing and his eyes were as expressive as buttons on a machine. He had a mustache-and-beard combination that looked like a skinny white caterpillar taking a lap around his mouth. On anybody else, his schoolboy smile might look pleasant, but he was about the ugliest, meanest-looking creature I'd ever seen. Still, if you didn't look at his head and considered the lower six feet or so, he could pose as the "after" advertisement for a body-building spa. Neither Stott nor Cortez wore any ribbons. Cortez had a small pocket-laser suspended in a magnetic rig, sideways, under his left armpit. It had wooden grips that were worn very smooth.

"Now, before I turn you over to the tender mercies of these two gentlemen, let me caution you again:

"Two months ago there was not a living soul on this planet, just some leftover equipment from the expedition of 1991. A working force of forty-five men struggled for a month to erect this base. Twenty-four of them, more than half, died in the construction of it. This is the most dangerous planet men have ever tried to live on, but the places you'll be going will be this bad and worse. Your cadre will try to keep you alive, for the next month. Listen to them . . . and follow their example; all of them have survived here for longer than you'll have to. Captain?" The Captain stood up as the Major went out the door.

"Tench-*hut*!" The last syllable was like an explosion and we all jerked to our feet.

"Now I'm only gonna say this *once* so you better listen," he growled. "We *are* in a combat situation here and in a combat situation there is only *one* penalty for disobedience and insubordination." He jerked the pistol from his hip and held it by the barrel, like a club. "This is an Army model 1911 automatic *pistol* caliber .45 and it is a primitive but effective weapon. The Sergeant and I are authorized to use our weapons to kill to enforce discipline, don't make us do it because we will. We *will.*" He put the pistol back. The holster snap made a loud crack in the dead quiet.

"Sergeant Cortez and I between us have killed more people than are sitting in this room. Both of us fought in Vietnam on the American side and both of us joined the United Nations International Guard more than ten years ago. I took a break in grade from major for the privilege of commanding this company, and First Sergeant Cortez took a break from sub-major, because we are both *combat* soldiers and this is the first *combat* situation since 1976.

"Keep in mind what I've said while the First Sergeant instructs you more specifically in what your duties will be under this command. Take over, Sergeant." He turned on his heel and strode out of the room, with the little smile on his face that hadn't changed one millimeter during the whole harangue.

The First Sergeant moved like a heavy machine with lots of ball bearings. When the door hissed shut he swiveled ponderously to face us and said, "At ease, siddown," in a surprisingly gentle voice. He sat on a table in the front of the room. It creaked but held.

"Now the Captain talks scary and I look scary, but we both mean well. You'll be working pretty closely with me, so you better get used to this thing I've got hanging in front of my brain. You probably won't see the Captain much, except on maneuvers."

He touched the flat part of his head. "And speaking of brains, I still have just about all of mine, in spite of Chinese efforts to the contrary. All of us old vets who mustered into UNEF had to pass the same criteria that got you drafted by the Elite Conscription Act. So I suspect all you are smart and tough but the Captain and I are smart and tough *and* experienced."

He flipped through the roster without really looking at it. "Now, as the Captain said, there'll be only one kind of disciplinary action, on maneuvers. Capital punishment. But normally *we* won't have to kill you for disobeying; Charon'll save us the trouble.

"Back in the billeting area, it'll be another story. We don't much care what you do inside. Grab-ass all day and screw all night, makes no difference . . . but once you suit up and go outside, you've gotta have discipline that would shame a Centurion. There will be situations where one stupid act could kill us all.

"Anyhow, the first thing we've gotta do is get you fitted to your fighting suits. The armorer's waiting at your billet; he'll take you one at a time. Let's go."

4

"Now I know you got lectured and lectured on what a fighting suit can do, back on Earth." The armorer was a small man, partially bald, with no insignia of rank on his coveralls. Sergeant Cortez told us to call him "sir", as he was a lieutenant.

"But I'd like to reinforce a couple of points, maybe add some things your instructors Earthside weren't clear about or couldn't know. Your First Sergeant was kind enough to consent to being my visual aid. Sergeant?"

Cortez slipped out of his coveralls and came up to the little raised platform where a fighting suit was standing. popped open like a man-shaped clam. He backed into it and slipped his arms into the rigid sleeves. There was a click and the thing swung shut with a sigh. It was bright green with CORTEZ stenciled in white letters on the helmet.

"Camouflage, Sergeant." The green faded to white, then dirty grey. "This is good camouflage for Charon, and most of your portal planets," said Cortez, from a deep well. "But there are several other combinations available." The grey dappled and brightened to a combination of greens and browns. "Jungle." Then smoothed out to a hard light ocher. "Desert." Dark brown, darker, to a deep flat black. "Night or space."

"Very good, Sergeant. To my knowledge, this is the only feature of the suit which was perfected after your training. The control is around your left wrist and is admittedly awkward. But once you find the right combination, it's easy to lock in.

"Now, you didn't get much in-suit training Earthside because we didn't want you to get used to using the thing in a friendly environment. The fighting suit is the deadliest personal weapon ever built, and with no weapon it is easier for the user to kill himself through carelessness. Turn around, Sergeant.

"Case in point." He tapped a square protuberance between the shoulders. "Exhaust fins. As you know, the suit tries to keep you at a comfortable temperature no matter what the weather's like outside. The material of the suit is as near to a perfect insulator as we could get, consistent with mechanical demands. Therefore, these fins get *hot*—especially hot, compared to darkside temperatures—as they bleed off the body's heat.

"All you have to do is lean up against a boulder of frozen gas; there's lots of it around. The gas will sublime off faster than it can escape from the fins; in escaping, it will push against the surrounding 'ice' and fracture it . . . and in about one hundredth of a second, you have the equivalent of a hand grenade going off right below your neck. You'll never feel a thing.

"Variations on this theme have killed eleven people in the past two months. And they were just building a bunch of huts.

"I assume you know how easily the waldo capabilities can

kill you or your companions. Anybody want to shake hands with the Sergeant?" He stepped over and clasped his glove. "He's had lots of practice. Until *you* have, be extremely careful. You might scratch an itch and wind up bleeding to death. Remember, semi-logarithmic response: two pounds' pressure exerts five pounds' force; three pounds' gives ten; four pounds' twenty-three; five pounds', forty-seven. Most of you can muster up a grip of well over a hundred pounds. Theoretically, you could rip a steel girder in two with that, amplified. Actually, you'd destroy the material of your gloves and, at least on Charon, die very quickly. It'd be a race between decompression and flash-freezing. You'd be the loser.

"The leg waldos are also dangerous, even though the amplification is less extreme. Until you're really skilled, don't try to run or jump. You're likely to trip, and that means you're likely to die.

"Charon's gravity is three-fourths of Earth normal, so it's not too bad. But on a really small world, like Luna, you could take a running jump and not come down for twenty minutes, just keep sailing over the horizon. Maybe bash into a mountain at eighty meters per second. On a small asteroid, it'd be no trick at all to run up to escape velocity and be off on an informal tour of intergalactic space. It's a slow way to travel.

"Tomorrow morning, we'll start teaching you how to stay alive inside this infernal machine. The rest of the afternoon and evening, I'll call you one at a time to be fitted. That's all, Sergeant."

Cortez went to the door and turned the stopcock that let air into the airlock. A bank of infra-red lamps went on to keep the air from freezing inside it. When the pressures were equalized, he shut the stopcock, unclamped the door and stepped in, clamping it shut behind him. A pump hummed for about a minute, evacuating the airlock, then he stepped out and sealed the outside door. It was pretty much like the ones on Luna.

"First I want Private Omar Almizar. The rest of you can go find your bunks. I'll call you over the squawker."

"Alphabetical order, sir?"

"Yep. About ten minutes apiece. If your name begins with Z you might as well get sacked."

That was Rogers. She probably *was* thinking about getting sacked.

5

The sun was a hard white point directly overhead. It was a lot brighter than I had expected it to be; since we were 80 A.U.s out, it was only 1/6400th as bright as it is on Earth. Still, it was putting out about as much light as a powerful streetlamp.

"This is considerably more light than you'll have on a portal planet," Captain Stott's voice crackled in our collective ear. "Be glad that you'll be able to watch your step."

We were lined up, single-file, on a permaplast sidewalk connecting the billet and the supply hut. We'd practiced walking inside, all morning, and this wasn't any different except for the exotic scenery. Though the light was rather dim, you could see all the way to the horizon quite clearly, with no atmosphere in the way. A black cliff that looked too regular to be natural stretched from one horizon to the other, passing within a kilometer of us. The ground was obsidian-black, mottled with patches of white or bluish ice. Next to the supply hut was a small mountain of snow in a bin marked OXYGEN.

The suit was fairly comfortable, but it gave you the odd feeling of being simultaneously a marionette and a puppeteer. You apply the impulse to move your leg and the suit picks it up and magnifies it and moves your leg for you.

"Today we're only going to walk around the company area and nobody will *leave* the company area." The Captain wasn't wearing his .45, but he had a laser-finger like the rest of us. And his was probably hooked up.

Keeping an interval of at least two meters between each person, we stepped off the permaplast and followed the Captain over the smooth rock. We walked carefully for about an hour, spiraling out, and finally stopped at the far edge of the perimeter.

"Now everybody pay close attention. I'm going out to that blue slab of ice"—it was a big one, about twenty meters away —"and show you something that you'd better know if you want to live."

He walked out in a dozen confident steps. "First I have to

heat up a rock—filters down." I slapped the stud under my armpit and the filter slid into place over my image converter. The Captain pointed his finger at a black rock the size of a basketball and gave it a short burst. The glare rolled a long shadow of the Captain over us and beyond. The rock shattered into a pile of hazy splinters.

"It doesn't take long for these to cool down." He stooped and picked up a piece. "This one is probably twenty or twenty-five degrees. Watch." He tossed the "warm" rock on the ice slab. It skittered around in a crazy pattern and shot off the side. He tossed another one, and it did the same.

"As you know you are not quite *perfectly* insulated. These rocks are about the temperature of the soles of your boots. If you try to stand on a slab of hydrogen the same thing will happen to you. Except that the rock is *already* dead.

"The reason for this behavior is that the rock makes a slick interface with the ice—a little puddle of liquid hydrogen—and rides a few molecules above the liquid on a cushion of hydrogen vapor. This makes the rock or *you* a frictionless bearing as far as the ice is concerned and you *can't* stand up without any friction under your boots.

"After you have lived in your suit for a month or so you *should* be able to survive falling down but right *now* you just don't know enough. Watch."

The Captain flexed and hopped up onto the slab. His feet shot out from under him and he twisted around in midair, landing on hands and knees. He slipped off and stood on the ground.

"The idea is to keep your exhaust fins from making contact with the frozen gas. Compared to the ice they are as hot as a blast furnace and contact with any weight behind it will result in an explosion."

After that demonstration, we walked around for another hour or so, and returned to the billet. Once through the airlock, we had to mill around for a while, letting the suits get up to something like room temperature. Somebody came up and touched helmets with me.

"William?" She had MCCOY stenciled above her faceplate.

"Hi, Sean. Anything special?"

"I just wondered if you had anyone to sleep with tonight."

That's right; I'd forgotten, there wasn't any sleeping roster here. Everybody just chooses his own partner. "Sure, I mean, uh, no—no, I haven't asked anybody, sure, if you want to . . ."

"Thanks, William. See you later." I watched her walk away and thought that if anybody could make a fighting suit look sexy, it'd be Sean. But even Sean couldn't.

Cortez decided we were warm enough and led us to the suit room where we backed the things into place and hooked them up to the charging plates (each suit had a little chunk of plutonium that would power it for several years, but we were supposed to run on fuel cells as much as possible). After a lot of shuffling around, everybody finally got plugged in and we were allowed to unsuit, ninety-seven naked chickens squirming out of bright green eggs. It was *cold*—the air, the floor, and especially the suits—and we made a pretty disorderly exit toward the lockers.

I slipped on tunic, trousers and sandals and was still cold. I took my cup and joined the line for soya, everybody jumping up and down to keep warm.

"How c-cold, do you think, it is, M-Mandella?" That was McCoy.

"I don't, even want, to think, about it." I stopped jumping and rubbed myself as briskly as possible, while holding a cup in one hand. "At least as cold as Missouri was."

"Ung . . . wish they'd, get some, heat in, this place." It always affects the small girls more than anybody else. McCoy was the littlest one in the company, a waspwaist doll barely five feet high.

"They've got the airco going. It can't be long now."

"I wish I, was a big, slab of, meat like, you."

I was glad she wasn't.

6

We had our first casualty on the third day, learning how to dig holes.

With such large amounts of energy stored in a soldier's weapons, it wouldn't be practical for him to hack out a hole in the frozen ground with the conventional pick and shovel.

Still, you can launch grenades all day and get nothing but shallow depressions—so the usual method is to bore a hole in the ground with the hand laser, drop a timed charge in after it's cooled down and, ideally, fill the hole with stuff. Of course, there's not much loose rock on Charon, unless you've already blown a hole nearby.

The only difficult thing about the procedure is getting away. To be safe, we were told, you've got to either be behind something really solid, or be at least a hundred meters away. You've got about three minutes after setting the charge, but you can't just sprint away. Not on Charon.

The accident happened when we were making a really deep hole, the kind you want for a large underground bunker. For this, we had to blow a hole, then climb down to the bottom of the crater and repeat the procedure again and again until the hole was deep enough. Inside the crater we used charges with a five-minute delay, but it hardly seemed enough time—you really had to go slow, picking your way up the crater's edge.

Just about everybody had blown a double hole; everybody but me and three others. I guess we were the only ones paying really close attention when Bovanovitch got into trouble. All of us were a good two hundred meters away. With my image converter tuned up to about forty power, I watched her disappear over the rim of the crater. After that, I could only listen in on her conversation with Cortez.

"I'm on the bottom, Sergeant." Normal radio procedure was suspended for maneuvers like this; nobody but the trainee and Cortez was allowed to broadcast.

"Okay, move to the center and clear out the rubble. Take your time. No rush until you pull the pin."

"Sure, Sergeant." We could hear small echoes of rocks clattering; sound conduction through her boots. She didn't say anything for several minutes.

"Found bottom." She sounded a little out of breath.

"Ice or rock?"

"Oh, it's rock, Sergeant. The greenish stuff."

"Use a low setting, then. One point two, dispersion four."

"God darn it, Sergeant, that'll take forever."

"Yeah, but that stuff's got hydrated crystals in it—heat it up too fast and you might make it fracture. And we'd just have to leave you there, girl, giblets and all."

"Okay, one point two dee four." The inside edge of the crater flickered red with reflected laser light.

"When you get about half a meter deep, squeeze it up to dee two."

"Roger." It took her exactly seventeen minutes, three of them at dispersion two. I could imagine how tired her shooting arm was.

"Now rest for a few minutes. When the bottom of the hole stops glowing, arm the charge and drop it in. Then *walk* out, Understand? You'll have plenty of time."

"I understand, Sergeant. Walk out." She sounded nervous. Well, you don't often have to tiptoe away from a twenty-microton tachyon bomb. We listened to her breathing for a few minutes.

"Here goes." Faint slithering sound of the bomb sliding down.

"Slow and easy now, you've got five minutes."

"Y-yeah. Five." Her footsteps started out slow and regular. Then, after she started climbing the side, the sounds were less regular; maybe a little frantic. And with four minutes to go—

"God!" A loud scraping noise, then clatters and bumps. "Oh—my—God."

"What's wrong, Private?"

"God!" Silence.

"Private, you don't wanna get shot, you *tell me what's wrong!*"

"I . . . God, I'm stuck . . . rockslide . . . God . . . . DO SOMETHING I can't move I God can't move I, I—"

"Shut up! How deep?"

"Can't move my God my legs HELP ME—"

"Then goddamnit use your arms—push!—you can move a ton with each hand." Three minutes.

Then she stopped cussing and started to mumble, in Russian, I guess, a low monotone. She was panting and you could hear rocks tumbling away.

"I'm free." Two minutes.

"Go as fast as you can." Cortez's voice was flat and emotionless.

At ninety seconds she appeared crawling over the rim. "Run, girl . . . you better run." She ran five or six steps and fell, skidded a few meters and got back up, running; fell again, got up again—

It looked like she was going pretty fast, but she had only covered about thirty meters when Cortez said, "All right, Bovanovitch, get down on your stomach and lie still." Ten seconds, but she didn't hear him or she wanted to get just a little more distance and she kept running, careless leaping strides and at the high point of one leap there was a flash and a rumble and something big hit her below the neck and her headless body spun off end over end through space, trailing a red-black spiral of flash-frozen blood that settled gracefully to the ground, a path of crystal powder that nobody disturbed while we gathered rocks to cover the juiceless thing at the end of it.

That night Cortez didn't lecture us, didn't even show up for night-chop. We were all very polite to each other and nobody was afraid to talk about it.

I sacked with Rogers; everybody sacked with a good friend, but all she wanted to do was cry, and she cried so long and so hard that she got me doing it too.

7

"Fire team A—move out!" The twelve of us advanced in a ragged line toward the simulated bunker. It was about a kilometer away, across a carefully prepared obstacle course. We could move pretty fast, since all of the ice had been cleared from the field, but even with ten days' experience we weren't ready to do more than an easy job.

I carried a grenade launcher, loaded with tenth-microton practice grenades. Everybody had their laser-fingers set at point oh eight dee one; not much more than a flashlight. This was a *simulated* attack—the bunker and its robot defender cost too much to be used once and thrown away.

"Team B follow. Team leaders, take over."

We approached a clump of boulders at about the halfway mark, and Potter, my team leader, said "Stop and cover." We clustered behind the rocks and waited for team B.

Barely visible in their blackened suits, the dozen men and

women whispered by us. As soon as they were clear, they jogged left, out of our line of sight.

"Fire!" Red circles of light danced a half-click downrange, where the bunker was just visible. Five hundred meters was the limit for these practice grenades; but I might luck out, so I lined the launcher up on the image of the bunker, held it at a 45° angle and popped off a salvo of three.

Return fire from the bunker started before my grenades even landed. Its automatic lasers were no more powerful than the ones we were using, but a direct hit would deactivate your image converter, leaving you blind. It was setting down a random field of fire, not even coming close to the boulders we were hiding behind.

Three magnesium-bright flashes blinked simultaneously, about thirty meters short of the bunker. "Mandella! I thought you were supposed to be *good* with that thing."

"Damn it, Potter—it only throws half a click. Once we get closer, I'll lay 'em right on top, every time."

"*Sure* you will." I didn't say anything. She wouldn't be team leader forever. Besides, she hadn't been such a bad girl before the power went to her head.

Since the grenadier is the assistant team leader, I was slaved into Potter's radio and could hear B team talk to her.

"Potter, this is Freeman. Losses?"

"Potter here—no, looks like they were concentrating on you."

"Yeah, we lost three. Right now we're in a depression about eighty, a hundred meters down from you. We can give cover whenever you're ready."

"Okay, start." Soft click: "A team, follow me." She slid out from behind the rock and turned on the faint pink beacon beneath her powerpack. I turned on mine and moved out to run alongside of her and the rest of the team fanned out in a trailing wedge. Nobody fired while B team laid down a cover for us.

All I could hear was Potter's breathing and the soft crunch-crunch of my boots. Couldn't see much of anything, so I tongued the image converter up to a log-two intensification. That made the image kind of blurry but adequately bright. Looked like the bunker had B team pretty well pinned down; they were getting quite a roasting. All of their return fire was laser; they must have lost their grenadier.

"Potter, this is Mandella. Shouldn't we take some of the heat off B team?"

"Soon as I can find us good enough cover. Is that all right with you? Private?" She'd been promoted to corporal for the duration of the exercise.

We angled to the right and laid down behind a slab of rock. Most of the others found cover nearby, but a few had to just hug the ground.

"Freeman, this is Potter."

"Potter, this is Smithy. Freeman's out; Samuels is out. We only have five men left. Give us some cover so we can get—"

"Roger, Smithy."—Click—"Open up, A team. The B's are really hurtin'."

I peeked out over the edge of the rock. My rangefinder said that the bunker was about 350 meters away, still pretty far. I aimed just a smidgeon high and popped three, then down a couple of degrees and three more. The first ones overshot by about twenty meters, then the second salvo flared up directly in front of the bunker. I tried to hold on that angle and popped fifteen, the rest of the magazine, in the same direction.

I should have ducked down behind the rock to reload, but I wanted to see where the fifteen would land, so I kept my eyes on the bunker while I reached back to unclip another magazine—

When the laser hit my image converter there was a red glare so intense it seemed to go right through my eyes and bounce off the back of my skull. It must have only been a few milliseconds before the converter overloaded and went blind, but the bright green afterimage hurt my eyes for several minutes.

Since I was officially "dead", my radio automatically cut off and I had to remain where I was until the mock battle was over. With no sensory input besides the feel of my own skin (and it ached where the image converter had shone on it) and the ringing in my ears, it seemed like an awfully long time. Finally, a helmet clanked against mine:

"You okay, Mandella?" Potter's voice.

"Sorry, I died of boredom twenty minutes ago."

"Stand up and take my hand." I did so and we shuffled back to the billet. It must have taken over an hour. She didn't say anything more, all the way back—it's a pretty awkward way to communicate—but after we'd cycled through the airlock and warmed up, she helped me undog my suit. I got ready for a mild tongue-lashing, but when the suit popped open, before I could even get my eyes adjusted to the light, she grabbed me around the neck and planted a wet kiss on my mouth.

"Nice shooting, Mandella."

"Huh?"

"The last salvo before you got hit—four direct hits; the bunker decided it was knocked out, and all we had to do was walk the rest of the way."

"Great." I scratched my face under the eyes and some dry skin flaked off. She giggled.

"You should see yourself, you look like . . ."

"All personnel report to the assembly area." That was the Captain's voice. Bad news.

She handed me a tunic and sandals. "Let's go." The assembly area/chop hall was just down the corridor. There was a row of roll-call buttons at the door; I pressed the one beside my name. Four of the names were covered with black tape. That was good, we hadn't lost anybody else during today's maneuvers.

The Captain was sitting on the raised dais, which at least meant we didn't have to go through the tench-hut bullshit. The place filled up in less than a minute; a soft chime indicated the roll was complete.

Captain Stott didn't stand up. "You did *fairly* well today, nobody got killed and I expected some to. In that respect you exceeded my expectations but in *every* other respect you did a poor job.

"I am glad you're taking good care of yourselves because each of you represents an investment of over a million dollars and one fourth of a human life.

"But in this simulated battle against a *very* stupid robot enemy, thirty-seven of you managed to walk into laser fire and be killed in a *sim*ulated way and since dead people require no food *you* will require no food, for the next three days. Each person who was a casualty in this battle will be allowed only two liters of water and a vitamin ration each day."

We knew enough not to groan or anything, but there were some pretty disgusted looks, especially on the faces that had singed eyebrows and a pink rectangle of sunburn framing their eyes.

"Mandella."

"Sir?"

"You are far and away the worst burned casualty. Was your image converter set on normal?"

Oh, shit. "No, sir. Log two."

"I see. Who was your team leader for the exercise?"

"Acting Corporal Potter, sir."

"Private Potter, did you order him to use image intensification?"

"Sir, I—I don't remember."

"You don't. Well as a memory exercise you may join the dead people. Is that satisfactory?"

"Yes, sir."

"Good. Dead people get one last meal tonight, and go on no rations starting tomorrow. Are there any questions?" He must have been kidding. "All right. Dismissed."

I selected the meal that looked as if it had the most calories and took my tray to sit by Potter.

"That was a quixotic damn thing to do. But thanks."

"Nothing. I've been wanting to lose a few pounds anyway." I couldn't see where she was carrying any extra.

"I know a good exercise," I said. She smiled without looking up from her tray. "Have anybody for tonight?"

"Kind of thought I'd ask Jeff . . ."

"Better hurry, then. He's lusting after Uhuru." Well, that was mostly true. Everybody did.

"I don't know. Maybe we ought to save our strength. That third day . . ."

"Come on," I scratched the back of her hand lightly with a fingernail. "We haven't sacked since Missouri. Maybe I've learned something new."

"Maybe you have." She tilted her head up at me in a sly way. "Okay."

Actually, she was the one with the new trick. The French corkscrew, she called it. She wouldn't tell me who taught it to her, though. I'd like to shake his hand. Once I got my strength back.

8

The two weeks' training around Miami Base eventually cost us eleven lives. Twelve, if you count Dahlquist. I guess having to spend the rest of your life on Charon, with a hand and both legs missing, is close enough to dying.

Little Foster was crushed in a landslide and Freeland had a suit malfunct that froze him solid before we could carry him inside. Most of the other deaders were people I didn't know all that well. But they all hurt. And they seemed to make us more scared rather than more cautious.

Now darkside. A flyer brought us over in groups of twenty, and set us down beside a pile of building materials, thoughtfully immersed in a pool of helium II.

We used grapples to haul the stuff out of the pool. It's not safe to go wading, since the stuff crawls all over you and it's hard to tell what's underneath; you could walk out onto a slab of hydrogen and be out of luck.

I'd suggested that we try to boil away the pool with our lasers, but then minutes of concentrated fire didn't drop the helium level appreciably. It didn't boil, either; helium II is a "superfluid", so what evaporation there was had to take place evenly, all over the surface. No hot spots, so no bubbling.

We weren't supposed to use lights, to "avoid detection". There was plenty of starlight, with your image converter cranked up to log three or four, but each stage of amplification meant some loss of detail. By log four, the landscape looked like a crude monochrome painting, and you couldn't read the names on people's helmets unless they were right in front of you.

The landscape wasn't all that interesting, anyhow. There were half a dozen medium-sized meteor craters (all with exactly the same level of helium II in them) and the suggestion of some puny mountains just over the horizon. The uneven ground was the consistency of frozen spiderwebs; every time you put your foot down, you'd sink half an inch with a squeaking crunch. It could get on your nerves.

It took most of the day to pull all the stuff out of the pool. We took shifts napping, which you could do either standing up, sitting, or lying on your stomach. I didn't do well in any of those positions, so I was anxious to get the bunker built and pressurized.

We couldn't build the thing underground—it'd just fill up with helium II—so the first thing to do was to build an insulating platform, a permaplast-vacuum sandwich three layers tall.

I was an acting corporal, with a crew of ten people. We were carrying the permaplast layers to the building site—two people can carry one easily—when one of "my" men slipped and fell on his back.

"Damn it, Singer, watch your step." We'd had a couple of deaders that way.

"Sorry, Corporal. I'm bushed, just got my feet tangled up."

"Yeah, just watch it." He got back up all right, and with his partner placed the sheet and went back to get another.

I kept my eye on him. In a few minutes he was practically staggering, not easy to do in that suit of cybernetic armor.

"Singer! After you set that plank, I want to see you."

"Okay." He labored through the task and mooched over.

"Let me check your readout." I opened the door on his chest to expose the medical monitor. His temperature was two degrees high; blood pressure and heart rate both elevated. Not up to the red line, though.

"You sick or something?"

"Hell, Mandella, I feel OK, just tired. Since I fell I been a little dizzy."

I chinned the medic's combination. "Doc, this is Mandella. You wanna come here for a minute?"

"Sure, where are you?" I waved and he walked over from poolside.

"What's the problem?" I showed him Singer's readout.

He knew what all the other little dials and things meant, so it took him a while. "As far as I can tell, Mandella . . . he's just hot."

"Hell, I coulda told you that," said Singer.

"Maybe you better have the armorer take a look at his suit." We had two people who'd taken a crash course in suit maintenance; they were our "armorers".

I chinned Sanchez and asked him to come over with his tool kit.

"Be a couple of minutes, Corporal. Carryin' a plank."

"Well, put it down and get on over here." I was getting an uneasy feeling. Waiting for him, the medic and I looked over Singer's suit.

"Uh-oh," Doc Jones said. "Look at this." I went around to the back and looked where he was pointing. Two of the fins on the heat exchanger were bent out of shape.

"What's wrong?" Singer asked.

"You fell on your heat exchanger, right?"

"Sure, Corporal—that's it, it must not be working right."

"I don't think it's working at *all*," said Doc.

Sanchez came over with his diagnostic kit and we told him what had happened. He looked at the heat exchanger, then plugged a couple of jacks into it and got a digital readout from a little monitor in his kit. I didn't know what it was measuring, but it came out zero to eight decimal places.

Heard a soft click, Sanchez chinning my private frequency. "Corporal, this guy's a deader."

"What? Can't you fix the goddamn thing?"

"Maybe . . . maybe I could, if I could take it apart. But there's no way—"

"Hey! Sanchez?" Singer was talking on the general freak. "Find out what's wrong?" He was panting.

Click. "Keep your pants on, man, we're working on it." Click. "He won't last long enough for us to get the bunker pressurized. And I can't work on the heat exchanger from outside of the suit."

"You've got a spare suit, haven't you?"

"Two of 'em, the fit-anybody kind. But there's no place . . . say . . ."

"Right. Go get one of the suits warmed up." I chinned the general freak. "Listen, Singer, we've gotta get you out of that thing. Sanchez has a spare suit, but to make the switch, we're gonna have to build a house around you. Understand?"

"Huh-uh."

"Look, we'll just make a box with you inside, and hook it up to the life-support unit. That way you can breathe while you make the switch."

"Soun's pretty compis . . . compilcated t'me."

"Look, just come along—"

"I'll be all right, man, jus' lemme res' . . ."

I grabbed his arm and led him to the building site. He was really weaving. Doc took his other arm and between us, we kept him from falling over.

"Corporal Ho, this is Corporal Mandella." Ho was in charge of the life-support unit.

"Go away, Mandella, I'm busy."

"You're going to be busier." I outlined the problem to her. While her group hurried to adapt the LSU—for this purpose, it need only be an air hose and heater—I got my crew to bring around six slabs of permaplast, so we could build a big box around Singer and the extra suit. It would look like a huge coffin, a meter square and six meters long.

We set the suit down on the slab that would be the floor of the coffin. "Okay, Singer, let's go."

No answer.

"Singer!" He was just standing there. Doc Jones checked his readout.

"He's out, man, unconscious."

My mind raced. There might just be room for another person in the box. "Give me a hand here." I took Singer's shoulders and Doc took his feet, and we carefully laid him out at the feet of the empty suit.

Then I laid down myself, above the suit. "Okay, close 'er up."

"Look, Mandella, if anybody goes in there, it oughta be me."

"Fuck you, Doc. *My* job. My man." That sounded all wrong. William Mandella, boy hero.

They stood a slab up on edge—it had two openings for the LSU input and exhaust—and proceeded to weld it to the bottom plank with a narrow laser beam. On Earth, we'd just use glue, but here the only fluid was helium, which has lots of interesting properties, but is definitely not sticky.

After about ten minutes we were completely walled up. I could feel the LSU humming. I switched on my suit light—the first time since we landed on darkside—and the glare made purple blotches dance in front of my eyes.

"Mandella, this is Ho. Stay in your suit at least two or three minutes. We're putting hot air in, but it's coming back just this side of liquid." I lay and watched the purple fade.

"Okay, it's still cold, but you can make it." I popped my suit. It wouldn't open all the way, but I didn't have too much trouble getting out. The suit was still cold enough to take some skin off my fingers and butt as I wiggled out.

I had to crawl feet-first down the coffin to get to Singer. It got darker fast, moving away from light. When I popped his suit a rush of hot stink hit me in the face. In the dim light his skin was dark red and splotchy. His breathing was very shallow and I could see his heart palpitating.

First I unhooked the relief tubes—an unpleasant business—then the bio sensors, and then I had the problem of getting his arms out of their sleeves.

It's pretty easy to do for yourself. You twist this way and turn that way and the arm pops out. Doing it from the outside is a different matter: I had to twist his arm and then reach under and move the suit's arm to match—and it takes muscle to move a suit around from the outside.

Once I had one arm out it was pretty easy; I just crawled forward, putting my feet on the suit's shoulders, and pulled on his free arm. He slid out of the suit like an oyster slipping out of its shell.

I popped the spare suit and after a lot of pulling and pushing, managed to get his legs in. Hooked up the bio sensors and the front relief tube. He'd have to do the other one himself, it's too complicated. For the nth time I was glad not to have been born female; they have to have two of those damned plumber's friends, instead of just one and a simple hose.

I left his arms out of the sleeves. The suit would be useless for any kind of work, anyhow; waldos have to be tailored to the individual.

His eyelids fluttered. "Man . . . della. Where . . . the hell . . ."

I explained, slowly, and he seemed to get most of it. "Now I'm gonna close you up and go get into my suit. I'll have the crew cut the end off this thing and I'll haul you out. Got it?"

He nodded. Strange to see that—when you nod or shrug in a suit, it doesn't communicate anything.

I crawled into my suit, hooked up the attachments and chinned the general freak. "Doc, I think he's gonna be okay Get us out of here now."

"Will do." Ho's voice. The LSU hum was replaced by a chatter, then a throb; evacuating the box to prevent an explosion.

One corner of the seam grew red, then white and a bright crimson beam lanced through, not a foot away from my head. I scrunched back as far as I could. The beam slid up the seam and around three corners, back to where it started. The end of the box fell away slowly, trailing filaments of melted 'plast.

"Wait for the stuff to harden, Mandella."

"Sanchez, I'm not that stupid."

"Here you go." Somebody tossed a line to me. That *would* be smarter than dragging him out by myself. I threaded a long bight under his arms and tied it behind his neck. Then I scrambled out to help them pull, which was silly—they had a dozen people already lined up to haul.

Singer got out all right and was actually sitting up while Doc Jones checked his readout. People were asking me about it and congratulating me when suddenly Ho said "Look!" and pointed toward the horizon.

It was a black ship, coming in fast. I just had time to think it wasn't fair, they weren't supposed to attack until the last few days, and then the ship was right on top of us.

9

We all flopped to the ground instinctively, but the ship didn't attack. It blasted braking rockets and dropped to land on skids. Then it skiied around to come to a rest beside the building site.

Everybody had it figured out and was standing around

sheepishly when the two suited figures stepped out of the ship.

A familiar voice crackled over the general freak. "Every *one* of you saw us coming in and not *one* of you responded with laser fire. It wouldn't have done any good but it would have indicated a certain amount of fighting spirit. You have a week or less before the real thing and since the Sergeant and *I* will be here *I* will insist that you show a little more will to live. Acting sergeant Potter."

"Here, sir."

"Get me a detail of twelve men to unload cargo. We brought a hundred small robot drones for *target* practice so that you might have at least a fighting chance, when a live target comes over.

"Move *now*. We only have thirty minutes before the ship returns to Miami."

I checked, and it was actually more like forty minutes.

Having the Captain and Sergeant there didn't really make much difference; we were still on our own, they were just observing.

Once we got the floor down, it only took one day to complete the bunker. It was a grey oblong, featureless except for the airlock blister and four windows. On top was a swivel-mounted bevawatt laser. The operator—you couldn't call him a "gunner"—sat in a chair that swiveled with the gun, holding dead-man switches in both hands. The laser wouldn't fire as long as he was holding one of those switches. If he let go, it would automatically aim for any moving aerial object and fire at will. Primary detection and aiming was by means of a kilometer-high antenna mounted beside the bunker.

It was the only arrangement that could really be expected to work, with the horizon so close and human reflexes so slow. You couldn't have the thing fully automatic, because in theory, friendly ships might also approach.

The aiming computer could choose between up to twelve targets, appearing simultaneously (firing at the largest ones first). And it would get all twelve in the space of half a second. The installation was partly protected from enemy fire by an efficient ablative layer. Didn't protect the human operator, of course—but then they *were* dead-man switches. One man above guarding eighty inside. The army's good at that kind of arithmetic.

Once the bunker was finished, half of us stayed inside at all times (feeling very much like targets), taking turns operating the laser, while the other half went on maneuvers.

About four clicks from the base was a large "lake" of frozen hydrogen; one of our most important maneuvers was to learn how to get around on the treacherous stuff.

It really wasn't too difficult. You couldn't stand up on it, so you had to belly down and sled.

If you had somebody to push you from the edge, getting started was no problem. Otherwise, you had to scrabble with your hands and feet, pushing down as hard as was practical, until you started moving, in a series of little jumps. Once started, you would keep going until you ran out of ice. You could steer a little bit by digging in, hand and foot, on the appropriate side, but you couldn't slow to a stop that way. So it was a good idea not to go too fast, and to be positioned in such a way that your helmet didn't absorb the shock of stopping.

We went through all the things we'd done on the Miami side; weapons practice, demolition, attack patterns. We also launched drones at irregular intervals, toward the bunker. Thus, ten or fifteen times a day, the operators got to demonstrate their skill in letting go of the handles as soon as the proximity light went on.

I had four hours of that, like everybody else. I was nervous until the first "attack", when I saw how little there was to it. The light went on, I let go, the gun aimed and when the drone peeped over the horizon—zzt! Nice touch of color, the molten metal spraying through the air. Otherwise not too exciting.

So none of us were worried about the upcoming "graduation exercise", thinking it would be just more of the same.

Miami Base attacked on the thirteenth day with two simultaneous missiles streaking over opposite sides of the horizon at some forty kilometers per second. The laser vaporized the first one with no trouble, but the second got within eight clicks of the bunker before it was hit.

We were coming back from maneuvers, about a click away from the bunker. I wouldn't have seen it happen if I hadn't been looking directly at the bunker the moment of the attack.

The second missile sent a shower of molten debris straight toward the bunker, Eleven pieces hit, and, as we later reconstructed it, this is what happened.

The first casualty was Uhuru, pretty Uhuru inside the bunker, who was hit in the back and the head and died instantly. With the drop in pressure, the LSU went into high gear. Friedman was standing in front of the main airco outlet and was blown into the opposite wall hard enough to knock him unconscious; he died of decompression before the others could get him to his suit.

Everybody else managed to stagger through the gale and get into their suits, but Garcia's suit had been holed and didn't do him any good.

By the time we got there, they had turned off the LSU and were welding up the holes in the wall. One man was trying to scrape up the unrecognizable mess that had been Uhuru. I could hear him sobbing and retching. They had already taken Garcia and Friedman outside for burial. The Captain took over the repair detail from Potter. Sergeant Cortez led the sobbing man over to a corner and came back to work on cleaning up Uhuru's remains, alone. He didn't order anybody to help and nobody volunteered.

10

As a graduation exercise, we were unceremoniously stuffed into a ship—*Earth's Hope*, the same one we rode to Charon—and bundled off to Stargate at a little more than one gee.

The trip seemed endless, about six months' subjective time, and boring, but not as hard on the carcass as going to Charon had been. Captain Stott made us review our training orally, day by day, and we did exercises every day until we were worn to a collective frazzle.

Stargate I was like Charon's darkside, only more so. The base on Stargate I was smaller than Miami Base—only a little bigger than the one we constructed on darkside—and we were due to lay over a week to help expand the facilities. The crew there was very glad to see us; especially the two females, who looked a little worn around the edges.

We all crowded into the small dining hall, where Submajor Williamson, the man in charge of Stargate I, gave us some disconcerting news:

"Everybody get comfortable. Get off the tables, though, there's plenty of floor.

"I have some idea of what you just went through, training on Charon. I won't say it's all been wasted. But where you're headed, things will be quite different. Warmer."

He paused to let that soak in.

"Aleph Aurigae, the first collapsar ever detected, revolves around the normal star Epsilon Aurigae, in a 27-year orbit. The enemy has a base of operations, not on a regular portal planet of Aleph, but on a planet in orbit around Epsilon. We don't know much about the planet: just that it goes around Epsilon once every 745 days, is about 3/4 the size of Earth, and has an albedo of 0.8, meaning it's probably covered with clouds. We can't say precisely how hot it will be, but judging from its distance from Epsilon, it's probably rather hotter than Earth. Of course, we don't know whether you'll be working . . . fighting on lightside or darkside, equator or poles. It's highly unlikely that the atmosphere will be breathable—at any rate, you'll stay inside your suits.

"Now you know exactly as much about where you're going as I do. Questions?"

"Sir," Stein drawled, "Now we know where we're goin' . . . anybody know what we're goin' to do when we get there?"

Williamson shrugged. "That's up to your captain—and your sergeant, and the captain of *Earth's Hope*, and *Hope*'s logistic computer. We just don't have enough data yet, to project a course of action for you. It may be a long and bloody battle, it may be just a case of walking in to pick up the pieces. Conceivably, the Taurans might want to make a peace offer"—Cortez snorted—"in which case you would simply be part of our muscle, our bargaining power." He looked at Cortez mildly. "No one can say for sure."

The orgy that night was kind of amusing, but it was like trying to sleep in the middle of a raucous beach party. The only area big enough to sleep all of us was the dining hall;

they draped a few bedsheets here and there for privacy,then unleashed Stargate's eighteen sex-starved men on our women, compliant and promiscuous by military custom (and law), but desiring nothing so much as sleep on solid ground.

The eighteen men acted as if they were compelled to try as many permutations as possible, and their performance was impressive (in a strictly quantitative sense, that is). Those of us who were keeping count led a cheering section for some of the more gifted members. Personally, I think their medic must have whipped them up some L-dopa or something.

The next morning—and every other morning we were on Stargate I—we staggered out of bed and into our suits, to go outside and work on the "new wing". Eventually, Stargate would be tactical and logistic headquarters for the war, with thousands of permanent personnel, guarded by half-a-dozen heavy cruisers in *Hope*'s class. When we started, it was two shacks and twenty people; when we left, it was four shacks and twenty people. The work was a breeze, compared to dark-side, since we had all the light we needed, and got sixteen hours inside for every eight hours' work. And no drone attack for a final exam.

When we shuttled back up to the *Hope*, nobody was too happy about leaving (though some of the more popular females declared it'd be good to get some rest)—Stargate was the last easy, safe assignment we'd have before taking up arms against the Taurans. And as Williamson had pointed out the first day, there was no way of predicting what that would be like.

Most of us didn't feel too enthusiastic about making a collapsar jump, either. We'd been assured that we wouldn't even feel it happen, just free fall all the way.

I wasn't convinced. As a physics student, I'd had the usual courses in general relativity and theories of gravitation. We only had a little direct data at that time—Stargate was discovered when I was in high school—but the mathematical model seemed clear enough.

The collapsar Stargate was a perfect sphere about three kilometers in radius. It was suspended forever in a state of gravitational collapse that should have meant its surface was dropping toward its center at nearly the speed of light.

Relativity propped it up, at least gave it the illusion of being there . . . the way all reality becomes illusory and observer-oriented when you study general relativity, or Buddhism.

At any rate, there would be a theoretical point in space-time when one end of our ship was just above the surface of the collapsar, and the other end was a kilometer away (in our frame of reference)—in any sane universe, this would set up tidal stresses and tear the ship apart, and we would be just another million kilograms of degenerate matter on the theoretical surface, rushing headlong to nowhere for the rest of eternity; or dropping to the center in the next trillionth of a second—you pays your money and you takes your frame of reference.

But they were right. We blasted away from Stargate I, made a few course corrections and then just dropped, for about an hour.

Then a bell rang and we sank into our cushions under a steady two gravities of deceleration. We were in enemy territory.

11

We'd been decelerating at two gravities for almost nine days when the battle began. Lying on our couches being miserable, all we felt were two soft bumps, missiles being released. Some eight hours later, the squawkbox crackled: "Attention, all crew. This is the Captain." Quinsana, the pilot, was only a lieutenant, but was allowed to call himself Captain aboard the vessel, where he outranked all of us, even Captain Stott. "You grunts in the cargo hold can listen too.

"We just engaged the enemy with two fifty-bevaton tachyon missiles, and have destroyed both the enemy vessel and another object which it had launched approximately three microseconds before.

"The enemy has been trying to overtake us for the past 179 hours, ship time. At the time of the engagement, the enemy was moving at a little over half the speed of light, relative to Aleph, and was only about thirty AUs from *Earth's Hope*. It was moving at .47c relative to us, and thus we would have been coincident in space-time"—rammed?—"in a little more than nine hours. The missiles were launched at 0719 ship's time, and destroyed the enemy at 1540, both tachyon bombs detonating within a thousand clicks of the enemy objects."

The two missiles were a type whose propulsion system itself was only a barely-controlled tachyon bomb. They accelerated at a constant rate of 100 gees, and were traveling at a relativistic speed by the time the nearby mass of the enemy ship detonated them.

"We expect no further interference from enemy vessels. Our velocity with respect to Aleph will be zero in another five hours; we will then begin to journey back. The return will take twenty-seven days." General moans and dejected cussing. Everybody knew all that already, of course; but we didn't care to be reminded of it.

So after another month of logy calisthenics and drill, at a constant two gravities, we got our first look at the planet we were going to attack. Invaders from outer space, yes, sir.

It was a blinding white crescent basking two AUs from Epsilon. The Captain had pinned down the location of the enemy base from fifty AUs out, and we had jockeyed in on a wide arc, keeping the bulk of the planet between them and us. That didn't mean we were sneaking up on them—quite the contrary; they launched three abortive attacks—but it put us in a stronger defensive position. Until we had to go to the surface, that is. Then only would the ship and its Star Fleet crew be reasonably safe.

Since the planet rotated rather slowly—once every 10½ days—a "stationary" orbit for the ship had to be 150,000 clicks out. This made the people in the ship feel quite secure, with six thousand miles of rock and 90,000 miles of space between them and the enemy. But it meant a whole second's time lag in communication between us on the ground and the ship's battle computer. A person could get awful dead while that neutrino pulse crawled up and back.

Our vague orders were to attack the base and gain control while damaging a minimum of enemy equipment. We were to take at least one enemy alive. We were under no circumstances to allow *ourselves* to be taken alive, however. And the decision wasn't up to us; one special pulse from the battle computer and that speck of plutonium in our power plant would fission with all of .01 % efficiency, and you'd be nothing but a rapidly expanding, very hot plasma.

They strapped us into six scoutships—one platoon of twelve people in each—and we blasted away from *Earth's Hope* at eight gees. Each scoutship was supposed to follow its own carefully random path to our rendezvous point, 108 clicks from the base. Fourteen drone ships were launched at the same time, to confound the enemy's anti-spacecraft system.

The landing went off almost perfectly. One ship suffered minor damage, a near miss boiling away some of the ablative material on one side of the hull, but it'd still be able to make it and return, as long as it kept its speed down while in the atmosphere.

We zigged and zagged and wound up first ship at the rendezvous point. There was only one trouble. It was under four kilometers of water.

I could almost hear that machine, 90,000 miles away, grinding its mental gears, adding this new bit of data. We proceeded just as if we were landing on solid ground: braking rockets, falling skids out, hit the water, skip, hit the water, skip, hit the water, sink.

It would have made sense to go ahead and land on the bottom—we were streamlined, after all, and water just another fluid—but the hull wasn't strong enough to hold up a four-kilometer column of water. Sergeant Cortez was in the scoutship with us.

"Sarge, tell that computer to *do* something! We're gonna get—"

"Oh, shut up, Mandella. Trust in th' lord." "Lord" was definitely lower-case when Cortez said it.

There was a loud bubbly sigh, then another and a slight increase in pressure on my back that meant the ship was rising. "Flotation bags?" Cortez didn't deign to answer, or didn't know.

That must have been it. We rose to within ten or fifteen meters of the surface and stopped, suspended there. Through the port I could see the surface above, shimmering like a mirror of hammered silver. I wondered what it could be like, to be a fish and have a definite roof over your world.

I watched another ship splash in. It made a great cloud of bubbles and turbulence, then fell—slightly tail-first—for a short distance before large bags popped out under each delta wing. Then it bobbed up to about our level and stayed.

Soon all of the ships were floating within a few hundred meters of us, like a school of ungainly fish.

"This is Captain Stott. Now listen carefully. There is a beach some 28 clicks from your present position, in the direction of the enemy. You will be proceeding to this beach by scoutship and from there will mount your assault on the Tauran position." That was *some* improvement; we'd only have to walk 80 clicks.

We deflated the bags, blasted to the surface and flew in a slow, spread-out formation to the beach. It took several minutes. As the ship scraped to a halt I could hear pumps humming, making the cabin pressure equal to the air pressure outside. Before it had quite stopped moving, the escape slot beside my couch slid open. I rolled out onto the wing of the craft and jumped to the ground. Ten seconds to find cover—I sprinted across loose gravel to the "treeline", a twisty bramble of tall sparse bluish-green shrubs. I dove into the briar patch and turned to watch the ships leave. The drones that were left rose slowly to about a hundred meters, then took off in all directions with a bone-jarring roar. The real scoutships slid slowly back into the water. Maybe that was a good idea.

It wasn't a terribly attractive world, but certainly would be easier to get around in than the cryogenic nightmare we were trained for. The sky was a uniform dull silver brightness that merged with the mist over the ocean so completely as to make it impossible to tell where water ended and air began. Small wavelets licked at the black gravel shore, much too slow and graceful in the three-quarters earth normal gravity. Even from fifty meters away, the rattle of billions of pebbles rolling with the tide was loud in my ears.

The air temperature was 79° Centigrade, not quite hot enough for the sea to boil, even though the air pressure was low compared to Earth's. Wisps of stream drifted quickly upward from the line where water met land. I wondered how long a man would survive, exposed here without a suit. Would the heat or the low oxygen (partial pressure one-eighth earth normal) kill him first? Or was there some deadly micro-organism that would beat them both . . .

"This is Cortez. Everybody come over and assemble on me." He was standing on the beach a little to the left of me, waving his hand in a circle over his head. I walked toward him through the shrubs. They were brittle, unsubstantial, seemed paradoxically dried-out in the steamy air. They wouldn't offer much in the way of cover.

"We'll be advancing on a heading .05 radians east of north. I want platoon one to take point. Two and three follow about twenty meters behind, to the left and right. Seven, command platoon, is in the middle, twenty meters behind two and three. Five and six, bring up the rear, in a semicircular closed flank. Everybody straight?" Sure, we could do that "arrow head" maneuver in our sleep. "OK, let's move out."

I was in platoon seven, the "command group". Captain Stott put me there not because I was expected to give any commands, but because of my training in physics.

The command group was supposedly the safest place, buffered by six platoons: people were assigned to it because there was some tactical reason for them to survive at least a little longer than the rest. Cortez was there to give orders. Chavez was there to correct suit malfuncts. The senior medic, Doc Wilson (the only medic who actually had an MD) was there and so was Theodopolis, the radio engineer: our link with the Captain, who had elected to stay in orbit.

The rest of us were assigned to the command group by dint of special training or aptitude, that wouldn't normally be considered of a "tactical" nature. Facing a totally unknown enemy, there was no way of telling what might prove important. Thus I was there because I was the closest the company had to a physicist. Rogers was biology. Tate was chemistry. Ho could crank out a perfect score on the Rhine extrasensory perception test, every time. Bohrs was a polyglot, able to speak twenty-one languages fluently, idiomatically. Petrov's talent was that he had tested out to have not one molecule of xenophobia in his psyche. Keating was a skilled acrobat. Debby Hollister—"Lucky" Hollister—showed a remarkable aptitude for making money, and also had a consistently high Rhine potential.

12

When we first set out, we were using the "jungle" camouflage combination on our suits. But what passed for jungle in these anemic tropics was too sparse; we looked like a band of conspicuous harlequins trooping through the woods. Cortez had us switch to black, but that was just as bad, as the light from Epsilon came evenly from all parts of the sky, and there were no shadows except us. We finally settled on the dun-colored desert camouflage.

The nature of the countryside changed slowly as we walked north, away from the sea. The thorned stalks, I guess you could call them trees, came in fewer numbers but were bigger around and less brittle; at the base of each was a tangled mass of vine with the same blue-green color, which spread out in a flattened cone some ten meters in diameter. There was a delicate green flower the size of a man's head near the top of each tree.

Grass began to appear some five clicks from the sea. It seemed to respect the trees' "property rights"; leaving a strip of bare earth around each cone of vine. At the edge of such a clearing, it would grow as timid blue-green stubble; then, moving away from the tree, would get thicker and taller until it reached shoulder-high in some places, where the separation between two trees was unusually large. The grass was a lighter, greener shade than the trees and vines. We changed the color of our suits to the bright green we had used for maximum visibility on Charon. Keeping to the thickest part of the grass, we were fairly inconspicuous.

We covered over twenty clicks each day, buoyant after months under two gees. Until the second day, the only form of animal life we saw was a kind of black worm, finger-sized with hundreds of cilium legs like the bristles of a brush. Rogers said that there obviously had to be some larger creature around, or there would be no reason for the trees to have thorns. So we were doubly on guard, expecting trouble both from the Taurans and the unidentified "large creature".

Potter's second platoon was on point; the general freak

was reserved for her, since her platoon would likely be the first to spot any trouble.

"Sarge, this is Potter," we all heard. "Movement ahead."

"Get down then!"

"We are. Don't think they see us."

"First platoon, go up to the right of point. Keep down. Fourth, get up to the left. Tell me when you get in position. Sixth platoon, stay back and guard the rear. Fifth and third, close with the command group."

Two dozen people whispered out of the grass, to join us. Cortez must have heard from the fourth platoon.

"Good. How about you, first . . . OK, fine. How many are there?"

"Eight we can see." Potter's voice.

"Good. When I give the word, open fire. Shoot to kill."

"Sarge . . . they're just animals."

"Potter—if you've known all this time what a Tauran looks like, you should've told us. Shoot to kill."

"But we need . . ."

"We need a prisoner, but we don't need to escort him forty clicks to his home base and keep an eye on him while we fight. Clear?"

"Yes. Sergeant."

"OK. Seventh, all you brains and weirds, we're going up and watch. Fifth and third, come along to guard."

We crawled through the meter-high grass to where the second platoon had stretched out in a firing line.

"I don't see anything," Cortez said.

"Ahead and just to the left. Dark green."

They were only a shade darker than the grass. But after you saw the first one, you could see them all, moving slowly around some thirty meters ahead.

"Fire!" Cortez fired first, then twelve streaks of crimson leaped out and the grass wilted black, disappeared and the creatures convulsed and died trying to scatter.

"Hold fire, hold it!" Cortez stood up. "We want to have something left—second platoon, follow me." He strode out toward the smoldering corpses, laser finger pointed out front, obscene divining rod pulling him toward the carnage . . . I felt my gorge rising and knew that all the lurid training tapes, all the horrible deaths in training accidents, hadn't prepared me for this sudden reality . . . that I had a magic wand that I could point at a life and make it a smoking piece of half-raw meat; I wasn't a soldier nor ever wanted to be one nor ever would want—

"OK, seventh, come on up." While we were walking toward them, one of the creatures moved, a tiny shudder, and Cortez flicked the beam of his laser over it with an almost negligent gesture. It made a hand-deep gash across the creature's middle. It died, like the others, without emitting a sound.

They were not quite as tall as humans, but wider in girth. They were covered with dark green, almost black fur; white curls where the laser had singed. They appeared to have three legs and an arm. The only ornament to their shaggy heads was a mouth, wet black orifice filled with flat black teeth. They were thoroughly repulsive but their worst feature was not a difference from human beings but a similarity . . . wherever the laser had opened a body cavity, milk-white glistening veined globes and coils of organs spilled out, and their blood was dark clotting red.

"Rogers, take a look. Taurans or not?"

Rogers knelt by one of the disemboweled creatures and opened a flat plastic box, filled with glittering dissecting tools. She selected a scalpel. "One way we might be able to find out." Doc Wilson watched over her shoulder as she methodically slit the membrane covering several organs.

"Here." She held up a blackish fibrous mass between two fingers, parody of daintiness through all that armor.

"So?"

"It's grass, Sergeant. If the Taurans can eat the grass and breathe the air, they certainly found a planet remarkably like their home." She tossed it away. "They're animals, Sergeant, just animals."

"I don't know," Doc Wilson said. "Just because they walk around on all fours, threes maybe, and eat grass . . ."

"Well, let's check out the brain." She found one that had been hit in the head and scraped the superficial black char from the wound. "Look at that."

It was almost solid bone. She tugged and ruffled the hair

all over the head of another one. "What the hell does it use for sensory organs? No eyes or ears or . . ." She stood up. "Nothing in that head but a mouth and ten centimeters of skull. To protect nothing, not a thing."

"If I could shrug, I'd shrug," the Doctor said. "It doesn't prove anything—a brain doesn't have to look like a mushy walnut and it doesn't have to be in the head. Maybe that skull isn't bone, maybe *that's* the brain, some crystal lattice . . ."

"Yeah, but the stomach's in the right place, and if those aren't intestines I'll eat—"

"Look," Cortez said. "This is all real interesting, but all we need to know is whether that thing's dangerous, then we've gotta move on, we don't have all—"

"They aren't dangerous," Rogers began. "They don't—"

"Medic! DOC!" Somebody was waving his arms, back at the firing line. Doc sprinted back to him, the rest of us following.

"What's wrong?" He had reached back and unclipped his medical kit on the run.

"It's Ho, she's out."

Doc swung open the door on Ho's biomedical monitor. He didn't have to look far. "She's dead."

"Dead?" Cortez said. "What the hell—"

"Just a minute." Doc plugged a jack into the monitor and fiddled with some dials on his kit. "Everybody's biomed readout is stored for twelve hours. I'm running it backwards, should be able to—there!"

"What?"

"Four and a half minutes ago—must have been when you opened fire—Jesus!"

"Well?"

"Massive cerebral hemorrhage. No . . ." he watched the dials. "No . . . warning, no indication of anything out of the ordinary; blood pressure up, pulse up, but normal under the circumstances . . . nothing to . . . indicate . . ." He reached down and popped her suit. Her fine Oriental features were distorted in a horrible grimace, both gums showing. Sticky fluid ran from under her collapsed eyelids and a trickle of blood still dripped from each ear. Doc Wilson closed the suit back up.

"I've never seen anything like it. It's as if a bomb went off in her skull."

"Oh Christ," Rogers said, "she was Rhine-sensitive, wasn't she?"

"That's right." Cortez sounded thoughtful. "All right, everybody listen up. Platoon leaders, check your platoons and see if anybody's missing or hurt. Anybody else in seventh?"

"I—I've got a splitting headache, Sarge," Lucky said.

Four others had bad headaches. One of them affirmed that he was slightly Rhine-sensitive. The others didn't know.

"Cortez, I think it's obvious," Doc Wilson said, "that we should give these . . . monsters wide berth, especially shouldn't harm any more of them. Not with five people susceptible to whatever apparently killed Ho."

"Of course, goddamnit, I don't need anybody to tell me that. We'd better get moving. I just filled the Captain in on what happened; he agrees that we'd better get as far away from here as we can, before we stop for the night.

"Let's get back in formation and continue on the same bearing. Fifth platoon, take over point: second, come back to the rear. Everybody else, same as before."

"What about Ho?" Lucky asked.

"She'll be taken care of. From the ship."

After we'd gone half a click, there was a flash and rolling thunder. Where Ho had been, there appeared a wispy luminous mushroom cloud boiling up to disappear against the grey sky.

13

We stopped for the "night"—actually, the sun wouldn't set for another seventy hours—atop a slight rise some ten clicks from where we had killed the aliens. But they weren't aliens, I had to remind myself—*we* were.

Two platoons deployed in a ring around the rest of us, and we flopped down exhausted. Everybody was allowed four hours' sleep and had two hours' guard duty.

Potter came over and sat next to me. I chinned her frequency.

"Hi, Marygay."

"Hi, William," her voice over the radio was hoarse and cracking. "God, it's so horrible."

"It's over now—"

"I killed one of them, the first instant, I shot it right in the, in the . . ."

I put my hand on her knee. The contact made a plastic click and I jerked it back, visions of machines embracing, copulating. "Don't feel singled out, Marygay, whatever guilt there is, belongs evenly to all of us . . . but a triple portion for Cor—"

"You privates quit jawin' and get some sleep. You both pull guard in two hours."

"OK, Sarge." Her voice was so sad and tired I couldn't bear it, I felt if I could only touch her I could drain off the sadness like a ground wire draining current but we were each trapped in our own plastic world—

"G'night, William."

"Night." It's almost impossible to get sexually excited inside a suit, with the relief tube and all the silver chloride sensors poking you, but somehow this was my body's response to the emotional impotence, maybe remembering more pleasant sleeps with Marygay, maybe feeling that in the midst of all this death, personal death could be soon, cranking up the procreative derrick for one last try . . . lovely thoughts like this and I fell asleep and dreamed that I was a machine, mimicking the functions of life, creaking and clanking my clumsy way through the world, people too polite to say anything but giggling behind my back, and the little man who sat inside my head pulling the levers and clutches and watching the dials, he was hopelessly mad and was storing up hurts for the day—

"Mandella—wake up, goddamnit, your shift!"

I shuffled over to my place on the perimeter to watch for god knows what . . . but I was so weary I couldn't keep my eyes open. Finally I tongued a stimtab, knowing I'd pay for it later.

For over an hour I sat there, scanning my sector left, right, near, far; the scene never changing, not even a breath of wind to stir the grass.

Then suddenly the grass parted and one of the three-legged creatures was right in front of me. I raised my finger but didn't squeeze.

"Movement!"

"Movement!"

"Jesus Chri—there's one right—"

"HOLD YOUR FIRE, f'shit's sake don't shoot!"

"Movement."

"Movement." I looked left and right and as far as I could see, every perimeter guard had one of the blind dumb creatures standing right in front of him.

Maybe the drug I'd taken to stay awake made me more sensitive to whatever they did. My scalp crawled and I felt a formless *thing* in my mind, the feeling you get when somebody has said something and you didn't quite hear it, want to respond but the opportunity to ask him to repeat it is gone.

The creature sat back on its haunches, leaning forward on the one front leg. Big green bear with a withered arm. Its power threaded through my mind; spiderwebs, echo of night terrors, trying to communicate, trying to destroy me, I couldn't know.

"All right, everybody on the perimeter, fall back, slow. Don't make any quick gestures . . . anybody got a headache or anything?"

"Sergeant, this is Hollister." Lucky.

"They're trying to say something . . . I can almost . . . no, just . . ."

"Well?"

"All I can get is that they think we're, think we're . . . well, *funny*. They aren't afraid."

"You mean the one in front of you isn't—"

"No, the feeling comes from all of them, they're all thinking the same thing. Don't ask me how I know, I just do."

"Maybe they thought it was funny, what they did to Ho."

"Maybe. I don't feel like they're dangerous. Just curious about us."

"Sergeant, this is Bohrs."

"Yeah."

"The Taurans've been here at least a year—maybe they've learned how to communicate with these . . . overgrown teddybears. They might be spying on us, might be sending back—"

"I don't think they'd show themselves, if that were the case," Lucky said. "They can obviously hide from us pretty well when they want to."

"Anyhow," Cortez said, "if they're spies, the damage has been done. Don't think it'd be smart to take any action against them. I know you'd all like to see 'em dead for what they did to Ho, so would I, but we'd better be careful."

I didn't want to see them dead, but I'd just as soon not see them in any condition. I was walking backwards slowly, toward the middle of camp. The creature didn't seem disposed to follow. Maybe he just knew we were surrounded. He was pulling up grass with his arm and munching.

"Okay, all of you platoon leaders, wake everybody up, get a roll count. Let me know if anybody's been hurt. Tell your people we're moving out in one minute."

I don't know what Cortez expected, but of course the creatures just followed right along. They didn't keep us surrounded; just had twenty or thirty following us all the time. Not the same ones, either. Individuals would saunter away, new ones would join the parade. It was pretty obvious that *they* weren't going to tire out.

We were each allowed one stimtab. Without it, no one could have marched an hour. A second pill would have been welcome after the edge started to wear off, but the mathematics of the situation forbade it: we were still thirty clicks from the enemy base; fifteen hours' marching at the least. And though one could stay awake and energetic for a hundred hours on the 'tabs, aberrations of judgment and perception snowballed after the second 'tab, until *in extremis* the most bizarre hallucinations would be taken at face value, and a person would fidget for hours, deciding whether to have breakfast.

Under artificial stimulation, the company traveled with great energy for the first six hours, was slowing by the seventh, and ground to an exhausted halt after nine hours and nineteen kilometers. The teddybears had never lost sight of us and, according to Lucky, had never stopped "broadcasting".

Cortez's decision was that we would stop for seven hours, each platoon taking one hour of perimeter guard. I was never so glad to have been in the seventh platoon, as we stood guard the last shift and thus were the only ones to get six hours of uninterrupted sleep.

In the few moments I lay awake after finally lying down, the thought came to me that the next time I closed my eyes could well be the last. And partly because of the drug hangover, mostly because of the past day's horrors, I found that I really just didn't give a shit.

14

Our first contact with the Taurans came during my shift.

The teddybears were still there when I woke up and replaced Doc Jones on guard. They'd gone back to their original formation, one in front of each guard position. The one who was waiting for me seemed a little larger than normal, but otherwise looked just like all the others. All the grass had been cropped where he was sitting, so he occasionally made forays to the left or right. But he always returned to sit right in front of me, you would say staring if he had had anything to stare with.

We had been facing each other off for about fifteen minutes when Cortez's voice rumbled:

"Awright everybody wake up and get hid!"

I followed instinct and flopped to the ground and rolled into a tall stand of grass.

"Enemy vessel overhead." His voice was almost laconic.

Strictly speaking, it wasn't really overhead, but rather passing somewhat east of us. It was moving slowly, maybe a hundred clicks per hour, and looked like a broomstick surrounded by a dirty soap bubble. The creature riding it was a little more human-looking than the teddybears, but still no prize. I cranked my image amplifier up to forty log two for a closer look.

He had two arms and two legs, but his waist was so small you could encompass it with both hands. Under the tiny waist was a large horseshoe-shaped pelvic structure nearly a meter wide, from which dangled two long skinny legs with no apparent knee joint. Above that waist his body swelled out again, to a chest no smaller than the huge pelvis. His arms looked surprisingly human, except that they were too long and undermuscled. There were too many fingers on his hands. Shoulderless, neckless; his head was a nightmarish growth that swelled like a goiter from his massive chest. Two eyes that looked like clusters of fish eggs, a bundle of tassels instead of a nose, and a rigidily open hole that might have been a mouth sitting low down where his Adam's apple should have been. Evidently the soap bubble contained an amenable environment, as he was wearing absolutely nothing except a ridged hide that looked like skin submerged too long in hot water, then dyed a pale orange. "He" had no external genitalia, nor anything that might hint of mammary glands.

Obviously, he either didn't see us, or thought we were part of the herd of teddybears. He never looked back at us, but just continued in the same direction we were headed, .05 rad east of north.

"Might as well go back to sleep now, if you can sleep after looking at *that* thing. We move out at 0435." Forty minutes.

Because of the planet's opaque cloud cover, there had been no way to tell, from space, what the enemy base looked like or how big it was. We only knew its position, the same way we knew the position the scoutships were supposed to land on. So it could easily have been underwater too, or underground.

But some of the drones were reconnaissance ships as well as decoys; and in their mock attacks on the base, one managed to get close enough to take a picture. Captain Stott beamed down a diagram of the place to Cortez (the only one with a 'visor in his suit) when we were five clicks from the base's "radio" position. We stopped and he called all of the platoon leaders in with the seventh platoon to confer. Two teddybears loped in, too. We tried to ignore them.

"OK, the Captain sent down some pictures of our objective. I'm going to draw a map; you platoon leaders copy." They took pads and styli out of their leg pockets, while Cortez unrolled a large plastic map. He gave it a shake to randomize any residual charge, and turned on his stylus.

"Now, we're coming from this direction." He put an

arrow at the bottom of the sheet. "First thing we'll hit is this row of huts, probably billets, or bunkers, but who the hell knows . . . our initial objective is to destroy these buildings—the whole base is on a flat plain; there's no way we could really sneak by them."

"Potter here. Why can't we jump over them?"

"Yeah, we could do that, and wind up completely surrounded, cut to ribbons. We take the buildings.

"After we do that . . . all I can say is that we'll have to think on our feet. From the aerial reconnaissance, we can figure out the function of only a couple of buildings—and that stinks. We might wind up wasting a lot of time demolishing the equivalent of an enlisted men's bar, ignoring a huge logistic computer because it looks like . . . a garbage dump or something."

"Mandella here," I said. "Isn't there a spaceport of some kind—seems to me we ought to—"

"I'll *get* to that, goddamnit. There's a ring of these huts all around the camp, so we've got to break through somewhere. This place'll be closest, less chance of giving away our position before we attack.

"There's nothing in the whole place that actually looks like a weapon. That doesn't mean anything, though, you could hide a bevawatt laser in each of those huts.

"Now, about five hundred meters from the huts, in the middle of the base, we'll come to this big flower-shaped structure." Cortez drew a large symmetrical shape that looked like the outline of a flower with seven petals. "What the hell this is, your guess is as good as mine. There's only one of them, though, so we don't damage it any more than we have to. Which means . . . we blast it to splinters if I think it's dangerous.

"Now, as far as your spaceport, Mandella, is concerned—there just isn't one. Nothing.

"That cruiser the *Hope* caulked had probably been left in orbit, like ours has to be. If they have any equivalent of a scoutship, or drone missiles, they're either not kept here or they're well hidden."

"Bohrs here. Then what did they attack with, while we were coming down from orbit?"

"I wish we knew, Private.

"Obviously, we don't have any way of estimating their numbers, not directly. Recon pictures failed to show a single Tauran on the grounds of the base. Meaning nothing, because it *is* an alien environment. Indirectly, though . . . we can count the number of broomsticks, those flying things.

"There are fifty-one huts, and each has at most one broomstick. Four don't have one parked outside, but we located three at various other parts of the base. Maybe this indicates that there are fifty-one Taurans, one of whom was outside the base when the picture was taken."

"Keating here. Or fifty-one officers."

"That's right—maybe fifty thousand infantrymen stacked in one of these buildings. No way to tell. Maybe ten Taurans, each with five broomsticks, to use according to his mood.

"We've got one thing in our favor, and that's communications. They evidently use a frequency modulation of megahertz electromagnetic radiation."

"Radio!"

"That's right, whoever you are. Primitive radio. Identify yourself when you speak. So, it's quite possible that they can't detect our phased-neutrino communications. Also, just prior to the attack, the *Hope* is going to deliver a nice dirty fission bomb; detonate it in the upper atmosphere right over the base. That'll restrict them to line-of-sight communications for some time; even those will be full of static."

"Why don't . . . Tate here . . . why don't they just drop the bomb right in their laps. Save us a lot of—"

"That doesn't even deserve an answer, Private. But the answer is, they might. And you better hope they don't. If they caulk the base, it'll be for the safety of the *Hope*. *After* we've attacked, and probably before we're far enough away for it to make much difference.

"We keep that from happening by doing a good job. We have to reduce the base to where it can no longer function; at the same time, leave as much intact as possible. And take one prisoner."

"Potter here. You mean, at least one prisoner."

"I mean what I say. One only. Potter . . . you're relieved of your platoon. Send Chavez up."

"All right, Sergeant." The relief in her voice was unmistakable.

Cortez continued with his map and instructions. There was one other building whose function was pretty obvious; it had a large steerable dish antenna on top. We were to destroy it as soon as the grenadiers got in range.

The attack plan was very loose. Our signal to begin would be the flash of the fission bomb. At the same time, several drones would converge on the base, so we could see what their antispacecraft defenses were. We would try to reduce the effectiveness of those defenses without destroying them completely.

Immediately after the bomb and the drones, the grenadiers would vaporize a line of seven huts. Everybody would break through the hole into the base . . . and what would happen after that was anybody's guess.

Ideally, we'd sweep from that end of the base to the other, destroying certain targets, caulking all but one Tauran. But that was unlikely to happen, as it depended on the Taurans' offering very little resistance.

On the other hand, if the Taurans showed obvious superiority from the beginning, Cortez would give the order to scatter: everybody had a different compass bearing for retreat—we'd blossom out in all directions, the survivors to rendezvous in a valley some 40 clicks east of the base. Then we'd see about a return engagement, after the *Hope* softened the base up a bit.

"One last thing," Cortez rasped. "Maybe some of you feel the way Potter evidently does, maybe some of your men feel that way . . . that we ought to go easy, not make this so much of a bloodbath. Mercy is a luxury, a weakness we can't afford to indulge in at this stage of the war. *All* we know about the enemy is that they have killed seven hundred and ninety-eight humans. They haven't shown any restraint in attacking our cruisers, and it'd be foolish to expect any this time, this first ground action.

"*They* are responsible for the lives of all of your comrades who died in training, and for Ho, and for all the others who are surely going to die today. I can't under*stand* anybody who wants to spare them. But that doesn't make any difference.

You have your orders, and what the hell, you might as well know, all of you have a post-hypnotic suggestion that I will trigger by a phrase, just before the battle. It will make your job easier."

"Sergeant . . ."

"Shut up. We're short on time; get back to your platoons and brief them. We move out in five minutes."

The platoon leaders returned to their men, leaving Cortez and the ten of us, plus three teddybears, milling around, getting in the way.

15

We took the last five clicks very carefully, sticking to the highest grass, running across occasional clearings. When we were five hundred meters from where the base was supposed to be, Cortez took the third platoon forward to scout, while the rest of us laid low.

Cortez's voice came over the general freak: "Looks pretty much like we expected. Advance in a file, crawling. When you get to the third platoon, follow your squad leader to the left or right."

We did that and wound up with a string of 71 people in a line roughly perpendicular to the direction of attack. We were pretty well hidden, except for the dozen or so teddy-bears that mooched along the line munching grass.

There was no sign of life inside the base. All of the buildings were windowless, and a uniform shiny white. The huts that were our first objective were large featureless half-buried eggs, some sixty meters apart. Cortez assigned one to each grenadier.

We were broken into three fire teams: team A consisted of platoons two, four, and six; team B was one, three, and five; the command platoon was team C.

"Less than a minute now—filters down!—when I say 'fire', grenadiers take out your targets. God help you if you miss."

There was a sound like a giant belch and a stream of five or six iridescent bubbles floated up from the flower-shaped building. They rose with increasing speed to where they were almost out of sight, then shot off to the south, over our heads. The ground was suddenly bright and for the first time in a long time, I saw my shadow, a long one pointed north. The bomb had gone off prematurely. I just had time to think that it didn't make too much difference, it'd still make alphabet soup out of their communications—

"Drones!" A ship came screaming in just above tree level, and a bubble was in the air to meet it. When they contacted the bubble popped and the drone exploded into a million tiny fragments. Another one came from the opposite side and suffered the same fate.

"FIRE!" Seven bright glares of 500-microton grenades and a sustained concussion that I'm sure would have killed an unprotected man.

"Filters up." Grey haze of smoke and dust. Clods of dirt falling with a sound like heavy raindrops.

"Listen up:

" 'Scots, wha hae wi' Wallace bled;
Scots, wham Bruce has aften led,
Welcome to your gory bed,
Or to victory!' "

I hardly heard him, for trying to keep track of what was going on in my skull. I knew it was just post-hypnotic suggestion, even remembered the session in Missouri when they'd implanted it, but that didn't make it any less compelling. My mind reeled under the strong pseudo-memories; shaggy hulks that were Taurans (not at all what we now knew they looked like) boarding a colonist's vessel, eating babies while mothers watched in screaming terror (the colonists never took babies; they wouldn't stand the acceleration), then raping the women to death with huge veined purple members (ridiculous that they would feel desire for humans), holding the men down while they plucked flesh from their living bodies and gobbled it (or would want to eat them) . . . a hundred grisly details as sharply remembered as the events of a minute ago, ridiculously overdone and logically absurd; but while my conscious mind was rejecting the silliness, somewhere much deeper, down in that labyrinth where we keep our real motives and morals, something was thirsting for alien blood, secure in the conviction that the noblest thing a man could do would be to die killing one of those horrible monsters . . .

I knew it was all purest soyashit, and I hated the men who had taken such obscene liberties with my mind, but still I could hear my teeth grinding, feel cheeks frozen in a spastic grin, bloodlust . . . a teddybear walked in front of me, looking dazed. I started to raise my laserfinger, but somebody beat me to it and the creature's head exploded in a cloud of grey splinters and blood.

Lucky groaned, half-whining, "Dirty . . . filthy bastards." Lasers flared and criss-crossed and all of the teddybears fell dead.

"*Watch* it, goddamnit!" Cortez screamed. "*Aim* those fuckin' things they aren't toys!

"Team A, move out—into the craters to cover B."

Somebody was laughing and sobbing. "What the fuck is wrong with *you*, Petrov?" Cortez cussing.

I twisted around and saw Petrov, behind and to my left, lying in a shallow hole, digging frantically with both hands, crying and gurgling.

"Fuck," Cortez said. "Team B! past the craters ten meters, get down in a line. Team C—into the craters with A."

I scrambled up and covered the hundred meters in twelve amplified strides. The craters were practically large enough to hide a scoutship, some ten meters in diameter. I jumped to the opposite side of the hole and landed next to a fellow named Chin. He didn't even look around when I landed, just kept scanning the base for signs of life.

"Team A—past team B ten meters, down in line." Just as he finished, the building in front of us burped and a salvo of bubbles fanned out toward our lines. Most people saw it coming and got down, but Chin was just getting up to make his rush and stepped right into one.

It grazed the top of his helmet, and continued on. He took one step backwards and toppled over the edge of the crater, trailing an arc of blood and brains. Lifeless, spreadeagled, he slid halfway to the bottom, shoveling dirt into the perfectly symmetrical hole where the bubble had chewed through plastic, hair, skin, bone and brain indiscriminately.

"Everybody hold it. Platoon leaders, casualty report . . . check . . . check, check . . . check, check, check . . . check. We have three deaders. Wouldn't be *any* if you'd have kept low.

So everybody grab dirt when you hear that thing go off. Team A, complete the rush."

They completed the maneuver without incident. "OK. Team C, rush to where B—hold it! Down!"

Everybody was already hugging the ground. The bubbles slid by in a smooth arc about two meters off the ground. They went serenely over our heads, and, except for one that made toothpicks out of a tree, disappeared in the distance.

"B, rush past A ten meters. C, take over B's place. You B grenadiers see if you can reach the Flower."

Two grenades tore up the ground thirty or forty meters from the structure. In a good imitation of panic, it started belching out a continuous stream of bubbles—still, none coming lower than two meters off the ground. We kept hunched down and continued to advance.

Then suddenly the bubbles stopped. "Everybody down and freeze," Cortez said. "Now let me have Rogers, Tate, Mandella, Bohrs. On my private freak."

I chinned him and reported. When all four of us were tuned in he said: "I'm going to defuse you. Listen up . . . 'All-right-knock-it-off.' " The bloodlust drained away and I could think of a Tauran as just a weird-looking creature again. I had an almost uncontrollable urge to rub my face vigorously.

"All right, you four are the prisoner detail. Don't fight, don't kill unless you absolutely have to.

"You'll be going into the Flower alone; going in first. Find a prisoner and hold him, keep him away from the others, until the battle's over. Bohrs, you're in charge. Everything clear?"

Yeah, it was clear. Just a run-of-the-mill, everyday suicide mission. "Sergeant, this is Mandella. Don't we have any support? Just the four of us?"

"Goddamnit Mandella just get in there and get me a prisoner! You'll get all the fucken help you need, if you need it." He switched to the general freak.

"Listen up. I've got four volunteers from C team, who're going to assault the Flower and try to take one of these mean fuckers prisoner. B team, you stay right outside the Flower. If I give you the word, follow the volunteers and *sterilize* that place. Roger?" Muted growl of assent.

"Let's go," said Bohrs. "Best done quickly." We jogged toward the Flower, B team right behind us. The rest of the company followed Cortez to the building with the antenna.

No resistance at all. The enemy camp was still, silent except for the pair of loud reports when the grenadiers took out the communications building.

We stopped at the nearest "petal" of the Flower. At the end was an outline of what had to be a door of some sort, a rectangle scribed in the otherwise seamless material. There was a small red circle in the exact center.

"Push the button, Tate."

"Come on, Bohrs. It's probably boobytrapped."

"So you're the booby this time. I'll take the next one."

Tate pressed the circle—all of us braced for disaster—and the door slid noiselessly into the ground. It was barely high and wide enough to admit a man in a fighting suit. It didn't seem to be an airlock; just a door opening on a long narrow corridor.

"Akwasi, you in charge of B team?"

"That's right."

"If this door closes, wait two minutes and burn it down. Otherwise, just hang around until you hear from me."

Akwasi roger'd him. "All right, volunteers. Let's go."

There was a slight resistance as I walked through the opening—evidently some sort of a field that served them instead of an airlock. Probably the same principle as the "soap bubble" that had been around the only Tauran we'd seen.

The corridor was lined with doors identical to the one we'd just opened. Bohrs hesitated, then pushed the red spot on the first one. It slid open to reveal a softly lit cubicle empty except for a strung wire hammock and what looked like a piece of abstract sculpture in one corner. He described it to Cortez, who said it leave it alone and go on to the next.

The next cubicle was exactly the same, and so were all the rest, along both sides of the narrow corridor. I would have gu ssed they were living quarters, but if they were, where was everybody?

Forced to walk single file, we approached the end of the corridor with caution. Corridors from all of the other petals converged there in a large circular hall. In the center was a vertical metal tube, two meters thick. I supposed it had something to do with the bubble generator.

We followed Bohrs into the hall and spread out along the wall. Still not a sound, no sign of life.

"Rogers, toss a grenade down that far corridor." He gestured across the hall. "Everybody down."

She was next to me, so I could watch the trajectory of the grenade out of the launcher. It sailed up the corridor and detonated where the wall and ceiling came together, about two meters from the exit. The noise was awesome, confined indoors and focused by the corridor. There was a satisfying amount of smoke and debris; the corridor ceiling started to collapse but only fell about a meter and held at a crazy angle.

"What the hell was that?" Akwasi.

"Nothing yet," Bohrs answered. "Just trying to get somebody's attention."

"Bohrs, this is Rogers. Shoot another one down?"

"No, not yet. Let's wait and—God!—what—"

Bohrs was floating about a half-meter off the ground and rising. I looked down and so was I; so was everybody else. There was no sensation of weightlessness. It was as if we were on a perfectly transparent platform. I scrambled to my feet.

"Everybody hold your fire. This is probably just some sort of freight elevator."

"Hey, Bohrs, this is Akwasi. What the hell is going on in there?"

"We can handle it, Akwasi. That door still open?"

"Sure it is, but—"

"Just keep your eye on it. If we need any help inside, I'll let you know"

"Roger." The bitterness was strong in his voice, even over the communicator. Hard to believe—Akwasi was normally such a gentle, sensible person. One Scotch poem and he was itching for bloody murder.

It took us almost two minutes to reach the second, top level; the center of the Flower. We stepped up onto a black platform ringing the center hall—or elevator—and looked around cautiously.

It was a single large circular room, and if I'd had to guess I would've said it had something to do with the production and/or guidance of the defensive bubbles. But nothing in its alien form gave any indication of the room's function.

The basic feature of the room was a kind of wire frame, from which hung metal plates about the size of a hand. The plates were distributed in a seemingly random way on the frames, sometimes overlapping one another, and were colored various shades of blue. After a few seconds I realized their colors were constantly, slowly changing, going from a pale sky-blue to almost black and back again.

The frames were arranged in concentric circles around the center pit, and grew in height as you moved out from the center, from about 50 centimeters to 2 meters. There were corridors from the center to the outside wall, spaced at irregular intervals. The outside wall appeared to be transparent.

Behind us, over the corridor Rogers had grenaded, the floor was slightly depressed and all of the shingles were a dull blue-black. Some had fallen to the floor and shattered.

"Looks like nobody home here, either," Bohrs said. "Rogers, you stay here. Everybody else follow me."

"Everybody else" seemed somewhat generous, describing two people. Tate and I followed him up the nearest corridor.

My external monitor was turned 'way up, but the aliens didn't make a sound until we were right on top of them. Bohrs stepped past the last row of frames and pointed his laserfinger to the right. "Look! There's—"

I moved up to him, heard a faint click to the left and saw the other Tauran, carrying a thing like a white suitcase, to which was attached a flexible metal tube. He was pointing the tube at us.

I shouted something and jumped back, but the warning was too late for Bohrs. The tube didn't make any noise in firing, but whatever it shot made loud explosions against Bohrs's suit. Stumbling back, I fanned my laser in the general direction of the alien—shattering hundreds of the little plates in the process—and hit him just as he was aiming my way. From the mouth-hole up he dissolved into flying char and crimson steam. I didn't have time to reflect that all God's children got haemoglobin.

Tate headed right, between the frames, moving down to the next corridor to flank the other Tauran. I called for Rogers to move up, but she was already halfway there.

I moved up to the last frame and peered around it. The remaining Tauran didn't seem to be armed, or even interested in what was going on. He was leaning against a railing, looking out over the base.

Bohrs must have died instantly. One shot had hit him in the center of the chest, blowing away the whole chest-plate of his fighting suit and his right arm, slimy litter of blood and bone and guts still moving, settling. The other shot had taken his left hand off at the wrist, scrambling the camouflage circuits of his suit so it flickered black-white-jungle-desert-green-grey. The devastation was so complete that it robbed his death of any sense of tragedy, of humanity . . . it wasn't Bohrs lying there, just a broken anatomy demonstrator in a harlequin suit. His blood welled to the corridor and mixed with Tauran blood.

"Bohrs! What the hell is going on up there?"

"Akwasi, this is Mandella." I marveled at the steadiness of my voice. "We had some trouble but I think everything is under control now. Stand by."

"I can't raise Bohrs."

"He's unconscious. Just stand by."

Rogers came up behind me. "My God," she whispered.

I chinned Cortez's private frequency, told him what had happened. "All right," he said, "send B team back to me; you three guard the prisoner. We're gonna get some of these bastards now."

I relayed the message to Akwasi and the three of us closed in on the Tauran. He made no sign that he knew we were even there. I wondered whether he might be in something like a state of shock.

We tried to tie him up, but the rope only encircled his protective bubble. The best we could do was to lash the bubble to the railing.

Tate took one look at what was left of Bohrs and was violently ill. In an oblique way I envied him. What was I becoming, that I could take a friend's bloody death in stride?

Once the Tauran—or at least his bubble—was secured, we

watched as Akwasi's team joined the others. They were about a hundred meters away, at the building Cortez had named the Sausage; a featureless white half-cylinder about thirty meters long by six wide.

The Tauran next to us moved for the first time. He folded pipestem arms over his bloated chest and rippled his fingers. Then he went back to the original position, both hands on the railing.

Suddenly the woods ringing the enemy camp boiled with activity, and hundreds—thousands of the teddybear creatures spilled out and stampeded toward the Sausage.

Cortez shouted orders and both teams turned, began firing into the advancing horde. It was a horrifying sight. At first they were too far away for effective laser fire, so the grenadiers laid down salvos along the teddybears' advancing edge. Ignoring their fellows killed or maimed in the blasts, the mass of creatures surged around and through the smoking craters and finally into range of sixty-seven high-powered lasers. The men started out choosing individual targets, but soon were just fanning back and forth, lasers evidently set on their highest power and lowest dispersion. A great rift of bodies and parts of bodies grew in a ring around the men, the Sausage at the center. The teddybears crawled up and over the mounds of their dead, seeming never to gain as much as a meter before being burned down. Still they gained, until the annulus of dead had come within some twenty meters of the humans.

Then both ends of the Sausage opened, dilating suddenly to make the building a tube open at both ends, and a mob of Taurans crowded out to attack the preoccupied soldiers.

I switched freaks and shouted out a warning—so did Tate and Rogers—but it was too late; at least half of the Taurans were armed with the suitcase-things and they came out firing.

Twenty, perhaps thirty of our men died in the first couple of seconds. Then they took what cover there was and began to return fire.

I was numb; had no feeling that those were my friends dying, that it could just as easily be me . . . it was like watching a news-tape of some natural disaster; the fact of death undeniable, but no sense of personal involvement. I looked at the Tauran and tried to feel hate for him, but there was nothing. He was just another part of the malevolent environment, along with Cortez and Stott—all the way back to Charon and Missouri and the Elite Conscription Act. It occurred to me that I was in shock and could probably snap out of it with a stimtab. That would technically be an overdose, of course. So I rationalized myself out of having to face reality.

Now the crowd of teddybears advanced unchecked, milling past the humans without seeming to pay much attention to them, dying with apparent unconcern whenever they got in the way of a Tauran or human weapon. They reached the center just as our grenadiers blew the Sausage apart with four nearly simultaneous hits. This destroyed forty or fifty of them, but that many and more tumbled in, in the next few seconds. Soon the battlefield was solid with teddybears and their corpses, which both humans and Taurans used as cover.

A couple of Taurans got to their broomsticks and mounted a short-lived but effective aerial attack. They had the advantage of surprise, but the vehicles weren't fast or maneuverable enough. I watched them caulk three humans before being burned down, and noticed that one of them didn't appear to have been hit at all; the laser just grazed his protective bubble, then he lost control of the broomstick and whirled crazily to the ground. And it was the same all over the battleground, many Taurans lying dead without a mark. None of the humans' deaths had been so sanitary.

The battle had been going for less than a minute when it became obvious that, having lost the initiative, the Taurans didn't have a chance. Their weapons required fairly accurate fire, and we gave them poor targets, hidden in the rifts of teddybear deaders. The live teddybears, who had given the Taurans the initial advantage, now were a hindrance—and just as that thought occurred to me, the creatures stopped their purposeless wandering and suddenly bolted away from the battleground. Too late to help the Taurans, though. In another minute well over a hundred Tauran corpses had been added to the general carnage, and as far as I could tell, the only live one left was the one standing next to me.

A positively revolting scene followed. While Cortez shouted encouragement, our people scampered from Tauran to Tauran, under the spell of the gory post-hypnotic suggestion, carving their bodies to smoking ribbons. Then they advanced at a run toward the other Sausage, on the opposite side of the Flower.

"My" Tauran watched all of this without any outward sign of agitation, and continued to stare at the same spot after the humans had left. It was a hellish sight, butchery on a surreal scale; nearly a half-kilometer of quivering meat, the ground between bodies a uniform slick red, shallow grenade-craters slowly filling with blood.

After the humans had disappeared from view, the Tauran slowly raised both hands to the top of his head, lacing his fingers together in a curiously human gesture. Then suddenly the shimmering bubble disappeared and the ropes dropped to the floor. The Tauran staggered a little and then lay down on the floor; then jack-knifed in obvious pain, his hands still locked over his head. Powerless, we watched him die, pink-flecked white foam oozing out of his mouth-hole.

I called Cortez and told him that the prisoner had committed suicide.

After some fluent cussing: "You three check out the rest of the Flower, see whether you can find another one of them. And Chrissake don't let it kill itself." Excellent advice.

We inspected the top floor without finding any cowering Taurans, then lowered ourselves with rope to the ground level to check out the six corridors we hadn't yet been through. It took most of an hour, wandering down one side of the corridor and back up the other, opening doors to reveal uninhabited cells all identical to that first one.

We didn't find any Taurans and, outside, neither did Cortez. We listened on the general freak while they checked out the other Sausage—empty—and buildings christened Box, North Thing, the Warrens, South Thing and so on, all the way across the enemy base to the bunker-things on the other side. Lots of curious structures but not a living thing, Tauran or teddybear.

So we had preserved lots of enemy structures and equipment, but failed in our main objective. No prisoner. Lots of raw material for comparative anatomy, though.

Cortez led the company back to double-check some of the places, and then sort through the pile of dead to see whether by some miracle they might have missed one. No luck. He called down the Star Fleet research team and said the "knock-it-off" phrase that countermanded the post-hypnotic suggestion.

It was pretty rough on the men and women who had done the actual killing. Suddenly the memory of blood murder multiplied hundreds of times, of glorying in needless butchery came rushing in—some few could accept it philosophically, or convince themselves that the memory belonged to someone else, but most required heavy sedation. I tried to raise Marygay and got only strained whimpering.

We waited in orbit while the research team salvaged what they could—the little black worms were quick-working, efficient scavengers—and, lacking a live Tauran, tried to find a teddybear. No luck; it was as if they had disappeared from the face of the planet. So all we knew about them, besides some gross anatomy, was the obvious fact that they had either been in league with or controlled by the Taurans. And that they had some kind of formidable mental power, and an apparent lack of concern over dying. We didn't even really know whether they were native to the planet although, as Rogers had pointed out, circumstantial evidence indicated that they were.

I suppose we won the battle. We certainly gained more information about the Taurans than they did about us, and knowledge of the enemy was going to be the most important weapon of the war. But with superior armament and the advantage of having the initiative, we'd managed to lose over half of our people. And most of the survivors would never fight again, unless the deep wounds to their psyches could be healed.

I had counted myself lucky to have witnessed the thing in an objective way, not to have been a murdering Hun . . . but a week later Marygay found me down in a storage locker, thumping my head against the wall and mumbling incoherently. When we left orbit I was in the hastily-equipped "restraint" ward, and it was another week before Dr. Martinez had brought me around to where I could return to limited duty.

In the ward, I'd had too much time to think. Our action on Aleph hadn't been inhuman; a few generations before, men would have done the same thing to other human beings, without benefit of hypnotic preconditioning. A scant twenty years of enforced peace, and here we were, forced back into the old mold again.

I had a feeling it was going to be a long war.

From HUMAN HISTORY, A HUNDRED SCANS (Baldwin, Sed 3, 2019 SA)

. . . the longest and, hopefully, the last war ever fought. A succession of several hundred skirmishes generally involving only the sterile companions of collapsars, the war required almost total mobilization of human resources from 40 (old reckoning, 1997) to 1240 SA, when the Laemonia (called "Taurans" during the war) finally were able to communicate with humanity, and the war ended abruptly.

The initial cause of the war was evidently fear on the part of the human military establishment that it was about to be phased out of existence. A "United Nations" (q.v.), along with several charismatic pacifist leaders, had kept humanity out of war for nearly a generation . . . there is evidence that, before the first face-to-face battle (Aleph-1, 52), the military, nominally in charge of interstellar exploration, had capitalized on a number of unfortunate colonizing accidents, leading human authorities to believe they had been caused by Laemonian belligerence.

. . . the following descriptions are excerpted from *The Forever War*, the autobiography of William Mandella, one of four soldiers who, through time dilation, experienced the full 1200 years of war . . .

AFTERWORD

THE YEAR OF THE BIG SPRING CLEAN

This year has been fine, but I am looking forward to next.

Maybe that is the way sf buffs live, and perhaps it is not the most comfortable way. It would be easier on all concerned to take time as it comes and keep in step with it. Nevertheless, I'm eager for next year.

Next year is when all the histories of science fiction appear!

Of course, publishing schedules fluctuate and plans could change, but at present it looks as if Scribner's will be publishing Alexei Panshin's history, while Prentice-Hall have James Gunn's *Alternate Futures* lined up for the Spring, at about the same time as Doubleday's publish my *Billion Year Spree*. I understand that Darko Suvin, Sprague de Camp, Lester del Rey, and Professor Tom Clareson are also working on histories, while Penguin Books have a contract for one with Peter Nicholls of the SF Foundation. No doubt others are hatching.

Is all this necessary, do I hear you asking?

Let me tell you why I think it is highly necessary.

To start with, although inevitabilities and necessities are by no means the same thing, there is something inevitable in this sudden concatenation of histories. Say what you like, it is sf-history time. An old epoch is closing, a new one opening.

One of the hallmarks of the new epoch is that science fiction is now much more broad-based. It is no longer all centred round big strapping heroes who can punch or blast their way through any planet in the universe you care to name. That was a pulp formula. It still goes strong, particularly in some outer branches of sf like sword-and-sorcery. But, happily, it no longer monopolises the field. Infallible heroes are useless as protagonists in novels of social criticism. For them, one needs fallible people who are only marginally better than the society in which they exist; that was the H. G. Wells tradition. It is, I believe, coming back into favour.

Two other factors account for the greater diversity of sf nowadays. Firstly, there is the economic situation. Popular sf is no longer a monopoly of a few magazines. The magazines that still exist have little financial power behind them—which implies, among other things, that they are likely to be conservative in nature and reluctant to innovate. The great experimental sf magazine of the sixties, *New Worlds*, was forced out of monthly publication, although it survives as a paperback. But paperbacks are issued by firms more financially secure than the magazines. They can afford to be slightly more adventurous (though signs of adventure are often hard to detect) and, of course, they reach a much wider market.

The other area of diversification stems from the fact that science fiction is now being taught as a subject in hundreds of colleges and universities. Readers in classrooms are a very different audience from readers on holiday! Altered audiences invariably effect changes on authors. So here too we see sf diversifying.

Bellows of complaint have thundered through this Afterword from time to time, but never a one against diversity. Our belief has always been the same: that those who try to freeze sf into any posture are—however ostensibly benevolent their intentions—the enemies of sf. Sf deals with change and must incorporate change. But it is undeniable that increasing diversity brings confusion with it, and confusion has little to recommend it.

The urge to write a history of science fiction grows from a hope that one can straighten out some of the confusion.

To give one example of confusion, perhaps the most obvious one. Who started science fiction? Was it Edgar Allan Poe, constantly referred to as The Father of Science Fiction? Was is Jules Verne, frequently referred to as The Father of Science Fiction? Was it H. G. Wells, often referred to as The Father of Science Fiction? Was it Hugo Gernsback, sometimes referred to as The Father of Science Fiction? Or was it perhaps some hitherto inadequately appreciated candidate, such as Herman Melville or Edgar Rice Burroughs?

Or, on the other hand, did science fiction begin long long

ago? Are the first examples in the Epic of Gilgamesh? Or in Homer? Or Genesis? How about Lucian of Samosata? What of Dante? Shakespeare? Nostradamus?

To give a clear answer to these questions is, in part, to define the functions of sf, if it can be reckoned to have any. We appreciate better where we understand functions. Obviously, a reader who thinks that sf began with Nostradamus's mystical predictions is going in with a widely differing set of assumptions from a reader who thinks that Hugo Gernsback started it all in order to sell radio sets.

My answer to the vexatious question set out above is contained in *Billion Year Spree.* No doubt James Gunn will have a different answer from mine.

A fine way to clear up the confusion, if even the historians do not agree!

Well, we still live in a democratic society, although the concept is always under threat. One of our freedoms is the freedom to disagree, and I see no harm if all the historians disagree (in fact, I shall be sorry if they agree). The value of more than one history is that the ground is then opened for debate. We hope that the best-reasoned case, the case that shows the greatest appreciation of past society, the subtlest ear for prose, the soundest understanding of technological implications, will eventually win the day, perhaps with modifications.

In any event, each historian will approach the subject from different aspects. Panshin and I, there is little doubt, will rarely see eye-to-eye; yet it is pleasing to hear that he believes, as I do, that one of the great disasters to science fiction occurred in 1926! So we would probably agree that that was one of the turning points for sf.

Of course, there are scraps of sf history about already. The most enjoyable is probably Sam Lundwall's light-hearted canter, *Science Fiction: What It's All About.* The work of Sam Moskowitz on individual writers and magazines is well known. And there is that hightly commendable book of I. F. Clarke's, *Voices Prophesying War*, which deals with one whole aspect of sf in an illuminating way. The criticisms of Damon Knight and James Blish—though they suffer from randomness—are accepted as standard. There are books which provide individual slants on the field, like Don Wollheim's *The Universe Makers*. And there is a pioneering work by J. O. Bailey, *Pilgrims Through Space and Time*, which seeks to classify science fiction into historical themes. But a unified history for a wide readership is another matter.

For one of the satisfying things about sf is that it does possess something like a unified history. My interest has mainly been in the past of the art. I discovered how avidly science fiction writers have always sought out other earlier science fiction writers. Francis Godwin, who wrote the first lunar voyage in the English language, knew Lucian's *True History*. Godwin's character, Gonzales, appears in Cyrano de Bergerac's *Voyage dans la Lune* by way of tribute, as does Campanella, author of a utopia whose English title is *The City of the Sun*. Cyrano also mentions Lucian in his preface.

Campanella's book is one of the privileged few volumes whose titles we glimpse in the library of Roderick Usher, of Poe's *Fall of the House of Usher*. On the same shelf stands the work by the Scandinavian author, Ludvig Holberg, *The Subterranean Voyage of Nicholas Klimm*.

Poe had also read Francis Godwin's book, as did his great successor, Jules Verne. And Verne, of course, expressed his admiration for Poe throughout his life, for all that one was a poet of the Indoors and the other of the Outdoors. Tradition! Verne's love of liberty is echoed in the writings of Jack London.

To back-track a bit to *Nicholas Klimm*, which had its influence on Lewis Carroll. *Klimm* owes a good deal to Swift's *Gulliver's Travels*.

Swift, that learned man, had read his Lucian. His great and unassailable story of Gulliver remains the classic satire in the English language. Its influence—and in particular the influence of the fourth book, the voyage to the country of the Houyhnhnms—has been strong on later writers of that sort of sf which is used as a medium for social criticism, most notably on Wells, Aldous Huxley, and George Orwell. In particular, Wells's splendid *Island of Dr. Moreau* and Orwell's *Animal Farm* both owe a debt of gratitude to Swift's terrifying and enlightening vision.

So it continues. Each generation inherits the wealth of the past. If the forthcoming histories direct attention back to the great works of past times, that will be a service worth performing.

They will also serve to show some of today's inflated reputations in better perspective. Some of the achievements of yesteryear rise like mountain peaks—but peaks which have been obscured by cloud over the intervening decades. My favourite example here is Olaf Stapledon's writing, *Star Maker* in particular. First published in England in 1937, *Star Maker* is one long exhilarating sweep of innovation and outrageous philosophical cosmological speculation from beginning to end. It not only describes this universe of ours, but shows it to be merely one of a series, the others in the series being described as well. For those who believe that sf should be about basics and first causes rather than technological gadgets, this is the definitive novel. Even the gadgeteers will not feel the same about other men's star empires once they have visited Stapledon's.

Stapledon is the intellectual's sf writer. But even the popular writers have scarcely been considered in a proper perspective until now. Take the case of Edgar Rice Burroughs. His faults may be many, but his virtues are many more, and no true estimate of his effect on the field can be gained until he is dealt with as part of the larger picture.

Indeed, it is true to say that many of the major figures in the field are due for reconsideration. So low has been the stock of science fiction in the past that many good writers have never received proper attention. This is true even of H. G. Wells, the man who could work miracles.

It is true also of Mary Shelley, whose novel, *Frankenstein; or, the Modern Prometheus* was travestied even in her own day. Since then, its central idea has been pillaged and vulgarised in dozens of bad movies. Yet the original novel is a striking and thoughtful piece of work. The paradox is, that since it contains science-fictional elements, it was precluded (by some magical bit of scholarly prestidigitation) from consideration as literature; while the horror element greatly exaggerated by Universal, Hammer and other film studios, has precluded its proper consideration as science fiction.

Jules Verne's reputation is also in need of restoration. His work, which consists of sixty-four volumes, spans roughly the last four decades of last century. The novels by which he is best known—those splendid journeys to the bottom of the sea, to the Moon, to the centre of the earth, around the earth, or off on a comet—all belong to his early optimistic period, when his faith in science and humanity was strong. But his vision grows darker in his later years, and he spawns satanic cities like Blackland and Stahlstadt the way Poe spawns underground chambers. Verne studies are much advanced in France, the country of his birth. They should be greatly assisted in the United States and England by the publication in London of a translation of Jean Chesneaux's *The Political and Social Ideas of Jules Verne*. This book is the greatest critical work to appear this year. If I admit that it has gripped my imagination more than any work of fiction this year, readers must excuse my specialised interest in the topic!

Another function that histories of science fiction can perform is to remind writers of the richness of their heritage and the variety of themes which can be handled in an sf idiom.

By its nature, modern sf is closely geared to trends. There are a few authors who have gained reputations—often flimsy ones—by wearing their social consciences on their sleeves. The latest scare that arises through channels that "popularise" (as they say) science, and these authors are on it. If they are old enough, then they wrote of mutants induced by nuclear radiation in the early fifties, then PSI powers getting out of hand, then World War III, then automated worlds, then a planet ruled by television, then (of course) an over-populated Earth, and now they are turning out novels on racial wars and/or ecological problems.

Such opportunism ruined the big sf film of the year, *Silent Running*. A fleet of three ships is going out to install ecological satellites in orbit near Saturn (why *there* is never satisfactorily explained). They are almost there, with Saturn looming large on the port bow, when the order comes to destruct satellites (*why* is never satisfactorily explained). The crew of four on one of the ships consists of a Jesus Christ figure (he puts on a Jesus robe to go and commune with the trees and rabbits) and three yobs (why is never explained, since the Jesus-figure proves capable of managing the ship on his own).

The forests in the ecological satellite are failing because the Jesus-figure is not ecologist enough (could one be ecologist less?) to know that trees need light and heat. His bunnies appear not to breed, and in the end a robot of anthropomorphic and whimsey habit is left tending the sequoias with a child's tin watering-can.

One may accept the Bible dictum that a child shall lead them without having to have the brat think for them.The film features a perfectly splendid spaceship, but all plot and sense have been thrown out in favour of a trendy and sentimental message. I was not alone in wishing that they had called in Robert Heinlein and kicked Joan Baez (who supplies the songs) out of the airlock.

The merely trendy is always open to such infections. As in the film, so in the writings of those authors in sf who always hunt the latest fashion.

These boys seize their inspiration from the day's newspaper which is why their writing is generally as ephemeral as a newspaper. Their writerly impulse is in direct contrast to that of one of today's masters of the field, Philip K. Dick. Dick has a central preoccupation, which may be roughly stated as a mistrust of material appearances, from which all his diverse themes grow organically; they are thereby related to and draw vitality from some mysterious central mode of his being. In a word, they approach literature rather than journalism. As a result, even his lesser novels are of interest to a Dick fan. Far flashier and trendier novels come and go and are forgotten.

Sf histories can remind readers and writers pleasurably of such facts. You may have to stand on your head to gather a crowd; you have to stand on your own two feet to keep it. The remarkable corrollary to which is that those writers in the field whose thought was remarkable for its independence in its time still remain remarkable today. Once on the shelf of Fame, their busts have a habit of remaining there.

Next year, the big spring clean!

Brian W. Aldiss

ACKNOWLEDGEMENTS

In the Matter of the Assassin Merefirs by Ken W. Purdy, copyright © 1972 by The Condé Nast Publications, Inc.; reprinted by permission of the author's agents, Scott Meredith Literary Agency, Inc. First published in *Analog Science Fiction/Science Fact*.

As for Our Fatal Continuity . . . by Brian W. Aldiss, copyright © 1971 by Brian W. Aldiss; reprinted by permission of the author. First published in *New Worlds 3*.
The Old Folks by James E. Gunn, copyright © 1972 by James E. Gunn; reprinted by permission of the author. First published in *Nova 2*.
From Sea to Shining Sea by Jonathan Ela, copyright © 1972 by The Sierra Club; reprinted by permission of the author. First published in *Sierra Club Bulletin*.
Weihnachtabend by Keith Roberts, copyright © 1972 by Keith Roberts; reprinted by permission of the author. First published in *New Worlds 4*.

The Years by Robert F. Young, copyright © 1972 by UPD Publishing Corporation; reprinted by permission of the author. First published in *Galaxy*.
Darkness by Andre Carneiro, translated by Leo L. Barrow; reprinted by permission of the author and translator. First published in *Nova 2*.
Cymbal Player and *Report from the Planet Proteus* by Lawrence Sail, copyright © 1972 by Lawrence Sail; reprinted by permission of the author. First published in *Cornudo*.

Columbus on St. Domenica by John Cotton, copyright © 1972 by John Cotton; reprinted by permission of the author. First published by the *Sceptre Press*.
After Death by Patricia Beer, copyright © 1972 by The Statesman and National Publishing Co. Ltd.; reprinted by permission of the author. First published in *New Statesman*.

Faex Delenda Est by Theodore R. Cogswell, copyright © 1972 by Theodore R. Cogswell; reprinted by permission of the author. First published in *Cornudo*.
Words of Warning by Alex Hamilton, copyright © 1972 by Alex Hamilton; reprinted by permission of the author. First published in *Flies on the Wall* by Alex Hamilton.

Out, Wit! by Howard L. Myers, copyright © 1972 by The Condé Nast Publications, Inc.; reprinted by permission of the author's estate and their agents, Scott Meredith Literary Agency, Inc. First published in *Analog Science Fiction/Science Fact*.

An Imaginary Journey to the Moon by Victor Sabah, copyright © 1972 by Victor Sabah; reprinted by permission of the author.

The Head and the Hand by Chistopher Priest, copyright © 1971 by Christopher Priest; reprinted by permission of the author. First published in *New Worlds 3*.
Hero by Joe W. Haldeman, copyright © 1972 by The Condé Nast Publication, Inc.; reprinted by permission of the author and his agent, Robert P. Mills Ltd. First published in *Analog Science Fiction/Science Fact*.

Grin And Bear It by Lichty, copyright © 1972 by Publishers-Hall Syndicate; reprinted by permission of Publishers-Hall Syndicate.